To

my neighbors
with very best wishes!

Mallewaer

Aug. 2013

Joseph M. Callewaert

Lights out
for
Freedom

A Diary

Four Years under the Nazi Boot

Copyright © 2010 by Joseph M. Callewaert

ISBN 0-7414-6047-5

Printed in the United States of America

Published July 2010

INFINITY PUBLISHING
1094 New DeHaven Street, Suite 100
West Conshohocken, PA 19428-2713
Toll-free (877) BUY BOOK
Local Phone (610) 941-9999
Fax (610) 941-9959
Info@buybooksontheweb.com
www.buybooksontheweb.com

Table of Contents

~~

In Memory
of René, Hector Callewaert
and Marie-Emilie née Devoldere
my parents,
who showed admirable fortitude
during very trying times.

September 1, 1939 - May 10, 1940

*Once more we hear the word
That sickened earth of old
No law except the sword
Unsheathed and uncontrolled.*

Rudyard Kipling

An angel wheeling down out of space any morning in the years before World War Two, in his flight to survey western Europe, would have been offered from Arras in France to Antwerp close to the Dutch border, the uninterrupted plain of Flanders, intensely cultivated, stretching as far as the eye could see into the misty distance.

Here and there, this angel would have been looking down on an industrial town, a very old village or a little group of farm buildings. The latter are usually arranged around a central courtyard strangely similar to the Roman villas that dotted the plain long, long ago. Their outer walls are practically windowless as if the present owners still counted on the possibility of a siege like those their ancestors often had to sustain against the wandering marauders who, for centuries, infested the countryside. Along every road and canal, and beside nearly every cross-country path, he could have seen long lines of trees set out at regular intervals, all bent in the same direction by the force of the western wind which blows from the impetuous North Sea, and cuts the landscape into sections of varying sizes and shapes. Now and then a little hamlet would be noticeable, its red-tiled roofs nestling close together and a tiny church steeple rising from the center.

Flying a little lower, the heavenly messenger might have encountered what any visitor to Flanders cannot ignore namely the vagaries of Flemish weather. In this part of Europe the weather records show that it rains more or less two hundred and sixty days in each year, and while there are many days when the showers are brief, and some periods when it is clear for several days, it is better to come prepared for anything. Somewhere in the direction of the English Channel there seems to exist a vast and secret cloud factory which, day after day, sends huge masses of clouds rolling slowing eastward or southward across the country. They are high overhead, with frequent intervals of brilliant sunshine, and the showers few and far between. At other times the clouds hang low and dark and the rain falls steadily, not in furious driving showers as occurs frequently in the United States in summertime, but with a monotonous continuity that is the despair of travelers who are equipped for fair weather. It is no exaggeration to state that one may look out of the window upon a cloudless sky and find that by the time he has descended to the street it is raining. Happily the reverse is equally possible. Frequently one can look out of the window while at breakfast to a curtain of rain and dripping roofs, only to find by the time he is ready to go out of doors that the shower is over and the is sky clear.

The year is 1938, the eleventh of July. On one of those rare days of beautiful sunshine, in a little town near the French border, in the sharp bend formed by the sluggish river Lys, the same angel would have noticed a little troop, heavily loaded, marching in single file along the one-track railroad path that leads to the railroad station close by the border.

The group consists of a mother, three of her daughters and all three sons. One of the boys by the name of Joseph-Michel is the author of this diary. At present, in charge of two small suitcases and a rucksack, I bring up the rear and keep an eye on my youngest sister, Marie-Thérèse, who carries a little bag full of her most precious possessions: a few picture-books and her favorite dolls. She is my favorite sister, partly because she does not try to boss me, as do my older sisters, an attempt which I resist fiercely. I like her graceful figure and soft brown eyes, not a flaunting beauty of course -not yet, not a rose, but a modest violet hiding her sweetness.

At the point where the rail curves to the right, the little band turns around for a last look at the big house, half a mile away, built on a slight rise sloping gently down to the river, which they are

2

leaving forever. Long-repressed tears now rush down the mother's cheeks and the older children begin to weep too. They send a final adieu to their lovely home with its big garden, beautiful flower beds and all the precious remembrances of this deeply united family. The mother clutching the last bouquet of roses freshly cut early in the morning gives one to each child murmuring: "Please, don't ever forget the wonderful years you spent in this house." And then she turns and throws away the rest of the flowers...

It is not, as you might think, the wrenching departure of a small group of early refugees. No! But it has to do with the clouds of war which have accumulated in the last five years and threaten to burst forth over Europe. During these years, as Father explains, the Western democracies have watched the growth of the Nazi movement in Germany and they don't like what they see. They have learned about the growth of persecution of men, women and children on racial and political grounds; they have heard of concentration camps and watched the swaggering Nazi leaders boasting and threatening in the newsreels. On the whole, the reaction of the common folk, if not of their elected rulers prone to panic, is that one day such people will become a threat to life and comfort and have to be eliminated. To the British, the Germans are proving what willing tyrants they can become under the wrong sort of leaders; to the Belgians and the French, les sales Boches are beginning to act up and are threatening again.

Father is concerned that democratic Europe is bereft of real leadership and that the men in power have neither faith in themselves nor in their compatriots; the stronger the threats from Germany, the more they are inclined to stick their heads in the sand hoping the menace will go away. As the Belgian regional representative with the French railroad system in this border town, Father wants to leave his post, afraid that this part of the country might again become a no-man's land in case of war. He is also anxious to provide his children with the best education they can get and this small town is not the place for it. Hearing about an interesting opening in the Brussels western district, he has applied for it and in view of his 20-years of dutiful services, he has been given the job.

After weeks of preparation, the Great Move, as we call it, is underway. I have mixed feelings about it. On the one hand, I am excited about discovering our capital and its great schooling opportunities; on the other, it is hard to leave my friends, the fields, the woods and the lazy river I know so well. Two days ago I took leave of the Headmaster of the grammar school I have attended in the town of Houplines, near Armentières, across the border in France. I also bade farewell to my friend Robert Leroy. We have been inseparable for years, playing and studying together to such an extent that we earned the nickname "The Twins".

It is a beautiful day. The sky filled with a luminous powder at dawn has now deepened in shades of blue. The countryside is laid out in checkered fields whose contrasted colors are patterns on the land, the fields separated by deep draining ditches. In a hollow, a dozen cows graze lazily: a pastoral scene at its best. The sun is hot and burning with popcorn clouds catching the incandescent light. The poppies and the cornflowers grow in profusion in the fields, a thrown carpet of vivid scarlet and intense blue moving gently in the wind.

Our little group is proceeding rather slowly along the slag-covered path. Presently we pass a cluster of concrete bunkers, overgrown with bramble and half inundated. This was the front for more than four years in the Great War. Next to these relics you find innumerable little ponds, remains of the craters created by the incessant pounding of artillery shells.

From here looking northwesterly, with the whole landscape bathed in soft light, one can see about fifteen miles away the hump of Mount Kemmel, the highest hill in Flanders: 526 ft. It is close to the town of Ypres, the site also of intense fighting from September 1914 to November 1918. As a consequence this part of the country is covered with British military cemeteries as well as war memorials and has become a center of pilgrimage for many English families.

We are now approaching the station, a rather busy place mostly for goods trains on account of the brickyards nearby. They go back to Roman times and probably earlier thanks to the excellent quality of the clay. Our train is waiting, the locomotive hissing and

Above left: The house we left in 1938. Right: The author at the age of 14.
Below: the Callewaert family. First row: Joseph, Marie-Thérèse, Lucien.
Second row: Father, Mother, Simone, Léona, Michel, Rosa.
Sister Marguerite had already left home for a career in nursing.

puffing with a pungent smell generated by steam-heated air and hot coals. The railroad employees greet the arrival of our little caravan with amused comments and waste no time in installing us in the compartment especially reserved for the family. Father has made sure we will be treated properly, at least until Kortrijk. After that we are on our own, for the connection to Brussels is not assured.

Nestled cosily in my favorite corner at the window, I am anxious not to miss any of the Flemish landscape that rolls lazily in wide undulations to the North Sea. After making sure that everyone is accounted for and all the luggage securely stored on the rack above our heads, Mother sits with a great sigh of relief in the opposite window corner facing me.

Her eyes smile in the soft light, half mocking, half friendly, cerulean blue and shining, the whites ultra-white. There is nothing wrong with the design of the eyebrows. The nose is rather long and straight, the mouth curved up at the corners and her cheeks showing faint hollows at the right places. Assembled, the components add up not to a standard type of beauty, but to a face of character and vitality. No anxiety, no inner confusion. A good deal of self assurance, knowing she looks attractive and that she has succeeded in the job of bringing up a loving brood of children.

We arrived safely in Brussels and were quickly established in our new surroundings. The transition to a big city environment, to a new school, new programs, keeps me extremely busy. I make new friends in the neighborhood and, for a full year, I pay very little attention to international events although the tension is great .

On the first of September 1939, however, as I prepare for a new school year to start in about two weeks, the news that Germany has invaded Poland turns me, almost overnight, from an unconcerned schoolboy into an interested teenager. I decide to follow the war events as closely as possible and to consign them in what I will call: My War Diary.

September 1, Friday. Germany invaded Poland today. Warsaw and many other Polish towns have been bombed by German warplanes.

6

As his troops marched into Poland, in an address to the Reichstag at the Kroll Opera House in Berlin, Hitler said that Poland attacked first, last night, and Germany has been shooting back "since 5:45, this morning." He added: "From now on bomb after bomb is falling."

September 2nd, Saturday. Great confusion. The Poles say they have repulsed the Germans; the latter don't say much except that they are bombing strategic targets.

I review Hitler's speech at the Kroll Opera and note the following:
- I (Hitler) am not going to ask help from Italy.
- The German Army today is better than in 1914.
- If anything happens to me, Göring is to be my successor and after him, Rudolf Hess.
- Only military targets will be bombed but if the enemy acts otherwise, the German Air Force will reply in the same way.
- An iron discipline is to be imposed on German women.

The last point leaves me perplexed. I discuss it with Father whose reply is: "Hitler is a mysogynist". I look up the word in the Larousse Dictionary and find "woman hater".

September 3, Sunday. Great Britain declares war on Germany at 11 o'clock . Six hours later France follows suit. Jules Wille, my brother-in-law, Sister Rosa's husband, has been called up on August 31st and has left to rejoin his regiment at Metz, in Eastern France.

September 5, Tuesday. This must be the first casualty of the war. The British ship Athenia, bound for Canada, with many Americans aboard, was torpedoed yesterday.

Not much news from Poland. The Nazis announce great victories but this must be pure propaganda. I read in the papers that the Poles are putting up a fierce resistance against 70 German divisions. My question: How many men in a division?

September 12, Sunday. The first British troops have arrived in France. The father of Robert Leroy must not be happy. As a volunteer in the Great War, he was in almost daily contact with "les Anglais" and didn't like the experience. They are lazy, he says, "they will not miss a tea break, and they leave the fighting to the French".

Here in Brussels, the newspapers mention an attack on a 20 km front in the Saarland by French troops.

September 18, Monday. The big news is that Russian armies marched into Poland yesterday to occupy a big chunk of Eastern Poland. This is what you can call a stab in the back and certainly, according to the papers, it is the end of that country.

An interesting point, to me at least, is the explanation given by the Soviet Government to explain its dastardly move: "We cannot leave these kindred peoples defenseless in view of the fact that the Polish Government has disintegrated".

September 23, Saturday. All the talk is still about Poland. The Soviet Union will gain two-thirds of the country, about 150,000 square km2 and Germany is getting 90,000 km2.
Furthermore, each of these pirate countries will lord it over 16 million inhabitants and over half of Warsaw.

October 6, Friday. Hitler has made the following declarations in his much-trumpeted "Peace Plan" speech to the Reichstag, today. The chief points are:
1. Return of the former German colonies to the Reich.
2. This colonial claim is justified by the necessity of a new distribution of the world's raw materials.
3. The creation of a just and enduring German frontier.
4. The status of the various races within Germany's sovereignty to be reappraised.
5. The building of a Polish State whose security will be guaranteed by Germany and the Soviet Union, whose respective governments will allow no intrigues against either countries.
6. Germany has no claims against France and no claims will ever be raised against France.
7. There can be only real peace in Europe and the world when Britain and Germany come to an agreement. "Never have I tried to oppose British interests".

8. If, however, the attitude of Mr. Churchill gets the upper hand, then we shall fight. Neither armed forces nor time will conquer Germany.

9. Fate will show who is right. One thing is certain, there have never been in the history of the world two victors, but there have often been two conquered. May those who reject my hand be prepared to accept the responsibility of defeat.

October 17, Tuesday. The British have announced, and it has been confirmed by Berlin, that German bombs fell on England yesterday for the first time since the war began. Actually, it appears that the bombs fell not on England but on Scotland.

November 2, Thursday. Trouble is brewing between Finland and the Russian Bear. The latter is asking that the Finnish port of Hangoe (Hanko in Finnish) be handed over to Russia.

I look up my map of Scandinavia and discover that the port is situated at the mouth of the Gulf of Finland, a very strategic point. The Finnish Foreign Minister had this to say: "A way can and must be found for Finland and Russia to live together, and no pressure can change our resolution. The country is determined to defend itself".

My question: Now that they have made peace with their arch-enemy Nazi Germany, will the Reds try to gobble up other neighbors?

November 9, Thursday. Thanks to Father I pay attention to Hitler's speeches. Yesterday, in Munich, he spoke as follows:

- No matter how long the war may last, Germany will never capitulate,
- England claims to be prepared for a three-year war. On the day when England declared war on Germany, I gave Göring orders to prepare for a war of five years.
- We have organized all Germany's resources down to the last detail. The enemy will never lay us low, economically or militarily. There can be only one victor and that is us.

Twenty-seven minutes after Hitler ended his speech at the Burgerbräu Cellar, the building was shaken by an explosion which killed six members of the Nazi Party's "Old Guard" and injured sixty others. Hitler had already left and consequently was not hurt. It looks like the Fùhrer is not universally loved in Germany.

Yesterday also, a dozen German planes flew over Belgium and apparently took photographs. Why doesn't the DTCA (anti-aircraft) shoot them down?

Another disturbing piece of news. It is rumored that Germany has asked Holland not only for the use of some Dutch military bases, but also for the control of the port of Vlissingen at the mouth of the Scheldt River. More rumors have it that a German attack on the Netherlands was planned but was cancelled at the last moment. Is this real or just propaganda to intensify "la guerre des nerfs" (war of the nerves)?

November 9, Thursday. King Léopold of Belgium and Queen Wilhelmina of Holland have come up with an offer of mediation and a plan for peace to resolve the European conflict. Pope Pius XII and the Kings of Norway and Sweden have endorsed this initiative. It doesn't seem, however, that the Great Powers are paying much attention.

November 11, Saturday. As a boy scout, I attend the ceremonies at the tomb of the Unknown Soldier at the Colonne du Congrès, rue Royale. I take part in the parade that marched past King Léopold; this is the first time I have seen him in person. The parade, for us, was all over in a few minutes.

Some news from a faraway country: Rumania! It appears that oil shares at the Bucharest Stock Exchange increased in value by 16% this Wednesday, in just one day. It is also pointed out that the price of these shares have doubled in the last two weeks as a result of Germany's attempt to corner crude oil supplies.

November 30, Thursday. Russia has broken off diplomatic relations with Finland. The Big Bear is trying to scare the Finnish Fox. From Helsinki comes the message that the Government of Finland, after Molotov's radio warning that "Russia will act", expects an invasion at any time now. The Finns are wondering where the Reds will strike first. It is reported that Soviet troops are being moved up to the border north of Leningrad.

The Russians in control of the Gulf of Finland and with a direct access to the Baltic? Isn't this a move that should concern the Nazis? Here is what the German radio says: "Soviet desire to have access to the Baltic is understood here. Since the beginning of the war, Britain has hinted she has claims to the islands of the Baltic. People in Berlin think that bases which were once Russian are more vital to Russia than to an independent Finland."

December 1, Friday. Not that I intend to sail to England soon, but I noticed the following item in the paper: After being suspended since early September, the Channel service between Belgium and England was resumed on November 29. One of the mailboats arrived safely at an English port that day with sixty-eight passengers.

December 18, Monday. Big news today! The British Navy has sunk the pocket battleship "Graf von Spee". It was neither a "pocket" ship nor a battleship but a heavy cruiser armed with six 11-inch turret guns and capable of 26 knots or more. This happened in the bay of Montevideo, in Uruguay.

December 19, Tuesday. Correction: "Graf von Spee" was not sunk by the British Navy, but was blown up by her crew rather than fight or surrender..

December 23, Saturday. The first term of the school year is over and my report card is not too bad. I am No. 2 in a field of 28. I am good at Math, French composition and elocution, German, History and Geography. I should do much better in English and don't understand what happened in that field. Father says it's good but I should try for number one. Why not?

1940

January 1, Sunday. The world is at war or at least Europe is. It is a "drôle de guerre", a strange war, a "phoney" war as the English say.

January 11, Thursday. Something peculiar happened yesterday near Mechelen-aan-de Maas. Due to bad weather, a German light aircraft was flown off-course and made an emergency landing just a mile or two inside the Belgian border. A gendarme approaching the small plane found an officer trying to set fire to some papers which the gendarme promptly seized. No official comment has been given about this incident.

January 23, Tuesday. The Vatican has condemned the German indemnity demand on Poland. Not only have the Nazis destroyed that country, they also want to exploit and impoverish it so that it will never be able to rise again. This conforms to Hitler's ideology expressed in Mein Kampf according to which the Slavs are an inferior race and to be treated as such.

March 13, Wednesday. Moscow has announced that the war in Finland which began with Soviet Army's invasion 104 days ago will end at midday. Although Helsinki so far has not confirmed it, Moscow claims that a peace treaty has been signed with Finland under the following terms:
1. Military operations to cease at once.
2. Finland to cede the whole of the Karelia Isthmus with the city of Viipuri (Viborg), the whole of Viipuri Bay with its islands.
3. Both countries give a pledge of non-aggression against each other.
4. Finland to lease to Russia the peninsula of Hanko for thirty years, with the area five miles south and east of Hanko.
5. Finland agrees to the establishment of a Soviet military base for protective purposes.
6. Russia obtains the right of free transit through the Petsamo region into Norway and back.
7. Soviet non-military planes obtain the right of free movement over the Petsamo region.
8. Russia agrees to withdraw all her troops from the Petsamo area.
9. Finland agrees to grant a right of way between Russia and Sweden by the shortest route.
10. The two countries undertake to negotiate a new trade treaty.

What is interesting in this treaty besides gathering the spoil of naked aggression, is the desire of the Russians for an ice-free port in Norway: Narvik or Tromsö?

March 15, Friday. I read in the papers that the British Expeditionary Force (BEF) in France is now more than 300,000 strong. This seems a lot but actually it is not much compared to the one and half million French troops and the 600,000 soldiers mobilized in Belgium. It is of course ridiculous for us to guard the border with France, but apparently as a neutral country in this conflict we have to be "impartial".

March 24, Sunday. The Défense Passive (Civil Defense) and the Red Cross have organized a "Be Prepared" day against enemy air raids. The Boy Scouts have been asked to cooperate. As a consequence I have been designated as a victim of a staged bombardment.

After the air raid warning alert, given by a series of long blasts of a siren lasting two minutes, I am told to go and lie down at the corner of the Boulevard de Smet de Naeyer and the Avenue de Jette, with a note indicating that as a result of a bomb blast I was suffering of a thigh wound, a broken arm and face lacerations. I dutifully laid down at the indicated spot and waited for my rescuers. It took them ten minutes to find me as they were looking in the wrong place. I had to stand up and shout and wave to attract their attention. In the meantime a small crowd had congregated around me wondering what this scene was all about.

I was efficiently taken care of, given first aid and conveyed by ambulance to the Brugmans Hospital where nice nurses and a young unshaven doctor took care of my "wounds". One hour or so later, after the all-clear signal given by a long and steady blast, I was released hale and hearty. The test was declared a success but this sort of thing always is, isn't it?

April 9, Tuesday. Today Germany occupied Denmark without a fight; it also invaded Norway in a lightning offensive on its southern and western coasts. A naval battle is underway off the Norwegian coast between the British fleet and units of the Kriegsmarine. There is great confusion and real news is hard to get. It seems that by late afternoon Oslo has been occupied.

The Germans have struck all the way to Narvik. (What will the Reds think of that?) They are in Stavanger, Bergen and Trondheim. If victorious the Nazis will have aerial and submarine bases just across the North Sea from Scotland and the big base of Scapa Flow.

April 11, Thursday. There is still fighting in Norway. The Nazis seem to have the upper hand. The Supreme Allied War Council met in London with both Premier Reynaud of France and his Defense Minister, Daladier, attending. The Allies have been surprised by the move. How will they react?

In the meantime, in the Balkans the German government has demanded that Yugoslavia, Hungary, Bulgaria and Rumania accept German river police along the entire length of the Danube in order to secure this vital supply route for Germany.

I slowly start to learn a little more about what is called "strategy". The Larousse dictionary defines it as the mobilization of a nation's or a group of nations' forces through long-range planning and readiness, to insure in times of peace, security; and in war, victory.

2

May 10 - August 27, 1940

May 10, Friday. I was awakened brutally this morning around 5:30 by the sound of anti-aircraft guns. Looking out of the window toward the northwest I saw a few rather large planes turning lazily to my left. In the distance one could hear muffled explosions covered at times by the loud reports of AA guns, nearby. "This is war" declares Mother who has known war in 1914-18, close to the front in Flanders.

The radio tells us that without a declaration of war the Germans have invaded Holland, Belgium and Luxemburg. Every airport in Belgium has been attacked by Nazi planes. Paratroops have landed in Holland and the Dutch have opened their floodgates. The Belgian army is resisting the German onslaught around the forts of Liège and along the Albert Canal. There is really no hard news.

Special editions of newspapers in both French and Flemish are available in late morning. Not much in them. Proclamation of a state of war by King Léopold and the Government and full mobilization of the reserve troops which should bring the total strength of the Belgian army to about 900,000.

Father has gone to work as usual. He comes back at his normal time and tells us that he is under mobilization orders and can be called up at any time, as a civilian, with the Belgian national railroad where he is employed.

The neighborhood is so quiet. The radio is on all day but there is very little news except cryptic announcements, martial music and bits of communiqués from the government: our troops are resisting; the forts of Liège are under heavy attack; the French and British troops are rushing to our help.

May 11, Saturday. Troop movements all day. The weather is unbelievably beautiful. Prime Minister Pierlot assures us on the radio that "the situation is stabilized" around Liège, but the Germans pursue their attacks towards the Ardennes using a great number of tanks and attack planes. Our air force is nowhere to be seen.

May 14, Tuesday. Despite all the governmental optimism, the situation is not clear. There is a big battle going on around Liège. The French tell us they are putting up a brilliant fight and their motorized units are clearly superior. They add that the Germans continue their mass attacks in the Ardennes region and mention that the enemy might have reached the Meuse River. This news I find very troubling.

May 15, Wednesday. Rumors, rumors, rumors. The feeling here is that the war is not going well for our side. The Belgian army is in retreat; the French are somewhere on the Meuse. I have seen a few British trucks on the road to Wemmel. People see German spies and saboteurs everywhere. It has become mass hysteria and the reason why I was on the road to Wemmel, "patrolling". The government has asked the Boy Scouts to help the police spot spies and traitors within our midst and to report them to the authorities. I didn't see anything suspicious, nothing but the normal activities of an army at war.

The situation is grave in central Holland. Nazi parachutists and glider troops have occupied that part of the country, and motorized forces from the German border are trying to get into contact with them.

May 16, Thursday. Depressing news. The Germans are advancing towards Brussels. People, in a panic, are starting to leave especially those who have cars. Others are leaving by cart or on foot.

Father has received orders to join a group of railroad officials in Oudenaarde. All young men, eighteen years and older, are ordered to assembly centers in Flanders. My brother Michel is assigned to the Ghent Army Depot. Should the rest of the family leave and take to the road? My mother has a short answer: NO! In Flanders, during the Great War, she was ordered to evacuate her home twice, and twice she lost almost everything. "Whatever happens, we stay put". This settles the matter.

In Great Britain, since May 10, there is a new government under the leadership of Mr. Winston Churchill. I never heard of him, except for brief mentions in the papers, but I have seen an extract of the speech he made at the House of Commons which does impress me very much:

"What is our policy? I say it is to wage war: war by sea, land and air; war with all our might and all the strength that God gives us... What is our aim? It is victory, victory at all costs, victory in spite of all terrors; victory however long and hard the road may be."

May 17, Friday. Total confusion... The Belgian communiqué this morning mentions heavy fighting on the Dyle river defense line from Antwerp to Louvain, to Gembloux, to Namur and then, along the Meuse, to Sedan. There is mention that the British are fighting at Louvain.

People are leaving in droves... I don my boy scout uniform and dutifully go on patrolling for spies. All I see are hundreds and hundreds of people fleeing towards Flanders and France. For the first time since May 10, I encounter unshaven and tired Belgian soldiers. But they are not front-line troops. They are reservists, they tell me, from Army depots in Tirlemont, Louvain and Mechelen (Mechlin). Why don't they suspect me as a spy and saboteur? I guess they are too weary to even think about the Fifth column that is: the enemy within. This is the general term used to encompass all activity that could help the Nazi aggressor.

In the evening, at intervals, we hear loud explosions. People are in the streets, eager for any bit of news they can gather. Someone tells me that the bridges on the Senne Canal are being blown up by the retreating troops.

May 18, Saturday. The explosions kept us awake during the night and this morning we learn to our astonishment and dismay that German troops did enter Brussels yesterday evening. I cannot believe we are occupied by the Nazis. The Burgomaster of the city Mr. van de Meulebroek, has spoken on the radio, which is now in

German hands. He advises the population to stay calm and do nothing that would invite reprisals from the Occupant.

I see my first German soldiers around noon on the Boulevard de Smet de Naeyer. Sister Léona is with me. A few people are watching the huge column of motor vehicles passing by at a steady but rather slow pace. Army trucks neatly camouflaged, articulated ones from the Reichsbahn, other obviously requisitioned civilian vehicles with inscriptions on their sides: "Spedition", "Fernspediteur" (long distance transportation) and the name of the firm. I notice that the drivers all wear a black uniform. They carry small discs, red with a narrow white band around the rim on one side, and green with a white band on the other side and use them to slow down, accelerate or stop. From time to time, a motorcycle with sidecar will speed by. The driver must be a scout or a traffic regulator. He is in full uniform with helmet and wears a greenish raincoat with ample sleeves. The helmet gives him a rather mean look.

An Army truck comes along with about twenty soldiers sitting or standing in the back. Seeing my sister, they wave and whistle but soon disappear around the corner. We don't move and show nothing but sullen looks: "We didn't ask you to come and invade us; we don't want you here; we will never accept you; you are the enemy, we hate you".

May 19, Sunday. The Belgian army is now fighting on the Scheldt river and the prospects are dismal. The Germans have announced the fall of Antwerp,

Yesterday afternoon, I went to my "collège"(high school) not far from home. I found it eerily empty. There have been no classes since May 10th. I had a chance to talk to the Deputy Director who told me he expects to reopen the school shortly. However, since most teachers have been called up, there is no telling whether we shall have enough teachers to finish the school year.

May 20, Monday. Long columns of troops continue to pass through Brussels day and night. There is no civilian traffic to speak of. All public transportation has been halted except in some privileged areas. The only way to move around is on foot or bicycle.

Someone tells me that the Dutch have surrendered on May 14, after only five days of fighting. But they were not well prepared for war.

Radio Brussels is on the air again both in Flemish and in French. Needless to say, it is controlled by the Nazis and broadcasts all Wehrmacht's communiqués. They mention that the German troops have reached Sedan and cut deep into France. Is this pure propaganda?

May 23, Thursday. Great surprise this morning: Father is back! Safe and sound. He followed his orders and got as far as Denderleeuw - a very important railroad center about 30 km from here. There he encountered utter confusion with conflicting orders and trains immobilized on side tracks going nowhere and exposed to bombing and strafing. Fortunately the dive bombers never appeared, being busy, we can assume, somewhere else.

Then the Germans overtook the whole area, but most of the rearguard of our army escaped during the night. The next day a German officer told all civilians to go back home with strict orders not to use the main roads reserved for enemy traffic.

Father has a few interesting stories to tell. He has walked all the way back at night, encountering German patrols ready to shoot. Fortunately, he speaks rusty German, a language he learned during the Great War from soldiers billeted at his home.
Father has no news about brother Michel. His destination was Ghent. Perhaps has he been able to find a military driver willing to take him along. For all we know he might at present be in Ghent or Bruges or even somewhere in France.

May 25, Saturday. Not much to report today. The battle of the Scheldt goes on unabated.

The Kommandatur, in Brussels, has issued a "Bekanntmachung" or proclamation to the public which has been posted in all towns and villages in occupied Belgium, in Flemish (Dutch) and in French. It lists all acts punishable under military law:
1. Aiding non-German soldiers in the occupied territory.
2. Aiding civilians to escape into unoccupied territory.

3. Transmitting news to persons or authorities outside the occupied territory if such transmission is prejudicial to the interests of the German armed forces and the Reich.
4. Communicating with prisoners of war.
5. Insulting the German Army and its Commanders.
6. Street meetings, distribution of leaflets, arrangement of public assemblies and parades without previous approval by the German Commander, as well as any other manifestation of hostility towards Germany.
7. Inducing work stoppages, malicious stoppage of work, strikes and lockouts.

May 28, Tuesday. I am dismayed, dispirited and profoundly discouraged. According to the news heard on the radio, the Belgian army, early this morning, has surrendered to the Germans. I cannot believe it and hope that the honor of the army is safe.

The Germans announced it first: "King Léopold III of the Belgians has decided to give up senseless resistance against German might and has asked for an armistice. In reply Germany demanded and received the unconditional surrender of the Belgian army."

Then, in France, Prime Minister Paul Reynaud, in a nationwide radio broadcast, revealed the Belgian capitulation in a bitter attack, excoriating King Léopold. Reynaud made no effort to conceal the seriousness of this surrender. He affirmed: "King Léopold has given up the fight without consideration for the Allies." And he accused the King of taking the decision against the unanimous advice of his ministers. (As far as I know, the Belgian government is somewhere in France.)

The British Prime Minister Winston Churchill has announced the surrender in the House of Commons adding "the House must prepare itself for hard and heavy tidings."

The British must be mad at us too but I notice that, in a broadcast to the British people the Minister of Information has asked the people of Britain to reserve judgment on King Léopold's act. This, in my opinion, is a good example of British "fair play".

May 29, Wednesday. The surrender continues to be the big item in the news. We learn that our army was, at the time, defending positions on the Scheldt and the coast northeast of Ostend. The ceasefire opened the way to Ypres, Furnes and Dunkirk, putting the French and the British in grave danger.

May 30, Thursday. Still the matter of capitulation. I look at a map published in the paper (under Nazi censorship). It shows the Germans at Abbeville. The Allies were encircled before the Belgian surrender!

Now the French acknowledge that at present the front is on the Somme and Aisne rivers. That is, the Nazis are in the town of Laon, 140 kms from Paris!! We, the Allies, are in big trouble. The French also announce heavy fighting in Lille and on the Lys river, including the town of Armentières where my sister Rosa lives. It is 1914 all over again.

May 31, Friday. I visit St. Pierre College where I meet with Fr. Desloover, the French teacher of both my brother Lucien's class and myself. No reopening of school yet. Fr. Desloover, who seems to have contact with people in high places, tells me that very soon Cardinal Van Roey, archbishop of the archdiocese of Mechlin (which includes Brussels) and the Primate of Belgium, is preparing a pastoral letter to defend the actions of the King. This letter will be read at all masses on Sunday in all churches of Belgium.

There seems to be a lull in the fighting in France. The front has stabilized except in the pocket of Dunkirk where the Luftwaffe is bombing the Allied troops all day long.

June 1st, Saturday. The British are evacuating their troops from the Dunkirk pocket. Nothing is said about the French. In any case the battle for Lille is over. We all hope that sister Rosa and her little son, Charles, are safe.

I want to mention here that the father of my brother-in-law, Jules, was killed in action in 1915. Now, twenty-five years later, Jules is in harm's way with a baby son by the name of Charles, a few months old, who has been named after his grandfather, a victim of the Great War.

We are also concerned about brother Michel who left us two weeks ago to join the army. Where is he now? Hopefully, there was no time for him to be inducted in the army and therefore he will not be treated as a prisoner of war.

June 4, Tuesday. Dunkirk is in the news today. The Nazi-controlled announcement was short: the battle of Dunkirk is over. The British and the French have fled. Numerous prisoners have been taken and the German army has taken possession of an enormous booty of vehicles, tanks, arms and ammunition. The French Admiralty communiqué together with the British War Office reveals that Dunkirk has been abandoned by the Allies "after the most remarkable withdrawal in military history."

In the House of Commons, Mr. Churchill has declared that no fewer than 335,000 British and French troops have been evacuated. The BEF (British Expeditionary Force) losses are 30,000 killed, wounded or missing; 1000 guns and all transport and armored vehicles lost.

In a special broadcast the German High Command says that the Nazi losses between May 10 and June 1st were: 10,222 killed, 8,463 missing, 42,523 wounded. During the same period, adds the same communiqué, 432 German planes were lost but the Luftwaffe shot down 1,841 enemy planes and at least 1,600 more were destroyed on the ground. This seems a lot to me. I am not even sure the Allies have or had that many planes. Perhaps someone in the Wehrmacht's statistics department is seeing double.

June 6, Thursday. The Italians are issuing warlike threats. Mussolini is rattling his wooden saber against France. The Italian cabinet had a meeting yesterday. The radio communiqué, in a strange way - or maybe the translation is incorrect - reads as follows: "Results of this meeting are by no means to be taken as an indication Italy has changed intentions. She is still prepared to take arms and fight for her rights at any time she sees fit."

June 11, Tuesday. First month of war and already so many battles and defeats. However, I strongly believe that France somehow will recover and defeat the Nazis. The German economy, I am told, cannot sustain for long this war effort. But perhaps I should be a little more careful in accepting this statement. Back in September 1939, it was claimed that the Nazis didn't have a chance, that Germany will crack up, that the populace will revolt and the soldiers, underfed, will defect at the next opportunity... And here they are!

Yesterday, the Italians took the plunge. As of midnight, their country is now at war with France and Britain.

June 12, Wednesday. Great joy for us today: brother Michel has returned in good shape and in high spirits after quite a few adventures and a lot of zigzags in Flanders. He walked back most of the way.

Bad news from France. The French General Headquarters has announced that German troops have crossed the Seine west of Paris. Violent fighting is continuing along the whole Weygand line. (Don't ask me about this Weygand line: I am only a civilian.) Paris has been placed in a "state of defense". Whatever that means. Sorry!

June 14, Friday. President Roosevelt has revealed that he has given the order "full speed ahead" to provide armaments to the Allies. This is the first time I hear about any American involvement in this war. Isn't it a little late?

June 15, Saturday. Fr. Victor Desloover gives me a mimeographed leaflet with extracts of Winston Churchill's speech to the House of Commons on June 4th, at the occasion of the withdrawal of the British troops from Dunkirk.

"Even if large tracts of Europe fall into the grip of the Gestapo and all the odious apparatus of Nazi rule, we shall not flag or fail. We will go on to the end and will fight in France, on the oceans and in the air. We will defend our island, whatever the cost, and will fight on the beaches and landing grounds, in the fields and streets and we shall never surrender.

"Even if this island or a large part of it were subjugated, our Empire abroad, armed and guarded by the British Fleet, would carry on the struggle until, in God's good time, the new world, with all its force and men, set forth to the liberation and rescue of the old world...

"We shall ride out the storms of war and outlive the menace of tyranny, if necessary for years. That is the resolve of the Government, every man of it, and that is the will of Parliament and the nation. The British Empire and the French Republic, linked together in their cause and in their need, will defend to the death their native soil, aiding each other like good comrades to the utmost of their strength."

It is said that a roar of cheers answered this wonderful speech full of superb and stark confidence. The great orators of the Ancient World, we study in school, would surely approve.

Last minute: The Germans have entered a deserted Paris this June 14 at around 5:30 p.m.

June 17, Monday. What a terrible month this June of 1940 seems to be. Now we hear that France has asked Germany for "peace with honor", but Hitler will accept nothing but complete capitulation. He will meet with Mussolini to discuss the French proposal broadcasted by the new Premier, Marshall Henri-Philippe Pétain. In the meantime the German armies pursue their advance through France. Orléans, on the river Loire, has fallen and German mechanized columns have reached the Rhône valley.

The British argue that the fight must go on, and that France should join other refugee governments to carry on the fight outside French soil, particularly since the French naval forces are so vital to Britain. Meanwhile, the German High Command has issued a communiqué stating that the troops have reached the Swiss border near Pontarlier, southeast of Besançon, thereby closing the ring around the French forces in Alsace-Lorraine. This completes the encirclement of all troops defending the Maginot Line, a zone in which upward of one million men are concentrated.

June 18, Tuesday. Here is the text of Marshal Pétain's broadcast.

"Frenchmen! At the request of the President of the Republic, I have assumed the Government of France.

"I am sure of the faith of our soldiers who have been fighting with admirable heroism against an enemy superior in numbers and in arms. I also think of those old combatants whom I commanded during the last war. I have given myself to France to better her situation at this decisive hour.

24

"At this moment I think of the unfortunate refugees, the men and women on the roads, driven away from their homes by the misfortunes of war. I express to them my sincerest sympathy and compassion.

"It is with a heavy heart that I tell you today that we must stop the fight. I sent a message to the enemy, yesterday, to ask him if he would meet with me, as between one soldier and another after the fight, and honorably, to seek a way to put an end to the hostilities.

"Let all Frenchmen gather around the government over which I preside during these sad hours. And let them do their duty during these difficult times, with faith in our destiny."

June 19, Wednesday. Marshal Pétain last night, we are told, ordered French and Allied combatants on land air and sea, to keep on fighting.

He said that armistice negotiations have not even begun and warned the Allied soldiers that German forces were using the white flag to take important positions without fighting.

My comment: yesterday Maréchal Pétain told the French "we must stop the fight." Today he says: "Oh yes! but you should go on fighting." Does the Maréchal think the average soldier will risk his life when he is told everything is lost and that the struggle will soon be over?

The Germans (and the Macaronis), Hitler and Musso the Benito (my nickname for the Italian dictator) after a four-hour conference in Munich, agreed on the attitude of both their governments toward France's request for armistice terms. The two dictators have ordered their armies to take positions for a final attack on France, if their terms should be refused. Berlin has declared that the terms would be unconditional surrender or destruction of the French system.

Mr. Winston Churchill, in a broadcast, announced: "The battle of France is over. I expect that the battle of Britain is about to begin. The news from France is very bad and I grieve for the gallant French people who have fallen into this terrible misfortune. Nothing will alter our feelings towards them or our faith that the genius of France will rise again...

"What happened in France makes no difference to British faith and purpose. We have become the sole champions, now in arms, to defend the world cause. We shall do our best to be worthy of this high honour. We shall defend our island and, with the British Empire around us, we shall fight on, unconquerable, until the curse of Hitler is lifted from the brows of men."

I get all this news courtesy of D. I. S., the Desloover Information System. It consists of having a person listen to the BBC and take down the communiqués and speeches by shorthand. It is then transcribed, typed, mimeographed and distributed among sure friends.

June 20 Thursday. Berlin announces that the French Armistice delegates will meet the Wehrmacht representatives on German-occupied territory. Italy will not be represented in these negotiations. (I guess Hitler feels that Musso has come a little too late in the game.)

June 22, Saturday. In the Far East, the Japanese have massed 30,000 troops at the border of the British Colony of Hong-Kong. Furthermore, Japanese warships, including aircraft carriers, are cruising in the vicinity of Indochina. In Tokyo, the Vice-Minister for Foreign Affairs has summoned the French Ambassador and asked that steps should be taken immediately to secure the voluntary suspension of assistance extended by French Indochina to the Chinese Chung-King government.

So you have it: After the Italian *HYENA* we get the Japanese *VULTURE.*

June 23, Sunday. The French plenipotentiaries have signed an armistice with Germany yesterday at 17h30 at Compiègne in the railroad carriage where the Armistice was signed in 1918. The Armistice will not take effect until a separate French-Italian agreement has been signed.

Mr. Churchill didn't wait long to issue a statement:
"The British Government has heard with grief and amazement that the terms dictated by the Germans have been accepted by the French Government at Bordeaux.

"They cannot feel that such or similar terms could have been submitted to by any French Government which possessed freedom, independence, and constitutional authority.

Such terms, if accepted by all Frenchmen, would place not only France but the French Empire entirely at the mercy and in the power of the German and Italian dictators.

"When Great Britain is victorious, she will, in spite of the action of the Bordeaux Government, cherish the cause of the French people, and a British victory is the only possible hope for the restoration of the greatness of France and the freedom of its people. Brave men from other countries overrun by the Nazi invasion are steadfastly fighting in the ranks of freedom.

"His Majesty's Government appeals to all Frenchmen, whoever they may be, to aid to the utmost of their strength the forces of liberation, which are enormous and which, faithfully and resolutely used, will assuredly prevail."

At least one Frenchman has already answered Mr. Churchill's appeal. In London, a certain General de Gaulle, who is or was Paul Reynaud's (the former Prime Minister) Military Adviser, broadcasting in French on the BBC, has appealed to all Frenchmen to rally and fight with the British - whatever the decision of the Pétain Government "which has no right to surrender."

June 24, Monday. Here are the terms of the French capitulation.
1. Germany will occupy the whole of the West Coast of France and all territory north of a line from Genève to Tours, on the Loire, and then all along the Loire River, to Nantes. France will pay for the occupation.
2. The French armed forces are to be demobilized and disarmed.
3. Germany may demand the surrender, in good condition, of artillery, tanks, aircraft and ammunition.
4. No French forces may leave French soil. No materiel may be conveyed to Great Britain. No French merchant shipping may leave harbor, and ships outside of France should be recalled.
5. All establishments and stocks must be handed over intact. The same applies to yards, railways and communications.
6. The French Government must facilitate transport of merchandise between Germany and Italy.
7. German prisoners of war must be released, but all French prisoners of war will remain in captivity until peace is signed.

8. The French Fleet is to be recalled to French territorial waters and there to be disarmed and interned under German and Italian control in ports which the German and Italian governments will specify.   .

9. The armistice will enter into force as soon as the French Government have concluded a similar agreement with the Italian Government.

10. The armistice is valid until peace is signed, but may be denounced at any moment by Germany if the French Government does not fulfill it.

June 28, Friday. Fr. Desloover with his contacts in high places, gives me a memo concerning Hitler's Plan for the future of Europe.

Hitler will call a European Peace Conference in Berlin as soon as a definitive settlement is reached with France. His plan will be outlined at that meeting, from which British and Russian representatives will be barred.

The Führer intends to establish his own model of a political and economic European federation divided into three or four groups of nations, each linked along economic and geographic lines. All governments will be modeled on Nazi lines and their national armies abolished.

The aim of the federation will be to checkmate the "Anglo-American economic bloc", because Hitler expects the United States to enter the war, which will mean prolonged hostilities.

Once the peace with France is finalized, Germany will concentrate on building airplanes and abandon tank construction, as an Anglo-American alliance will threaten to achieve superiority in the air.

In the meantime, Germany intends to break England's resistance mainly by violent aerial bombardments.

July 2nd, Tuesday. The "shooting" war is less than two months old and already three countries have been overwhelmed: Holland lasted but a few days, Belgium resisted for 18 long days and France was on her knees, beaten in only 45 days!

How the mighty have fallen! This to me is incomprehensible. France had the best army in the world. It was supposed to be far superior to the German armed forces which, I was told, were suffering from all kinds of shortages from raw materials to food to textiles; that the civilians in Germany were on tight rations, going hungry, afraid to issue any complaint for fear of the secret police.

July 4, Thursday. Absorbed by so many portentous events, I have failed to mention that classes have resumed at school on Monday June 17. Quite a few of my classmates have not shown up because they have fled to France and have not yet come back. Most teachers are present so that, despite the five weeks hiatus in the normal curriculum, we will be able to make up for lost time. Furthermore, summer vacation is being postponed until Saturday, August 3rd.

July 6, Saturday. There is no class in the afternoon and I decide to go downtown to have a look around. The streetcars are back in operation except that some lines have to be diverted from their normal routes because of bridge destruction. I have a choice of routes 9, 14 and 11 but the latter makes a long detour and also requires me to use a connection. I take tram 14 which brings me to the destroyed bridge spanning the Canal of Willebroek at the Place Sainctelette. A narrow footbridge has been built on the broken arches and the crossing is slow. I am not much delayed however because at that point the canal is not very wide.

Approaching the center I notice quite a few German soldiers who seem to be coming from the barracks of the 6th Infantry Division called "Caserne du Petit-Château". Curious, I make a detour making sure to stay on the opposite side of the boulevard. Yes! the Germans are occupying the buildings; at the entrance stands a helmeted, armed guard in the sentry box still painted in the Belgian colors: black, yellow and red.

It is late afternoon, the sun is low but still warm and a light wind blows from the tree-shaded boulevards. Downtown the enemy soldiers are to be seen in cafés and especially in the shops. They buy everything in sight, mostly women's clothing, so I am told. They have plenty of money to spend, the rate of exchange having been arbitrarily fixed at one Reichsmark to twelve and a half Belgian francs.

At the corner of the Boulevard Anspach and the rue Neuve, near

29

the department store "L'Innovation", I see my first German officer. He is a caricature of a Prussian, with his yellow hair, pale eyes, and angular jaw perfectly shaped for the duelling scar that, mysteriously, doesn't adorn it. The common soldier passing by salutes him smartly except, when his hands are encumbered with packages, his whole body stiffens and the head turns toward the officer acknowledging his presence.

This is the Army of Occupation. Its members are strictly correct towards the civilian population. But most of the time they ignore us and we ignore them; we will never accept their presence on our soil. Currently there is not much we can do except present a sullen countenance, with the hope against all hope that England will prevail.

The sky beyond the huge windows fronting the Rue Neuve is now beginning to show the first faint tint of dusk. Time to go. I walk back a good part of the way feeling rather sad and upon reaching home, mother, sensing my discouragement, pours me a large bowl of chicken soup while Minouche, the cat, comes slowly out of the shadow and places a black satin head on my knees and yawns pinkly.

July 9, Tuesday. Mr. Van der Linden is our math teacher, demanding and hard to please. But, at times, his tough attitude softens somewhat and then for a few minutes he comments on the news. Today he mentioned that over the weekend he went to visit a friend, professor at the University of Louvain. The town has suffered badly during the fighting on the Dyle front, two months ago. The magnificent library, that had been put to the torch by the Germans in 1914 and rebuilt with American help, has been destroyed again. A few million books have gone up in flames together with a unique collection of incunables as well as arabic and medieval manuscripts which can never be replaced.

Nobody knows how it happened and who the perpetrators are: The British who defended the town or the Nazi attacker? We all think the latter: he had done it in 1914, why not again? It seems that the St. Peter's medieval church as well as the 14th-century Town Hall have escaped serious damage.

July 11, Thursday. We work hard in school with classes starting at 8h15 to noon and from 13h30 to 16h30, Monday through Saturday. On Tuesdays and Thursdays, however, we have the afternoon off.

Today after morning classes and a light lunch, I take my bike and ride towards the park of Laeken and the Castle, which in normal times is the residence of King Léopold. He still resides here at present, but as a prisoner of war. The castle is off-limits. As I walk close by, pushing my bike, I notice the swastika flying on top of the palace and two German soldiers on guard at the entrance. How humiliating for the King and for us! Could we have fought better to avoid this defeat? As far as I am concerned, the answer is NO. The Dutch were finished in five days; we held on for eighteen, and the Allies, French and English, with all their might could not stop the juggernaut.

On my way back I notice that the Germans have posted their own road signs and they flourish everywhere: Kommandatur, Ortskommandatur, Kriegslazaret, Soldatenkino, Zum Luftschutzraum, NSKK, Bezirkstelle, Feldgendarmerie, Arbeitsamt, etc.

July 14, Sunday. More and more refugees are coming back. There was a first wave just after the capitulation. Then a trickle and finally, after the fall of France, a second wave more important and persistent. The tale of some refugee-friends is a somber one: heat, dust, hunger, thirst, bombing, death, and hostile reception by the French, who blame their defeat on the Belgians in general and on the "traitor" King in particular.

An interesting item: almost all my friends point to the correctness of all representatives of the Wehrmacht they came in contact with. Compared to the French, the Germans are "good guys."

Some refugees unfortunately will never make it back from the Exodus. They were killed, about 12,000 of them I am told, not by the bad Frenchmen but by the bullets and bombs of the "good" Germans. Let's not forget it.

July 16, Tuesday. From the Nazi-controlled radio commentaries and newspaper articles one can deduct that the Germans are confident they have won the war. There is still England but, with a little push, the English people will understand that the game is over. What can they oppose to the victorious German Army, if Hitler launches his troops againt their island?

July 20, Saturday. Yesterday, speaking before the Reichstag, Hitler offered England "peace or destruction".

"I feel myself obliged to make one more appeal to reason to England, not as a victor but for the triumph of the common sense".

I listened to part of his speech in a radio rebroadcast. I understand the language, thanks to my two years of German in school, rendered easier by my knowledge of Flemish, a related language. It was, however, rather difficult to follow Hitler in his harangue, not because of his shouting and ranting, there was very little of that, but because of his harsh accent coming I guess from his Austrian background. I could make out his attack against Churchill (which he pronounces Shoorshill) and his prophecy that a great Empire will be destroyed.

This morning in the newspaper I note the end of the speech:

"In this hour I feel it to be my duty before my own conscience to appeal once more to reason and common sense in Great Britain as well as elsewhere. I consider myself in a position to make this appeal since I am not the vanquished begging for favors, but the victor speaking in the name of reason.

"I can see no reason why the war must go on. I am saddened to think of the sacrifices it will demand. I should like to prevent them, also for my own people".

July 21, Sunday. Belgian National Holiday. All patriotic demonstrations including flying the flag .have been forbidden. I think people will keep a low profile: they don't want to taunt the Germans and create a tense situation that could lead to clashes and reprisals.

The Nazi papers are full of praise for Hitler's "magnanimous" and "generous" offer for peace. The British people surely, in spite of some of their "unscrupulous politicians", will accept this last chance to get out of the war and achieve peace with apparently no conditions attached.

July 23, Tuesday. Yesterday and the day before, every Nazi commentator was elated, optimistic, confident that England would not turn down Hitler's peace offer. The war is practically over.

Hitler is the master of Western Europe and the British are not crazy. They will recognize there is no sane alternative. They will choose peace.

Today, they are mad. First, the BBC without consulting the government said NO. This was later confirmed by Lord Halifax. The war will go on. The British are our only chance that one day we will be freed from this Nazi dictatorship.

July 28, Sunday. Father tells us that at a meeting with the top brass of the Belgian National Railroads, high officials of the Deutsche Reichsbahn have demanded a detailed and complete inventory of the rolling stock (locomotives, goods- and passengers cars), equipment, personnel, with emphasis on losses incurred during the eighteen days of the invasion, including all railroad bridges destroyed during that period.

The Reichsbahn wants to integrate the Belgian rail network, very dense in our country, with their own system. This demand, Father adds, make sense if the Nazis decide to invade England. This is not a rumor. Father got the news from an excellent source.

Well, if it's not to invade Albion it certainly will help greatly in the plunder of Belgium'd resources and that of other occupied countries.

August 3, Saturday. To get some exercise I went pedaling along the Boulevard de Smet de Naeyer up to the Chaussée Romaine or Roman Road which, two thousand years ago, connected Gesoriacum (Boulogne), Castellum Menapiorum (Cassel) to Atuatuca Tongrorum (Tongeren) and Colonia Agrippinensis (Cologne). I know this because in school we studied and discussed the Roman roads in Belgium and Northern France.

As usual, the Roman Road is built on the high ground so that, from here, one has a good view of Brussels and its western suburbs. As I sat down under a tree enjoying the scenery, the noise of airplanes turned my attention to the aerial activity north and north-west of the city where the Belgians had two Air Force bases: Evere and Grimbergen.

Planes were coming in and going up in an almost incessant shuttle; I cannot very easily identify the types of aircraft above Evere but the ones landing at Grimbergen, on their approach for landing, pass directly above me allowing a good look.

I have not yet learned to recognize all types of Nazi aircraft but I can readily identify at least three of them. The easiest one is the Junkers JU-87, better known as the STUKA, a dive-bomber that played an important role in the Polish campaign and in the battle of the West. Its fixed landing gear, wings configuration, relatively low speed and protruding cockpit makes it easily recognizable. Further, we have the DORNIER or "flying pencil", with its stubby nose, straight body and double empennage; it is a cinch even for an amateur. And finally, there is the HEINKEL 111 bomber, perfectly streamlined, almost like a bullet, with on top a bubble for the crew and another one, underneath, for a gunner as defense.

The plane's underside is painted for camouflage in patches of dark and light green colors. These monsters were bombing or strafing us two months ago and are now being made ready to terrorize the Brits into submission.

I ride back home in almost complete darkness. In the imposed and enforced blackout the stars glitter more brightly in the sweep of the sky. There is no moon...

August 6, Tuesday This Sunday we had our first "official" scouting meeting since May 10th. Some informal meetings have been held in the last three months but were lightly attended because of the circumstances. It was nice to get together again. No one is missing except for one of our Troop leaders now a prisoner of war in Germany.

I joined the Boy Scouts in October 1938 and I love it. I like the friendship, the outdoor activities and the discipline freely accepted. It has also helped me discover and improve some of the skills I didn't know I had, such as ability for leadership, organization and even excellence in Morse signaling, to which I can add quick reflexes and good speed in track and field. I have honed these skills as a young boy in France, as a member of the athletic society: L'ALERTE.

A regular meeting starts with Mass at the parish church followed by breakfast, after which we normally go on an outing for the day, very often to the Forest of Soignes. It is a superb forest covering 11,000 acres south of the city and is a leftover of the immense woods that, in pre-Roman times, covered the land situated between the Scheldt and the Sambre rivers. It was later used by the

Romans, as a source of wood to manufacture charcoal which was exported all over the western part of the Empire.

We take tram No 16 to Watermaal-Boitsfort, the end of the line. A group of about forty, we fill a good part of the streetcar, equipped with rucksacks containing our provisions for the day. Our uniform consists of a felt hat with a leather band, like the one Baden Powell, the Founder, wears in his pictures. The front is adorned with an enameled, ruby red Jerusalem Cross, at the center of which is a white fleur-de-lys. We wear a dark blue sweater over a lighter blue shirt, a leather belt, short navy blue pants, gray knee-high socks and good comfortable walking shoes. Around the neck, a scarf, in the colors of the Troop, neatly folded to leave only a small triangle, falls neatly at the back of the neck. In our case, the 26th Troop-Brussels, it is green with a bright yellow edge.

Both sweater and shirt are adorned on the left breast with the embroidered Jerusalem Cross; on the right you find the rank insignia.

August 9, Friday. We received today an incredible letter from Sister Rosa. It was posted in Belgium but since she lives in Armentières, a town smack on the border, it is quite easy to get to a Belgian mailbox. The incredible news is that Jules Wille, our brother-in-law, was taken prisoner near Lille and directed to go on foot to a transit camp very near Armentières. The great confusion resulting from the unusual number of POWs allowed Jules to slip away and go straight home... in uniform! Unfortunately, after a few hours he returned to the camp, fearful that the Germans would look for him, perhaps with disastrous consequences for himself and the family.

This might well be. We are of the opinion, however, that in the utter confusion, the Germans would not have even known of his existence. The only problem would have been a denunciation. It could be avoided by staying in hiding for a month or two.

August 12, Monday. André Renard and his brother Gustave are fellow Boy Scouts. They live in Strombeek-Bever, a big village situated very close to the Grimbergen airfield now used by the Luftwaffe.

In the last few days, André tells me, there has been a great deal of activity at the airfield. The air above Strombeek and

35

Brother Lucien and the author were proud of and active in the
Scouting Movement

surrounding communities is filled with twin-engine planes, mostly Heinkels, Dorniers and some Junkers 88 (not Stukas). "Something big is brewing" is the comment in the street. We shall see...

August 15, Thursday. The "street" was right. The latest news is that twin-engine bombers are hitting some ports in England in preparation, one can assume, of the big invasion. We see more and more of these planes, with the distinctive black cross outlined in white, flying low above our heads. Lots of rumors have spread. The latest would let you believe that the British have developed a secret weapon against German airplanes. It is supposed to be a gun shooting shells which, when they explode, extend big nets to snare enemy aircraft. I don't believe a word of it but it shows the type of nonsense people propagate for lack of solid information.

The Nazi radio meanwhile announces tremendous victories over the Royal Air Force or RAF. They shot down, they say, seventy-one British planes and admit nineteen of their own aircraft missing. Could it be that we are witnessing the beginning of the Invasion of Great Britain?

August 19th, Monday. The Nazi propaganda machine is all geared up and triumphant. The German air blitz has swept the length of south-east England on August 15th in the greatest air attack of the war. According to the Nazis, the Luftwaffe used more than a thousand bombers and fighters in the attacks. Greater London was hit as well as other cities.

The latest rumor (could it be true?) is that Hitler has arrived at Western Headquarters to supervise the predicted offensive against Great Britain.

August 24, Saturday. It is common knowledge that the Germans are assisting the refugees trekking back from the unoccupied zone of France. The troops are in a good mood and acting in a very efficient and courteous way, as mentioned earlier. It is of course a ploy, a means to ingratiate themselves with the civilian population, to keep it docile and willing to collaborate with the new powers.

As a consequence, there has been a third wave of returning refugees in Brussels and, through the Boy Scouts National Center, there has been a call for volunteers to help at the reception areas.

I did volunteer and was asked to report to one of these centers situated near the church of Les Sablons. The building has been fitted with bunk beds, three high, in all available rooms. There must have been over seventy persons, men women and children. But they are not mere refugees; they are people who have nowhere to go, being moved here and there, until a permanent abode can be found for them.

My first surprise in entering the premises was the pungent smell of unwashed bodies emanating from the rooms. There was no ventilation despite the fact that the windows can be opened at will. Although the weather has not been that great over the last few days, it is decidedly not cold. I find out very soon that most people here have lost hope and are in a state of apathy. They move slowly around like automata and stare at me with lusterless eyes, rendered dim and melancholy, it seems, by despair and undernourishment.

Nobody, I find out, seems to be in charge. I take over and round up a few boys who seem to have some energy left. I tell them to open at least one window in every room. Despite a few protests, in twenty minutes time the air is breathable again. Next comes the kitchen. It is not as messy or dirty as expected. I soon found out why. No food is prepared here. Three times a day the Red Cross shows up to feed the group. The ladies bring everything: food, drinks, plates and cutlery. No time is lost: five minutes to line up, thirty minutes to eat, ten minutes or so for cleanup and cutlery recovery and they are gone.

I found a few brooms and some cleaning products in a closet and in no time I have two women per room cleaning floors and bathrooms. Two hours later the building is a little better place to live.

In late afternoon, an official-looking gentleman shows up to take over for the night. He is a large man, heavy, full at the belt, a trifle bald and very slow in speech. He politely asks me to come back the next morning. I tell him that I am not free tomorrow and the day after but can come back on Tuesday. It's a deal.

As I walk back to the streetcar that will bring me back home, I notice the cloudy sky. I know, however, that as the wind holds, there is not much likelihood of rain; I am glad, for I don't want rain after a day of gloom and doom.

August 27, Tuesday. I show up at the Sablons Center, as it is called, bright and early this Tuesday only to find out that the City of Brussels has decided to move the refuges to a better organized camp near Antwerp. My services are no longer needed but I am asked to escort an Italian couple and their young boy to the North Railroad Station.

The fellow introduces himself but I don't quite get the name, something like "Gastella". His wife, in the foulest of moods, with eyes glowing like lamps, greets me with the choicest imprecations which, although I don't understand them, leave me with a clear comprehension of their meaning, so deep are the feelings of her Latin soul.

They are immigrants being repatriated to Italy and they hate it. But there is no choice. Musso has decided to bring back, *ins Heim*, all the Italians scattered in Nazi-occupied territories, no matter what. How this couple landed at this refugee center I cannot fathom.

With three suitcases, two bags and a few toys, we take the tram at the Sablons in the direction of the Porte de Schaerbeek. The idea is to catch a connection to the North Station, but for some reason all streetcars pass us by as full as pregnant whales. So we walk down the Boulevard Botanique, pausing now and then to rest our stiff arms.

The little boy is carrying his toys, a task he can't handle very well. As a consequence we have to stop more often than we wish to help him gather the precious treasures he keeps scattering around. About half-way down the hill, at a new stop his mother, exasperated, takes one of the toys, a tattered stuffed bear, and throws it over the balustrade into the park. Some stroller in the garden must have been very surprised to see a worn-out present landing at his feet, or perhaps on his head.

We make it to the station and are led, after many queries, to the "Office Italien de Rapatriement", a big name for such a small, dusty cubicle stuck in a forgotten corner of the station. It is empty. A handwritten sign tell us that the repatriation representative will be back soon.

I feel that my assignment is over and prepare to take leave of my charges but they want me to stay, to make sure they will be taken care of in a proper fashion. I acquiesce to their wish and we all sit down on a very hard wooden bench. Mr. "Gastella" is not too happy with the Italian repatriation scheme. As an immigrant in northern France he had a nice job with a transport company until the day he was told to return to his homeland. He sold everything he had at a great loss but hopes to be compensated for it. His great fear is to be, at 32, enlisted in the armed forces. He shows me a three-day old copy of "La Voce d'Italia," where a Signor Maida, speaking of Greece, declares that "it will not be many days before the British find themselves up against some new surprise".

Our little talk is interrupted by the representative's return. He is a Nazi. I know it because he is wearing on his lapel the badge of the NSDAP, a black swastika on a white background with red edge. Being of the superior race he offers no greetings, checks the couple's papers, declares them in order and writes up tickets and reservation slips for a train to Venice via Cologne, Frankfurt, Munich and Innsbruck. Plus restaurant vouchers for the trip.

Job done, after a rather emotional farewell to the couple, not forgetting the unhappy looking little boy, I leave the crowded station and head for home. Thinking of the arrogant Nazi, I reflect that a face such as his has not been fashioned by a lifetime of good works and pious thoughts.

3

September 2, 1940 - May 29, 1941

September 2, Monday. I have not noted much war news in the last two weeks, because it is so difficult to get reliable information. We refuse to believe the Nazi propaganda although I guess there is some truth in it, especially now that the Germans are winning. The news from London is certainly more reliable and we eagerly listen, sometimes several times a day, to the BBC. This is strictly forbidden by the "Militärsbefehlhaber für Belgien und Nordfrankreich", but nobody pays attention. To make sure we don't listen to the British news, the Nazis have started jamming the airwaves. Even when there is no German intervention, the reception can be pretty bad because of the weather conditions. There are days when we can't hear a thing and have to rely for news on other sources, mostly unreliable.

September 3, Tuesday. The Nazis have been bombing England for almost three weeks and now it appears that the RAF and the British ground defenses have forced the Luftwaffe to the conclusion that massive air attacks by day have not gained the quick results required. Will they bomb under the cover of darkness?

British bombers in the meantime have attacked targets in Germany by night. Stuttgart and Berlin have been hit. This is confirmed by Goebbels but, he says, the damage is minimal.

We had an air raid warning last night; the FLAK gunfire kept everybody awake and what a racket it was! The British planes could be heard but no bombs fell. They were, no doubt, on their way to Germany.

September 5, Thursday. As an employee of the Belgian Railroad, Father is entitled to a certain number of free trips for himself and every member of the family. This year, for the obvious reasons, very few tickets have been used. To get rid of me, because I prove to be so restless, he offers me a round trip ticket and suggests I visit my godfather in Izegem, a medium-sized town (18,000 inh.) in the West Flanders province. I accept with alacrity and get ready.

September 12, Thursday. Here are a few notes about my visit to my godfather, Joseph Devoldere, my mother's brother, and his wife Jeanne. Izegem is special to me because it is the birthplace of my mother Marie-Emelie Devoldere.

My godfather is about my height. Solid of body, dark hair sprinkled with grey smoothly brushed back. About forty-five years old. Chin freshly shaved, everything immaculate.

At first, I didn't recognize my aunt, but then women can change their appearance at will. She appeared to me with silver-blond hair under a blue head scarf, fair eyelashes, a firm friendly mouth and a composure which gave her an air of graceful reserve.

It is evening. After an early dinner we are sitting in the little garden enjoying the balmy weather looking out at the splendor of the sky overhead. Sunset is staining the sky when there is a knock at the front door and the sound of heavy boots in the hall. To my astonishment there appears, framed by the door, a German soldier, quite at ease, with a big smile on his face. I am dumbfounded. For the first time since the beginning of the war, I see the ENEMY close by, and cannot believe it.

His name is Kurt and he is billeted here because of the great influx of troops in the region. There are simply not enough barracks, schools and other public buildings to accommodate them all. Hence the billet system which the Germans used also in the Great War, exactly in the same area.

My godfather tells me that he had no choice but to accept the presence of Kurt. He finds himself quite lucky to have drawn "a good number" as Kurt happens to be a quiet, very polite and unobtrusive "guest". He is not tall, five foot eight or nine and wiry; he probably never weighed more than 140 lbs. with his boots on and after the biggest meal of his life. He has blond wavy hair with auburn tints, a thin aquiline nose and assertive hazel eyes. He displays a deep tan acquired, I found out later, during the battle of France. He smiles mostly with his eyes, perhaps because he is sensitive about his discolored teeth. He is a member of the armies that, from Walcheren in Holland and all along the Belgian and French coasts up to Boulogne, are mustered in preparation for the invasion of England. Or so I surmise.

The conversation with the young soldier is somewhat desultory. He speaks "nur Deutsch"; my godfather speaks reasonably good German, my aunt very little but the Flemish language helps. Although I understand most of what he says, I have no fluency and cannot contribute much to the conversation.

My godfather mentions that Kurt is with an artillery battalion. This I know already because the black epaulettes with red piping distinguish him from the infantry wearing forest green epaulettes (like the rest of the uniform) with light green piping. We talk about the military situation but he has even less information than we have. All he can say is repeating a line of the war song "Und wir fahren gegen England", the equivalent of the British (and French) "We're gonna hang out the washing on the Siegfried Line" as the introduction fanfare announcing a new German victory.

On Sunday, September 8, my godfather and I, with a group of his friends, travel east of Izegem, to the outskirts of the town of Kortrijk (Courtrai in French) to attend a competition at the Longbowmen Guild of St. Sebastian. The Guild is a very old association of archers whose foundation goes back to 1323, only 617 years ago!

The competition is held in the corner of a meadow with easy access to the road. The triangular area consists of a pole, fifty feet tall, which can be lowered by means of a counterweight balanced on an iron rod at its base. At the top is perched a big triangle made of three horizontal bars on which are affixed several heavy feathers, called doves, of different colors: green, blue, red and at the very top, gold. The goal is to shoot down one or more of these feathers and receive prizes matched to the colors. The longbowman who topples the golden dove is declared "King" for the year. A roll of drums will announce the feat amidst great excitement and rejoicing.

Waiting for this happening is a young maiden, dressed all in white, holding a crown of orange flowers. Around her waist she wears a belt of same color to which are affixed four separate ribbons, also orange, held by four sturdy young men, her guard of honor. She is the one who will bestow on the new King the crown and the heavy "collar" made of heavy damask (a fabric manufactured in Kortrijk that goes back to Roman times and perhaps earlier) on which are attached silver cockles of great antiquity and a beautifully crafted silver dove dangling at its end.

The ceremony completed, everyone gets ready for the back- to-town procession, arranged in a rigid order of precedence, while the drummers beat the rhythm. Colorful flags are waved and tossed up in the air in an intricate ballet of arabesques and caught again with amazing dexterity. A horseman meanwhile gallops to the home of the newly crowned King bringing the great news to his wife and family. She expresses her thanks by offering the messenger a five-frank coin.

The cortège is now ready to start. First come the drummers then the flag bearers swinging their banners, followed by a rider carrying with immense pride the great flag of the guild. It is a square standard made of silk, at least six foot by six decorated long ago with floral decorations and a huge Burgundian Cross in the form of a St. Andrew cross. At the top one can distinguish the arms of the Holy Roman Empire, at the bottom a scene representing the martyrdom of St. Sebastian, the patron-saint of the guild and a date: 1668.

Next comes the happy King proudly wearing the badge of honor followed by a compact group. These include the president of the guild elected for life, the four members of the board, the elders and deans; next the main body of the association in the midst of which, holding aloft a heavy frame representing the patron saint, is a small group surrounded by young boys carrying flaming torches.

We join the cortège, my godfather providing commentary, and soon we reach the banquet place in the guild's premises, close to the parish hall and even closer to the tavern De Zwarte Leeuw (The Black Lion) which provides food and drink.

The women join us there. In peacetime, the feast would last three days with the womenfolk attending only on the second day. In view of the war restrictions however, the ceremonies are reduced to a single day.

Godfather Seph (that's his nickname) reminisces about the "good old days" when, over a three-day period, lots of beer was absorbed and lots of victuals dispensed. The scene reminds me of Pieter Brueghel's famous painting: *The Flemish Kermis*. It is more decorous of course but, except for the clothes, we have the same solid farmers with their rubicund wives, the farm hands, much leaner, the trade people, the "ambachtsleden" or craftsmen: the painters, weavers, spinners, fullers as well as the woodcarvers, carpenters, locksmiths, bricklayers and many others.

I am offered one of those Belgian beers, so delicious if drunk lukewarm, and a meal in itself, brewed by one of those small breweries which abound in Flanders. We are not a member of the guild and cannot attend the banquet, but nevertheless the experience was delightful and memorable!

On the appointed day for my return home, I consult the railroad timetable. I am advised that the way by Bruges or Ghent is unsafe. In the last few weeks the RAF has kept a close watch on the invasion preparations and has bombed and strafed the Belgian coast, especially around Ostend and Zeebrugge. Bruges, only nine miles from this last town and about sixteen from Ostend, could easily be hit. So can Ghent, although there is less danger. The RAF is targeting railroad junctions, air bases and ship concentrations. I decide to detour via Kortrijk, Oudenaarde, Zottegem and Denderleeuw. The return was uneventful and I arrived safely at home late in the evening.

September 14, Saturday. The Luftwaffe is conducting very heavy air raids upon London and other English towns. This is confirmed by the BBC. The Nazi propaganda calls it the "England Blitz" or, more often, Der London Blitz.

Prime Minister Churchill, in a broadcast, two nights ago, has given warning that the invasion may be attempted soon and made this call to his people: "Every man and woman will therefore prepare himself to do his duty, whatever it may be, with special pride and care. With devout but sure confidence I say that God defends the right."

September 17, Tuesday. The Germans, with long-range guns on the French channel coast have begun to shell Dover and, apparently, also London, much further away.

It is a surprise for me. I don't know of any such guns except "Die grosse Bertha" of the Great War. Would the Germans still have it and be fit for re-use? Does it have the range to reach London?

Is it pure Nazi propaganda?

September 18, Wednesday. We have started the new school year 1940-41. I am in class 4A meaning another four years of high school. Some new faces but mostly the same schoolmates as last year. Quite a few new teachers, however, but this is not a consequence of the war. A simple reshuffling; the school system, in Brussels and suburbs, has not suffered from the invasion. As long as there is no overt action against the German Army, the Occupant leaves us alone. The secret police however must be watching.

We have a very tight class schedule, six days a week, Monday through Saturday, with a half-day off on Tuesdays and Thursdays, as I have said earlier. The courses include: French (composition, literature, diction/public speaking); Flemish (with same subdivisions); Latin, English, German, Math, History (lots of it), Geography, Sciences and Religious Education.

September 22, Sunday. As usual, on Sunday, we have our Troop meeting at the headquarters located in two of the unused classes at the St. Michael school. Today, we spend the morning performing various activities, repairing and cleaning the premises.

In the afternoon, we march toward the Abbaye de Dielegem and its park. The Abbey no longer exists but the "demeure abbatiale" or abbot's residence is still standing. It had been restored in the 18th century. The abbey itself was founded 800 years ago at about the same time as the neighboring town of Brussels.

Our Troop, has the reputation of being a culture-oriented unit and I approve. Yes, we like the outdoor and we are not afraid of a long march, or a rigorous exercise. We, however, combine these activities with visits to museums, small churches, impressive cathedrals, medieval castles and other monuments.

October 8, Tuesday. The impact of war and occupation, after the big blow of the May events, are felt every day like a mass of pinpricks to be suffered and pondered. The blackout however which is a daily occurrence is more than that. It has changed our way of life more thoroughly than anything we might have dreamed of only a few months ago.

In the first place, every evening we have to spend five to ten minutes blacking out our home. If we leave a chink visible from the street, an irate policeman will ring the bell furiously and threaten us with heavy fines. Or worse - it happened to us - a German patrol, fully armed and aggressive, will bang at the door with their rifle butts. One or two of them will enter, investigate our blackout arrangements and yell at the top their lungs in their harshest German, terrorizing the whole family. They will then leave in a big show of clanking of rifles against their gas mask canisters and the crunching noise of their hobnailed boots. Funny, I have noticed that our dear occupants, when on duty, always carry their gas masks attached to the belt, in the back, mostly on the left side. This must be army regulation and a display of a fear of gas attacks. Will it come to that?

I remember struggling on May 10th with brown paper, cut in strips and applied with adhesive made of white flour and water, to all windows in regular squares of about 8 by 8 inches. Everybody in the neighborhood was performing the same task and all houses seemed to be transformed into medieval dwellings looking through their mullioned eyes.

Nor is this the end of it. At night, to make one's way from street to back street, whether in the suburbs or the center of town, is a prospect fraught with depression and even danger. Accidents have risen sharply. People walk into trees, break an ankle stepping inadvertently from the sidewalk into the road or toppling from railroad platforms. Most injuries as the result of blackout are not serious of course, but it is painful enough to stub a toe on an unseen curb, crash into invisible trash cans, or bouncing off corpulent pedestrians...

So people turn to flashlights. They are allowed as long as the glass or lens is painted blue, unfortunately diminishing their usefulness.

Civilian cars, there are fewer and fewer of them, and military vehicles are fitted with masked headlights, the light coming through a narrow horizontal slit which must make driving at night rather difficult and hazardous.

47

Not that many people go out in the dark. We are under permanent martial law decreed by the Militärbefehlshaber General Baron Alexander von Falkenhausen. That means that the Occupant can do pretty much what he wants: requisition food, vehicles, horses and all kind of industrial products. And also impose a curfew every night starting from 11 pm or midnight to 5 am. Only essential services with special permits may be on the road within this time period. As a consequence all nightlife has gone. Restaurants close up early and so do theatres, cinemas and concert halls. People stay at home and listen to radio Brussels (French or Flemish) which broadcasts classical and light music as well as the bombastic and biased German communiqués. Most Belgians however try to follow the BBC programs in English, French or Flemish. Or they read books, lots of them, play cards, dominoes and any other games that can relieve the atmosphere of impotence and even despair which too often grips the population.

October 16, Wednesday. The Nazis continue their heavy bombing raids over England with the hope of breaking the morale of the common people. Their news reports over the radio are more and more hyperbolic. The Luftwaffe has now started to bomb Great Britain at night. We can hear, after sunset, the rumble of the bombers leaving the airfields in the north and returning, flying low, several hours later.

October 28, Monday. Our dear friend Musso has invaded Greece. His troops have attacked from bases in Albania, a country he invaded on Good Friday, April 7, 1939.

Ever since my encounter with the Italian couple and their little son, I have taken some interest in Italy. I had not, up to that point, paid any attention to that country except through Roman history and the Pope in Rome.

The question is what is Benito up to? First, I discover that he has been dictator and master of his country since 1922, a full eleven years before Hitler. Second, Musso is trying to unify his country of fifty provinces all of which, deeply rooted in their own past, want to follow their own independent course. Third, to achieve this unity, in the midst of latent anarchy, he tries to revive the glory and splendor that was Rome, the Roma Aeterna, the Immortal Empire. Fourth, to instill some nationalistic pride in the

Italian psyche, the Duce favors an expansionist policy. Hence the Mare Nostrum, the conquest of Abyssinia, the takeover of Albania, the attack on France and now the invasion of Greece. The last move puzzles me: what is the reasoning behind this action? Greece is a poor country with no raw materials and its strategic importance cannot be overwhelming.

Could we apply to Musso the Latin proverb: *Fax mentis, incendium gloriae*? (A burning desire for glory is a torch to the mind.)

What then? I guess it is an attempt to stir up public opinion at home. He also wants to show Hitler, of whom he must be extremely jealous, that he can line up a few additional conquests of his own.

November 3, Sunday. No troop meeting today. It was held on November 1st, on all All Saints Day. Yesterday, November 2, day of Commemoration of All Departed Souls, we went as a group, to visit the tomb of a schoolmate François Renard, the oldest brother of André and Gustave Renard, who died of meningitis, a little more than a year ago, aged 16. The Renard parents were attending and cried their eyes out. The little ceremony was extremely moving.

November 12, Tuesday. Yesterday was Armistice Day. All ceremonies and displays of flags were forbidden by the occupation authorities but there were sporadic demonstrations downtown and in other Belgian cities. Nothing spectacular however. It is interesting to note that these manifestations are the first public gesture of defiance against the German occupation.

November 16, Saturday. Coventry has been the victim of the most concentrated raid, and perhaps the worst, since the beginning of the blitz against Great Britain.

The Nazi radio claims that 500 planes took part and 500 tons of explosives as well 30,000 incendiary bombs were dropped. The same source adds that the raid caused tremendous devastation; fires were visible from the channel, 220 km away. I look at the map and find that Coventry is an industrial town, southeast of Birmingham, and an important arms manufacturing center.

The BBC confirms the news and mentions that the center of town as well as the cathedral have been destroyed.

November 18, Monday. The RAF continues its attacks on Berlin. Their first bombing of the Nazi capital took place on the night of August 25. I am told that the Nazis don't like it a bit. The confidence of the four million Berliners must have been shattered. Göring had promised the Germans that no enemy bomb would fall on German soil.

And then, on September 4, at the Sportpalast in Berlin and, before an audience of nurses and social workers, Hitler, mentioning the bombings of the capital, did assure his people that: "When the British air force drops two or three or four thousand kilograms of bombs, then we will, in one night, drop 150, 250, 300 or 400 thousand. kilograms!"

The massive night attacks on London, Coventry and other cities of England for sure look like the reprisals announced by Nazi-in-chief, also known as Little Mustache.

November 22, Friday. Benito is stuck in the mountains of the Greek-Albanian front. His efforts to conquer Greece have not been more successful than the offensive against France, in June. The Macaronis are decidedly not very good fighters, or perhaps they are poorly led and badly equipped. The result is the same. In some parts of the front the Greeks are now fighting on Albanian soil. Truly, it is the fight of David against Goliath: 50 million Italians against 8 million Hellenes.

The BBC tells us that President Roosevelt has pledged aid to Greece. This is nothing but posturing and empty promises. How can America concretely help Hellas?

November 27, Wednesday. Brother Michel and I share the same bedroom and, at night, before we go to sleep we talk about our daily activities and experiences until Mother shouts at us from the floor below that it is high time we stop the cackling and keep quiet. It seems that, at times, we are a little loud in our arguments. Michel, four years older than myself, is an avid reader always willing to impart his acquired knowledge. The other day he shared with me his enthusiasm for a book he is reading over and over again. The title: Trois Hommes dans un Bateau, the French translation of Jerome K. Jerome's classic: *Three Men in a Boat.* He has read it so often and so thoroughly that he can recount by heart the most famous passages of this delightful book. I read it and loved it too. Two weeks ago, I chose to present it in English class and it was quite a success.

When we talk about war events, Michel calls me a "stratège en chambre", that is "an armchair strategist". I am not sure whether he means it as a compliment. All I know is that I try to understand what is happening, realizing that due to lack of experience, historical knowledge and accurate information, I might reach the wrong conclusions. I often consult with my history teacher who is wise, learned and has access to not readily available news. The latter comes from his contacts with politicians, past and present (inactive for the time being) and professors at the University of Louvain. And other sources?

December 2, Monday. Yesterday I came up with the following item for discussion with brother Michel. (I call him Mich', pronounced Mish in English). "Will Hitler invade England soon?" The answer is NO! Winter is here and the weather in the Channel is very bad at this time of the year making it impossible for an armada of ships, to make an orderly and successful crossing. Furthermore, Hitler might understand that he should not fall into the trap of attempting an overseas invasion without a strong navy.

December 10, Tuesday. Sister Léona and I called on a few friends who live near the new Basilica, under construction since 1904 and far from being finished. It was the hour after sunset when we came back. The pale moon was straight up overhead, three-quarters full. There was still some milky blue in the sky and only the evening star hung in the west, yellow as candlelight.

In the distance one could hear the droning of airplanes, German aircraft we assumed, on their way to bomb London. Or rather, as the sound of the heavy throb of the bombers was approaching, aircraft coming back from England. Suddenly, without warning, searchlights start to cross the sky in stiff awkward arcs, plunging thousands of feet in the air, each terminating in a kind of nebulous mist. The anti-aircraft guns start to blaze away with every ounce of energy they can muster. The noise mingled with the sorrowful wail of the siren announcing, belatedly, an air raid, was hideous. The lightning and crack of explosions right above our heads make us beat a hasty retreat into the recess of a deep doorway. A few seconds later we can hear the clatter of shrapnel on the roof followed by a shower of fragments bouncing at our feet in a spectacular display of sparks. I ring the bottom bell of our shelter but no one answers. A few minutes later the cannonade ceases as abruptly as it started. Impassive, the RAF planes continue on their way to Germany.

The all clear sounds soon after and as I step down on the sidewalk, my foot touches a piece of shell fragment which I scoop up and immediately drop with an "Ouch!" as it is still very hot. I wrap it in my handkerchief and we reach home safely, commenting on the fact that anti-aircraft guns are as dangerous to people on the ground as they are to planes up in the sky. The recovered shrapnel, with the sharpest edges I have ever seen, measures about four inches long by about a third of an inch thick and looks deadly. I will keep it as a souvenir.

December 13, Friday. At school, we have started the first quarter exams and we will be very busy until December 19. On the 21st, at noon, Christmas vacation will begin.

I am not too concerned about these exams. The courses I like, because I study them with enthusiasm, will need no special preparation. The rest will be the object of intense cramming and, with the help of a good memory, I usually come out all right. The classes I favor are history, including Church history in religious education, all languages as well as French composition and literature.

December 14, Saturday. Today we get half a day off to study for next week. We have seven exams in five days. This break gives me an opportunity to catch up with the news.

I discover that Benito's invasion of Greece is now turning into a disaster. Hitler must be experiencing a nice feeling of German "Schadenfreude" (malicious pleasure). He (Adolf), must also grow anxious about the situation. He cannot possibly let the Greeks inflict a serious defeat on the Italians.

December 16, Monday. Speaking of defeat. I hear that the Brits have attacked the Italians in North Africa; in Cyrenaica to be precise. They have regained the town of Sidi-el-Barrani they had lost in September.

December 20, Friday. The exams are over. Everybody relaxes; the teachers are in a good mood. Tomorrow we will get the results of our efforts or our laziness and then two weeks of *far niente*. (I am still pursued by the Italian ghost!) We return to school on Monday January 6.

December 24/25, Tuesday-Wednesday. Midnight Mass with the Troop at Our Lady of Lourdes' parish. The church was jammed. We had thereafter ersatz coffee and small cakes and I returned home before curfew. The "midnight" Mass really started at 7:30 pm and was over by 9 o'clock.

The day had been cold and misty. On the way back, without warning, a fog fell upon the town and snatched it from reality, swathing it in choking bands that snuffed out the blue lights and curtained off each man from his neighbor in a cocoon-like isolation. The fog rolled and heaped itself along the silent streets in grotesque configurations. Sounds turned secretive, unidentifiable; shapes loomed in the dark. There was a hazard at every step, a threat at every corner.

Without warning, a "gentleman", as drunk as a lord, bumped into me; I was about to consign him to a very warm spot when it occurred to me that all God's creatures have their uses!

1941

January 6, Monday. Back to school. Very cold and not much heating in the classroom. The Germans appropriate most of our coal for themselves. The rumors have it, and nowadays we live on rumors, that stricter rationing is in the offing. This would include meat, fish, eggs, bread, sugar, potatoes, butter, vegetables, soap and fuel. Coffee has disappeared and is now a luxury only the rich can afford. Food rations have been, so far, very adequate but this will change. The occupation troops have to be fed and we have lots of them! Readying for the invasion? No, as I said before. The weather in the North sea at this time of the year doesn't allow it. And this is nothing compared to the destructive storms one can expect in February.

The Luftwaffe activities, weather permitting, have not slowed down too much. The province of West Flanders and the coastal area of northern France are now a gigantic air base.

On December 30th, a huge air raid was conducted against London, the BBC announced; more than a thousand bombers were used and tens of thousand of incendiaries were dropped. It was the biggest night attack on London, since September.

Poor, courageous Englishmen. This is their New Year's present: terror and death.

January 9, Thursday. I missed President's Roosevelt's address in late December in which he pledges more aid to Britain and declares that the Axis forces will not win the war. This, coupled with another piece of news, makes me slightly more optimistic about the outcome of this conflict.

Here it is. The U.S. Defense Commission has announced the approval of contracts worth 2,500,000,000. Yes, two billion five hundred million pounds sterling! A staggering number. Furthermore, monthly production in the United States war industry has risen to 2,400 aircraft engines, 700 war planes, 100 tanks and 10,000 automatic rifles. This, in my opinion, is not enough.

But wait! Present British and American orders at hand total 50,000 planes, 130,000 aircraft engines, 9,200 tanks, 2,055,000 guns, 380 naval vessels, 200 merchant ships, 50,000 trucks and all kinds of other equipment. This is reassuring but will some reach Britain in time?

January 15, Wednesday. With the tightening of food supplies and the talk of tougher rationing, a number of experts are discussing what would be sufficient to maintain the health and the basic metabolic needs of the average Belgian citizen. They have come up with the following basic diet.

Minimum daily diet

300 gr. of bread - about 10 oz.
500 gr. of potatoes - about 1 lb.
1/3 liter of milk – a little less than 1 pint.
150 gr. of vegetables - 5 oz.
60 gr. of starches such as oatmeal - 2 oz.
100 gr. of meat or starches rich in proteins - about 4 oz.
30 gr. of fat, (butter, margarine, vegetable oils) - 1 oz.

The above can be supplemented with small amounts of cheese, fish, sugar and fruit. I discuss this list with Mother and express my concern that, as a growing boy, I don't find this diet very satisfactory. She reassures me: "Don't worry, if all our efforts to provide you with nourishing food fail, I can still serve you an excellent bowl of piled brick!" This is what I consider a sick sense of humor.

January 23, Thursday. The British are doing very well against the Italians in North Africa. It was announced yesterday that the town of Tobruk has fallen. I should mention however that it was not the British but the Australians who accomplished this feat.

I have never heard of Tobruk of course and I take a look at the map. I discover it to be an important port in Cyrenaica, not far from the Egyptian border. I also find out that Sollum and Sidi Barrani are small towns on the Egyptian side, liberated a few weeks ago. The Italian losses are heavy.

February 3, Monday. We must consider ourselves lucky, here in Belgium. So far we have not been too much of a target for the RAF despite the fact that the western part of the country is a base for the Wehrmacht and especially the Luftwaffe from where it raids England in considerable numbers, resulting in many deaths and extensive damage. The RAF responds by the bombing of Berlin and other German towns. They also attack the ports and bases of the invasion fleets. And although Brussels has several air bases, we have, up to now, been spared, any British incursion.

February 10, Monday. More great news from North Africa and it gives us a tremendous morale boost. In the last seven weeks, the "Imperial Army of the Nile" has advanced 700 kms from Marsa Matruk to Benghasi. They are now at the door of Libya. In between they took Bardia, Tobruk, Derna and Cyrene, all well-defended strongholds. The British or rather the "Imperial" troops have taken more than 110,000 prisoners. The morale of the latter is said to be very low. In their place mine would be too.

February 13, Thursday. At school, we are all excited about the British advance in Cyrenaica. We ask our geography teacher, who is always running around to his classes with big cardboard-backed maps, to show us where these events take place. He complies with alacrity.

We get a full-scale overview of Italy's imperial designs. It starts with the present colony of Libya/Cyrenaica the Italians are in the process of losing. Then also in Africa, we have Erythrea and neighboring Abyssinia. To this add Albania and Greece; they would also love to get Illyria they know as Dalmatia. And one should not forget Rhodes with the rest of the Dodecanese the islands off the southwest coast of Turkey, part of Italy since 1912. To cap it all, staged student demonstrations assemble on a regular basis, in front of Mussolini's palace in Rome, howling: *Tunisia, Jibuti, Corsica.*

A good lesson in political geography.

February 19, Wednesday. Field Marshal Milch is Göring's deputy for the Luftwaffe and probably runs the show. A few days ago, in a speech that was broadcasted over all German radio stations, he warned that "danger hovers over everybody in Germany". He also hinted that the Germans may expect more intensified raids by the Royal Air Force.

He had however, some consoling words! "If our night repose is sometimes disturbed, you may rest assured that during the day preceding the alarm, London had six alerts and then an uninterrupted raid from 6 p.m. to 6 a.m. "On the whole," he pursued, "Germany has suffered merely pinpricks" .He regretted that the German workers sometimes have to spend half of their nights in shelters and have to work the day.

To me these sleepless nights are not mere "pinpricks".

March 3, Monday. Hitler must not be very happy with the situation in Libya. To help the Italians who are in a complete rout, he is sending German troops to avoid utter collapse. In the meantime, the British with a battalion of Belgian troops, are attacking the Italian possessions in East Africa. They are winning and there is nothing the Germans can do about it. Mogadishu, in Abyssinia, has been liberated.

March 4, Tuesday. I have a hard time keeping up with the events. It is now axiomatic that every move by Musso is doomed to defeat unless Adolf intervenes to save the situation. It has happened in Libya, it is happening now in the Balkans. To help out the Italians in Greece, German troops have entered Bulgaria and are now marching towards the Greek-Bulgarian frontier. And to get to Bulgaria, the Nazis had to march through Rumania and you can be sure they were not too diplomatic about it: "Let us get through or else..."

March 10, Monday. During the weekend we moved to 192, Chaussée de Wemmel. It is a bigger house with more kitchen space for Mother and a laundry room. I have my own small bedroom under the roof, rather cold now and probably hot in the summer. I will miss the conversations with my brother Mich', but I am glad to have my private little space.

There is also a bigger garden where my parents intend to grow vegetables in the approaching spring. Behind the house is a municipal soccer field with the particularity of having in a corner, guess what? a tall pole for longbow archery! Now that the Nazis have forbidden the possession of any firearm, archery may become popular again.

March 14, Friday. The situation in the Balkans is not improving. Yugoslavia is under pressure to let German troops cross their country to join forces with the Italians and smash the Greek resistance; and at the same time, to kick out the British advisers who have come to help the Hellenes.

The overwhelming sentiment of the Yugoslav people and their armed forces are known to be against any surrender to the Nazis. It is obvious, however, that the Germans are working hard on wavering politicians to produce the country's compliance with their wishes.

March 15, Saturday. A footnote to history. (I wonder how many historical notes I will miss in this forever expanding war).

British warships have on Tuesday March 4 raided the Lofoten islands, a German-controlled fish oil center, off the coast of Norway, above the Arctic circle. The fish oil is important to the Nazis as it is used as glycerine in the manufacturing of explosives.

The warships destroyed a number of fish oil factories and a power station at each of the four principal ports of the islands and oil storages were set on fire. The ships came back with 215

German prisoners and about 300 Norwegian emigrants, the latter happy to escape the Nazi occupation.

Is this important news? Probably not. But a small victory is what we need at present to remind us that the German war machine is not perhaps as omnipotent and invincible as it seems to be.

March 21, Friday. The Lend-Lease law was voted by the U.S. Senate and signed into law on March 9th. This is great news. It will allow Great Britain to survive, fight on and win thanks to American arms, ammunition, planes, ships, tanks and trucks.

Doesn't this sounds like the introduction to a propaganda leaflet?

March 25, Tuesday. We had a "Fliegeralarm" (air raid) last night and we all took refuge in our "Luftschutzraum" (air shelter) in the basement. The warning came just before midnight, a wail rising and falling for two minutes in a sorrowful and depressing tone. There was not one siren but a series, as the note was taken up from sector to sector. Still half asleep we went down to the vaulted cellar that had been reinforced with a few solid beams and outfitted with picks and shovels, a few flashlights and water bottles. This is all of a psychological benefit of course, as a close hit would simply pulverize the house. In our neighborhood and I guess in the rest of the city, no solid, concrete air shelters have been built. Any heavy bombing of our area could turn into grave damage and serious loss of life.

The FLAK or "Feldluftabwehrkanone" (field anti-aircraft guns) turn into action. The shells shriek, wang! wang! wang! with great reverberation and the splinters bounce off the roofs, sidewalks and cobblestones. Then abruptly the guns become silent. Fifteen minutes later the all-clear sounds. We go back to bed and fall into a deep sleep almost instantly.

April 2, Friday. What a week, this past week! On March 25, under heavy pressure from the Nazis, Yugoslavia adheres to the tripartite pact with Hungary, Rumania and Bulgaria. The German troops can cross the country to attack the Greeks and the British. The same day however: coup d'Etat! The signature of the Pact has brought a public outcry of indignation in all of Yugoslavia; the Army and Air Force overthrow the government and place the Crown Prince on the throne as Peter II.

Hitler must be mad. It will not be long before he takes revenge for this affront. Like Napoléon, he will take this rebuff personally and act spitefully and perhaps irrationally. Dictators are all the same. It is said that Napoléon in his frequent fits of rage was chewing his hat; Hitler is said to be eating the carpet.

April 7, Monday. It had to happen. Hitler has invaded Yugoslavia starting with the bombing of Belgrade though it had been declared an open city. The Luftwaffe has dive-bombed the capital three times in the first day of war (yesterday), so says the Nazi propaganda.

Yugoslavia, not a small country, is about half the size of France. After a look at the map it seems obvious that the Wehrmacht will attack along the Sava and Danube valleys and reach Belgrade using blitzkrieg tactics. The rest of the country however is very mountainous and will be much more difficult to conquer.

The same day, April 6, in Moscow Stalin signed a pact of friendship with Yugoslavia. It says that in the event either signatory becoming the victim of aggression by a Third Power, the other party undertakes to maintain a friendly policy toward the first. (It doesn't engage Russia too much, does it?)

Hitler must have taken note and is probably chewing on another carpet.

Late news. The Germans have attacked Greece through Bulgaria.

April 9, Wednesday. Thessaloniki, in Greece, has fallen to the Germans. The British are rushing troops to help but I am afraid it will be too late.

April 11, Friday. Back in Eastern Africa the Imperial troops have occupied Addis Ababa, the capital of Abyssinia.

In Libya, the German troops under General Rommel, sent to help the Italians, have counterattacked from Tripoli and are now advancing rapidly towards Cyrenaica. Not good!

A footnote: According to the BBC, on April 7, London had its 17th bomb-free night. The Luftwaffe is too busy in other places such as Greece and Yugoslavia.

April 13, Sunday. Double celebration today. It is Easter Sunday and also my birthday. Mother insists that actually I was born on April 12 but, the next day, Father flanked by two witnesses, declared me at the Registry office without mentioning that I was born the day before. I am therefore one day older than the records show. Posterity, sadly to say, will never know this important fact!

April 19, Saturday. The Yugoslavs have capitulated. Blitzkrieg and terror bombing have once again prevailed. I am surprised however by the swiftness of the collapse in such a mountainous country with poor roads and communications. It took the Germans eighteen days to overrun Belgium which is mostly flat land with an area of only 12,000 square miles. In eleven days, Yugoslavia was brought to its knees.

April 23, Wednesday. By order of Himmler, the Gestapo chief, all public dancing in Germany has been banned. The ban was to take effect immediately. Poor Germans! It is no fun to live in Grossdeutschland anymore! I recommend that they all emigrate to occupied countries where public dancing is still permitted. But not beyond curfew time...

Another footnote - Around mid-April, the Americans have occupied Greenland, the Ice Country. As it is part of Denmark now under the Nazi boot, I am not surprised by the move. A huge island of 840,000 square miles, or about a quarter of the area of the United States, its strategic value is evident.

April 26, Saturday. I went to the movies (free of charge) to see "Sieg im Westen" (Victory in the West), the official Nazi documentary of the German conquest of France, Belgium and Holland. The film is pure propaganda and has panorama shots of the endless rows of German soldiers standing at attention in full war gear, at early dawn, and being addressed by their commander off screen: Kameraden, Soldaten, die Zeit ist gekommen! (Camarades, soldiers, now is the time!) And there is the footage of the Stukas diving, sirens screaming. Later in the movie we see the German infantry marching along the French roads singing. Their song begins with the words: Kameraden, Soldaten die Zeit is gekommen!.

May 1st, Thursday. How good it is to waken in the month of May, when birds are singing in the early morning and the first sounds of a new day come through the open window. It is good too, to draw the curtains and to see the sun shining in a blue sky, giving each tree an immense shadow on the grass.

Then comes the return to reality: to war, oppressive occupation, intense longing for liberation and freedom which cannot come any time soon.

May 5, Monday. We are back in school since April 30 after 17 days of Easter vacation.

Things are getting better: the classrooms are no longer frigid ice-boxes where, to keep warm, one has to keep a coat on and wear woollen gloves, with the top of the right thumb and index cut off, to facilitate writing. Everyone is in a better mood including the teachers who no longer have to fight to ventilate the rooms between classes as in winter. These rooms were slowly made a little more comfortable by body heat. The teachers, coming from the outside, used to object to the body smell! Warmth however was our priority.

May 7, Wednesday. The Wehrmacht has smashed all resistance in Greece. Athens fell on April 7 and the whole country, except for Crete and a few islands, has been occupied.

May 10, Sunday. First anniversary of the Nazi invasion of Belgium. I spent most of the day at a Scout meeting. We ran up the colors and sang the national hymn with great feeling. But inside because all public demonstations are strictly forbidden. Our Scout Master delivered a marvelous patriotic speech.

Later, we went in small groups to lay flowers at the foot of the War Memorial in front of our district Town Hall. The local police were present to prevent such demonstrations, by order of the Occupant, but upon our arrival, they promptly disappeared and came back after we left... Good people!

May 13, Tuesday. Very strange events are happening in Germany. The German radio, yesterday, broadcast the news that Rudolf Hess, Hitler's deputy and designated successor, has gone mad, vanished in a plane and is believed to have committed suicide. Berlin radio added that Hess left messages stating his intention to kill himself. Later that night however a message from the British Government blew the German statements sky high: Rudolf Hess has landed in Scotland in a Messerschmidt 110 and given himself up. It can be summarized as follows:

On the night of Saturday 10, an Me 110 was reported to have

crossed the coast of Scotland flying in the direction of Glasgow. Later a similar plane crashed near that town with its guns unloaded. Shortly afterwards a German officer was found with his parachute, suffering from a broken ankle. He was taken to a hospital in Glasgow. Here he first gave his name as Horn. Later he stated that he was Rudolf Hess. He brought several photographs of himself at different ages, apparently in order to establish his identity.

May 14, Wednesday. The talk of the day everywhere is, quite naturally, the arrival in Great Britain of Rudolf Hess.

Here is the official Nazi communiqué:

"Party comrade Rudolf Hess who had been forbidden by the Führer to undertake flying because of his illness which had been getting worse for many years, succeeded in defiance of this order by gaining possession of a plane.

"Last Saturday at 6 p.m. Rudolf Hess took off from Augsburg on a flight from which he has so far failed to return. The letter which he left was so confused that it shows signs of mental disturbance."

This letter leads to the assumption that Hess fell victim to madness." Who will believe this?

May 22, Thursday. Many Rudolf Hess anecdotes are making the rounds and the interesting fact is that these jokes are said to come straight from Germany.

1. The 1000-year Reich has now become a 100-year Reich: one zero is gone.

2."That our [German] government is mad is something that we have known for a long time; but that they admit it, that is something new."

3. Churchill asks Hess: "So you are the madman? -No, only his deputy."

May 26, Monday. The British government has acknowledged the German claim that the British battle cruiser Hood has been sunk by the Nazi battleship Bismarck, somewhere between Iceland and Greenland. The Hood, world's largest battleship, was struck a fatal blow in one of its ammunition magazines and the ship exploded. All his 1,341 officers and men are said to be lost.

May 29, Thursday. The Royal Navy has avenged the Hood.

Germany's great new battleship has been sent to the bottom. Here is what happened.

The Bismarck (45,000 tons) and the cruiser Prinz Eugen sailed from the Norwegian port of Bergen, where they had been based, in a northwestern direction. Dispositions were taken by the British Admiralty and, on May 23, the two Nazi ships were detected in the Denmark Straits between Greenland and Iceland, proceeding at high speed south-westwards.

The weather was bad and visibility very poor. Early in the morning of May 24, however, the Hood and the Prince of Wales made contact with the enemy. Action was immediately joined.

During the ensuing engagement the Bismarck received damage but the Hood received a hit in the magazine and immediately blew up. The chase was continued on a south-easterly course with the Norfolk and the Suffolk maintaining contact with the enemy despite all his efforts to shake off the pursuers.

The Bismarck was now heading from the northern seas for the French ports of Brest or St. Nazaire, shadowed and hounded by naval airplanes. Four torpedoes crashed into the battleship which was brought to a standstill. Then British warships came up to finish off one of the shortest-lived capital ships ever.

The statement of the Oberkommando der Wehrmacht (OKW) says: "The thoughts of the entire German people are full of pride and grief for Admiral Lutjens, Captain Lindeman and all the members of the brave crew of the battleship Bismarck, who succumbed in their glorious fight off Iceland."

A footnote: The Germans say that the Bismarck sank at about 47 degree Latitude N and 17 degree longitude W. The German communiqué is wrong. My calculations show that the Bismarck sank much farther south at about 20 degree longitude W.

4

June 2 - October 26, 1941

June 2, Monday. More important news.

First. The troops of General Rommel, since their initial attack on March 24th, have destroyed the British 2nd Armored Division, captured the port of Benghazi, surrounded the Australian Division in the port of Tobruk and sent the rest of the British Army fleeing in disorder. And now Rommel stands at the frontier of Egypt!

Second. The Germans, in the past few weeks, have been attempting to conquer the island of Crete and a huge naval and aerial battle is in progress. Crete is of great strategic importance to Hitler if he wants to gain control of the Mediterranean. It will be a menace to Egypt if the island can be used as a bomber base, especially to Alexandria which, I am told, is the base of the British Eastern Mediterranean Fleet, no more than 300 miles away.

June 5, Thursday. It seems that the battle for Crete is over. After two weeks of fighting, the German airborne invasion has succeeded. The cost has been high for the Nazi paratroopers. The Germans took over the airfields and pushed the Imperial troops out of the island. This is a grave defeat. Hitler is now in possession of Crete and his armies are victorious in North Africa,

The Italians have Rhodes. If Hitler can take over Cyprus, all of Egypt and the Middle East are in serious trouble. As an "armchair strategist" this is what I deduce from a learned discussion between two gentlemen who know a lot more than I do. They supply the brains and I bring the maps in the form of a huge, heavy, detailed Atlas published in Leipzig, Germany, before the Great War.

June 8; Sunday. I am tutoring François Dodeur, a classmate, at his mother's request. Not that he is dumb or stupid, just a little lazy. We study together at his brand new home, airy and comfortable, reviewing mostly math and history. The results are pretty good and the parents are delighted.

François' father owns a gingerbread factory using as basic ingredients a lot of sugar, honey and flour. The other day he came back with a pail full of artificial honey and offered it to me as a token of gratitude for the service I render to his son.

I am delighted with the gift; it couldn't have come at a better time because at present, we have run out of anything resembling fats or sugary products.

The pail is too heavy and François' father offers to bring me home in the small company van. As practically all cars have disappeared from the roads (Mr. Dodeur tells me there are probably no more than 6,000 cars still on the road in Belgium); it feels strange to ride in a car again. It is exhilarating; I wish we could drive around for an hour or more in these almost empty streets, listening to the sounds of the engine and the crunching of the gears.

Soon however we are at our destination. The whole family greets me like a hero and Mother prepares a special dish and gives a double ration to a growing young man who is perpetually hungry.

June 10, Tuesday. Two important items.
1. The United States has occupied the island of Iceland. This cannot come as a surprise after the takeover of Greenland, another Danish possession. The affair of the Bismarck shows how important strategically those frozen countries are for access to the Denmark Straits.
2. British and Gaullists forces have moved into Syria. No surprise here either. With Crete gone and Cyprus in great danger, Churchill had to act against Vichy as Syria is or was under the latter's control.

Strange that I keep bumping into one nationality after the other since the May invasion. First it was the Germans, the Occupant; then the British, our sole hope for liberation; a little later, my encounter with the Italian couple had my interest switched to Italy. Now the French: Vichy/Germany; de Gaulle/England. I don't know much about de Gaulle. He is a relatively obscure general who refused the Armistice, took refuge in London and established a French Government-in-exile with the help of the British. His popularity is growing among the French people, especially in occupied France.

June 21, Saturday. The Burgomaster of Brussels is a gentleman by the name of François, Joseph van de Meulebroeck, who as a patriot does the best he can to defend the population against the demands of the Kommandantur. For the last few months it has been a game of cat and mouse but now it has developed into a full-blown crisis. A short while ago the German authorities requested through a "moderate" collaborator, by the name of Romsée, that he (v.d.M.) accept the nomination of four municipal councillors more favorable to the New Order. The Burgomaster refused. Yesterday, unable to communicate with his fellow citizens through the press, v.d.M. had a public notice printed and posted all over the city, to explain his refusal to obey the order. The Germans immediately ordered the notices removed and torn to shreds. But the contents were soon known and a great crowd assembled around the venerable Town Hall (built in the 13th century) to express support, but was promptly dispersed by German troops.

I am trying to get the full text of the Burgomaster's proclamation.

June 22, Sunday. At four o'clock this morning, the Nazis have attacked the Soviet Union. It was announced with great fanfare by the OKW a few hours later. I learned the news at the Scout meeting.

At night, I listen to the German communiqués and to the "Post Office" (a euphemism for the BBC), but it is much too early to get some hard news.

I have now a new assignment. After Germany, England, Italy and France, I must take up the study of Soviet Russia. This war is now encompassing half of the world!

In the warm spring evening we have dinner out of doors, watching the sun sink behind the darkening horizon. Moment by moment it is changing its color in a phantasmagoria of hues starting with shell pink, turning to rose pink, and deepening into rich purples before the light fades and the stars come out. I suddenly remember that today is the Summer solstice.

June 23, Monday. The Germans announce that their armies, in twenty-four hours, have taken ten thousand prisoners, destroyed around twelve hundred Russian aircraft and advanced more than fifty miles.

Churchill in a broadcast had this to say: "The Nazi regime is undistinguishable from the worst features of communism. No one has been a more consistent opponent of communism than I have for the last twenty-five years. I will unsay no word that I have spoken about it."

And then he adds: "The cause of any Russian fighting for his hearth and home is the cause of free men and free people in every quarter of the globe."

June 24, Tuesday. Burgomaster van de Meulebroeck has been arrested together with some of his collaborators as well as the printers who prepared the proclamation.

The German troops are advancing rapidly into Soviet Russia. In two days they have taken hordes of prisoners and seized many bridges intact. There seems to be no organized resistance. But then, we get very little concrete news.

June 27, Friday. This is strange. The new war in the East seems to be going well for the Nazis but very little information is available, as if it were a sideshow. Even the "Grossdeutscher Rundfunk" has not much to say.

June 29, Sunday. I spent the whole day with the Troop in the Forest of Soignes, one of our favorite spots. This time we went all the way to Groenendael, the "green valley", to the site of the former abbey. It is surrounded by large ponds dug by the monks ages ago which supplied them with an abundance of fish. The abbey was built around 1200 and was destroyed at the end of the 18th century by the French revolutionaries. Here lived and died the great mystic Jan van Ruusbroec (or Ruysbroeck), known also as "the Admirable."

In early afternoon, the sun was warm and bright, the sky clear, a perfect day for hiking along the narrow paths of these beautiful woods. The forest of Soignes in summer is an unmatched blessing. Upon my return home, Father mentions that radio Brussels has all day long, in hourly communiqués, broadcasted spectacular victories at what they now call the "Ostfront" or Eastern front.

I am too tired to discuss the news in detail and go to bed early.

June 30, Monday. Yesterday, in ten special communiqués at

hourly intervals, the OKW announced that the Nazi forces had knifed through the Soviet defenses and captured Minsk. Advance units have driven on to a point within sight of Smolensk only 250 miles on the way to Moscow. A German column advancing on Leningrad has taken Libau, a naval base on the Latvian coast. Other forces have captured Lvov (Lemberg) on the road to Kiev.

If true, these victories seem to justify the highest hopes for the Nazis. Today, the German radio announces that tens of thousands of prisoners were taken and there seems to be no meaningful resistance as German tanks burst through Soviet lines and roam at will.

Except for Leningrad and Moscow, I am not familiar with these towns and I have to resort to my atlas for a better understanding of the situation.

In order to better follow the events on the Russian front I decide to buy a map of European Russia (to the Ural mountains) published by R. De Rouck in Brussels. I still have the use of my atlas but the map is easier as I can pin it on the wall and stick little flags showing the German progression.

July 4, Friday. I am told that Hitler has attacked Russia the same day Napoléon invaded that country 129 years ago. Is it a bad omen?

I am not sure: the Grande Armée crossed the Niemen on June 23 and Hitler's Wehrmacht went to the offensive a day earlier. The comparison however is interesting. Against Napoléon's 450,000 men, the Russians had initially only 160,000 soldiers under Barclay de Tolly with the later addition, in the South, of the army of Bragation, with 60,000 men.

So let us talk numbers. How many divisions has Hitler in the east? With how many men and equipment can the Soviets oppose him? We will probably never know.

July 8, Tuesday. We are approaching the last exams of the school year and I have decided not to listen to the radio, all week, to better concentrate on my studies. Should something important come up, people will tell me. At night I go to the basement where I have a little room, to get away from the hustle and bustle of a large family, and cram.

July 11, Friday. Today is Flanders' National holiday

commemorating the Flemish victory over the French on July 11, 1302 in the vicinity of Kortrijk (Courtrai). It is known as the Battle of the Golden Spurs in which the French knights were beaten by the craftsmen of Ypres, Ghent and Bruges commanded by Pieter de Coninck.

There is no special celebration except for here and there a few Flemish flags, a black lion with red claws on a yellow background, the same flag under which my ancestors fought in 1302.

July 15, Tuesday. Summer vacation has started! Classes resume September 17. I am planning for a one-week camping trip with the Scouts, and a visit with sister Rosa and my friend Robert Leroy in northern France.

July 17, Thursday. The German troops continue to make progress in Russia but more slowly than in the first days of the attack. Propaganda chief Goebbels claims that the Wehrmacht has pierced the "Stalin Line" at "all decisive points". Since I don't know where the Stalin Line is located this information is of no great help. I gather however, from German and Russian communiqués, that the front after three weeks of fighting runs from the Black Sea along the Dniester river up to Mogilev-Podolsk, then straight north to a point midway between Novgorod-Volynsk and Kiev; through the Pripet marshes to Minsk, Polotsk, Vitebsk, Ostrov, Pskov and close to Leningrad.

On July 3rd, Stalin broke an ominous silence and in a broadcast to the Russian masses announced a "scorched earth" policy and calling for the formation of partisan groups behind the German lines.

My history teacher opines that Hitler will encounter the three problems which defeated Napoléon in Russia: time, distance and weather.

July 21, Monday. Belgium's national holiday. All public demonstrations are forbidden. I don't expect any outpouring of patriotic feelings. The Nazis have all the guns. Why stand up to them, pay dearly for it and make things a lot worse than they are?

It doesn't mean that the population is pro-German or in favor of the New Order. Far from it! But the resistance should take the form of "civil disobedience" in small matters that cannot be easily detected but are nevertheless effective. There is no doubt that the passive resistance of an enormous number of magistrates, government officials, police officers, railroad workers and postal clerks can be more effective against the occupying power than any other activity. There is no way the Nazi occupiers can control every Belgian, Frenchman, Dutchman, whoever! Resist, yes, but in a prudent and effective way.

July 24, Thursday. When I ask people "who should know" about the invasion of Soviet Russia, I find that most of them are glad the attack took place. Their reasons are that it gives a new dimension to the war by the losses it is sure to inflict upon the Nazis, the arrival of a potentially powerful ally, Russia, and the hope of some relief from the monotonous series of defeats. These friends are all strong opponents of the atheistic, soul-destroying regime of the USSR. They like the idea that the two dictatorships will destroy each other and their peoples will be freed. Wishful thinking?

The Germans meanwhile continue their advance but at a slower pace. It is now clear that the Soviets forces are fighting back with a hitherto unknown determination and even savagery.

August 5, Tuesday. From July 27 through August 3, I went on a short camping trip with almost the full complement of our Troop. It was not easy to organize because the German authorities keep a sharp eye on all youth organizations in general and the scouting movement in particular. One day we are authorized to meet at will and do whatever we please. Another time, we are allowed to get together but without uniforms, no flags and meetings held indoors. Sometimes we are outlawed altogether. And the cycle starts all over again.

All is ready, at last! We leave using today's only reliable mode of transportation: bicycles. Our goal? A beautiful Renaissance castle in the little village of Humbeek, near Grimbergen. The owners have graciously allowed us to use, not their mansion of course, but part of their barn complex where we establish our sleeping facilities. What, no tents? No. Camping under tent is forbidden, period. We are lodged in a vast loft, well lighted and ventilated (no smoking, please!) above the shed that shelters the farm's agricultural machinery and other implements. From my dormer window I have a partial view of the castle, a full view of

Above: Camping with boy scouts on the grounds of the 16th century
Humbeek Castle. The author is at the left with hands behind his back.
August 1942.
Below: Camping in the Ardennes after Belgium's Liberation. Late
September 1944.

the lawn in front of it, the large pond and the thickly wooded part where we will spend most of our time. We occupy the loft only for sleeping.

Our headquarters and kitchen facilities are located downstairs. There is a primitive washroom with one very asthmatic pump which needs resuscitation every time we use it. A large stone basin helps us to keep clean (almost).

The weather, oh miracle! is fine and warm, allowing us to spend many hours in the park and on hikes in the surrounding villages. The night of our arrival as we were getting ready for bed with the help of flashlights (there is no electricity here), a black cat came to join us and was immediately adopted by the company. We gave him the name of Ron-ron because of its laud purring (ronronner, in French). He has four white feet and a white tip to his plumed tail. Later on, Ron-ron decided there was too much disturbance for comfort. He rose, stretched, yawned pinkly, slowly walked to the heavy door and waited. I hastened to open it and he stalked out pretending not to see me.

On the third day, in late afternoon, our hosts invited us for a visit. A little marvel of the late Renaissance, the castle is three stories high, surrounded by a moat and accessible via an elegant bridge. Built in layers of pink bricks alternating with bands of white stones, it is pierced with high double or triple mullioned windows. At both ends of the façade rise square pavilions surmounted by small rounded turrets and lanterns; the broken line of the roof is further relieved by dormers and windows.

This is by no means a medieval building, strong and dark. It was built at the time when castles had lost their fortress-like character and became residences of royalty, nobles and wealthy bourgeoisie.

After partaking of a light cake and other refreshments, we were taken on a short tour of the first floor through the dining room, arms room, library and banquet room, whose decorations and furnishings are all in a style of rich and sober elegance. One of the most interesting items was the extraordinary wallcovering in the library and another room, made of "repoussé" leather of fine workmanship, raised in relief by hammering on the reverse side. It was probably made in the town of Malines (Mechlin), famous in the 16th and 17th centuries for this kind of leather which is known as "cuir de Cordoue" or Cordoba leather.

Not a single episode of note, not a tragedy, not a scandal has ever been associated with the Château of Humbeek. Its annals are of that simple type that, if they do not make history, do at least make happiness.

In the midst of the tumults of this war that are throwing their dark shadows in our present time, one is glad to carry away as a last impression the picture of a fair and stately mansion standing amidst its lawns and flowerbeds bathed, in the sweet sunshine.

The Count and the Countess have five children; the oldest is a girl of sixteen who was delighted by the sudden arrival of a group of boys her own age; her name is Marie-Françoise.

She was an instant success with us and became a permanent visitor to the camp. We treated her like a little queen and she reveled in the myriads of daily attentions. Soon she fell in love with our Assistant Troop Master. She was often seen with him in long conversations, with the consequence that his services to the Troop were reduced to a very minimum.

On the evening before our departure, she came to say goodbye by the last light of the day during the campfire. She was beautiful with her dark hair, her lovely features and these solemn brown eyes filled with deep sadness.

The sun went down at last, a circle of liquid fire, turning first to bronze and then to a deep blood orange as it slid toward the horizon, its rays refracted by an evening mist that promised further and greater heat to come.

The next day a fresh breeze came over the woods and bustled small clouds out of the sun's path. The earth was soft beneath us and a shower had left the grass and trees with a share of summer's greenness. Life was good.

In the morning, the Troop chaplain came to celebrate Mass at an outdoor altar made of sticks and rope. All were in attendance including our hosts and children. This was a solemn Mass with Gregorian chant, very beautiful, thanks to a competent choir master who was no other than Henri Martin, our Assistant Scout Master, recently renamed "Romeo" by a majority of our group. At the end, André Renard, who has an excellent voice, sang a capella the magnificent Panis Angelicus of Mozart. We were left speechless.

We broke up camp right after breakfast, cleaned everything in sight and said our goodbyes to Ron-ron who gave us his best rendition of a prolonged purr in cat minor. He then withdrew to a ledge where he washed his face with velvet paws and stared stonily at our strange activitities.

In a corner of the courtyard, Henri and Marie-Françoise, holding hands, said farewells as lengthily as Romeo and Juliet, with many promises of meeting again. We departed at last and by mid afternoon I was back home, tanned, mentally refreshed and in need of a good scrub.

Mother inquired about the quality of the food and I must say it was excellent. Henri, yes our Romeo, was our cook-in-chief and did an excellent job in the use of the disparate types of food we had brought with us: rice, beans, peas, potatoes, smoked fish, dried meat, flour, sugar, bread as good as anything a good mother could squeeze from a reluctant grocer or a black market "dealer".

August 8, Friday. We have received several letters from sister Rosa in the last two months. All is well on the surface, but mother doesn't like the tone of the last few notes; she decides that a member of the family ought to visit her. I volunteer gladly and plan to leave on the 21st to return on the 27th.

August 16, Saturday. "The President of the United States and the Prime Minister of the United Kingdom have met at sea." This dramatic news was announced to the world a few days ago. In view of the danger arising from the policy of military conquest by the Hitlerite government of Germany, the President and the Prime Minister have proceeded with a joint statement of war aims in eight points:
*Great Britain and the U.S. have no aims of territorial aggrandizement for themselves.
*They desire to see no territorial changes that do not accord with the freely expressed wishes of the people concerned.
*They respect the right of all peoples to choose their own government.

*They want all peoples to have access on equal terms to trade and raw materials.

*All nations should collaborate in the economic field with the object of securing for all improved labor standards, economic advancement and social security.

*Peace should bring freedom from fear and want.

*Peace should bring disarmament of the aggressors pending the establishment of a wider and more permanent system of general security."

I have read this statement several times and cannot grow very enthusiastic about it. It sounds like an electoral program with very little real thinking behind it. I will have to discuss this with my mentors.

August 21, Thursday. I am on my way to visit Rosa in Armentières, France. But first I pay a visit to my friend Robert Leroy who lives with his parents in Houplines a suburb of Armentières.

Robert and I first met in the kindergarten class of Mademoiselle Georgette - we were then five years old - and soon became inseparable. The fact that my family has moved to Brussels has not severed the bonds of friendship. We have kept contact by correspondence and a visit I made in August, 1939.

The train trip was uneventful. I proceeded from Brussels to Courtrai to Comines to Houplines. I notice that there are fewer German troops and no wonder; they have all gone to the Russian front. My godfather wrote that "Kurt" is gone too. Robert's parents receive me with open arms. He is an only child and they treat me as a second son. The father, Albert Leroy, is the manager of a textile plant owned by the well-known Motte family. The family Leroy lives in a nice apartment above the office.

Much has changed since 1939. First, the plant is a beehive of activity, manufacturing cotton goods for the Wehrmacht and occasionally also for the French population. Second, the place is almost unrecognizable. All plant buildings as well as the adjacent streets have disappeared under an impressive camouflage job. From the air, the complex is quite invisible to eventual British bombers.

Not that the textile mill is that important. What the Germans want to protect is the group of buildings next door, requisitioned by the Wehrmacht, now a huge tank depot and repair shop. The townspeople who work at the facility mention that most of the work is done on captured French tanks which are refitted and repainted with the black German cross on a white background. The finished tanks then rumble toward the train station close by, to be loaded on flatbed railroad cars, destination unknown, but you can guess.

Another part of the immense complex is used to refit hundreds and hundreds of French military trucks and, the job once completed, they follow the path of the tanks. The camouflage and tight security in and around the plant is proof of the importance the Germans give to this site. This is confirmed by the fact that parts of the complex are strictly "verboten" to the French workers and accessible only to military mechanics and other German experts.

It is strange to live under a camouflage canopy made of strands of wire and thousands upon thousands of multicolor burlap strips, brown, green, pale blue, yellow, giving the houses and the street below a permanent alchemical autumn sunlight.

August 22, Friday. Monsieur Albert Leroy, born in 1900, was a volunteer in the French Army in 1917. This experience, not a happy one, has marked him for life. He is anti-German, anti-English, anti-Government, anti-Army and anti about everything else. This attitude I find in many French war veterans. They read (or used to read) the "Canard Enchaîné" and also "Gringoire" both very aggressive weeklies, politically. Monsieur Leroy has no sympathy for fascism or communism; he is in some kind of limbo waiting for events to deliver him from his deep frustration. The defeat of June 1940 has not helped in any way. He had, at first, hoped that Maréchal Pétain would be the man who would save France. This hope didn't last long.

It is obvious that Pétain is a very old man who is manipulated, like the politicians of the Third Republic, by dark forces, but also by something more ominous: the murderous Nazis. Where should one turn? There is a general, totally unknown before June 1940; his name is Charles de Gaulle. He fumbled for a while but he seems now to have attracted the attention of quite a few

Frenchmen, including Albert Leroy. "There is no one else I can turn to," he sighs.

I read some of the de Gaulle's proclamations to the French people. He affirms that France has lost a battle but not the war; France will rise again. "Forget the defeat," he urges, "France is and will remain a Great Power." Strangely enough he rarely mentions England and I wonder how France can be free again without the help of the British. Do I detect a bit of Anglophobia? This is for de Gaulle and the French to figure out.

August 23, Saturday. May I introduce Madame Leroy? She has smooth black hair, fair eyelashes, direct dark eyes, a firm friendly mouth and a composure that gives her an air of graceful reserve. She comes from a Flemish family who emigrated to this part of France during the potato crop failure of 1867-68. She is totally assimilated and doesn't speak a word of Flemish.

She has one great quality, a very important one in the eyes of any Frenchman: she is a fantastic cook and every meal is a delight. That means she spends a lot of time in the kitchen. This is not an hindrance for kitchen and living room form one big area. She can thus keep watch over her cooking pots and at the same time be part of the conversation, ever so lively.

This afternoon we went to visit the big garden bordering the river Lys which at that point constitutes the border with Belgium. I used to live on the Belgian side. The gardener is Firmin Maertens, also of Flemish descent, who speaks fluent Flemish (Dutch) and somewhat halting French. He is the kind of character who seems to have stepped out of the Middle Ages by some regrettable mistake.

He is a terrifying mountain of a man, perpetually hungry. One has always the feeling that, when he stares at you from under the dark overhang cliffs of eyebrows, the expression in his eyes is that of a Bengal tiger mentally tucking in his napkin, before launching himself on the thirty-foot leap that is to culminate in lunch. He has a massive head with thick, somewhat graying hair and a strong square jaw; but there isn't enough real life stamped on his face for a man in his late forties.

Firmin's appetite is legendary. He can, in one setting, absorb the contents of two bottles of wine, or a generous amount of beer, plus delicious hors-d'oeuvres, a big fish, slabs of beef, platter of vegetables, salads, cheese and fruit, and still look hungry, I am certain that Pomona, the Goddess of Plenty, keeps an affectionate eye on Firmin who so bountifully enjoys the fruits of the earth.

In the evening Robert and I go to pay a visit to Joseph Mandin, the Headmaster of the elementary school where we spent so many years learning to master the French language, arithmetic, history, geography and other subjects, which now help us so wonderfully.

Monsieur Mandin is a short, stocky middle-aged man, prematurely gray and of ecclesiastical appearance. His face is gravely beautiful and dignified, though his eyes, reflecting a domineering manner, are like a piercing steel blade. Deep lines running from the corners of his nose to his chin gives his expression a look of strong willfulness. To me he looks like one of God's senior angels and, should he know, he would certainly agree with this sentiment. He is an educator of the old school: a strict disciplinarian and a marvelous teacher. He did instill in us a love of learning and gave us the solid base on which we now build our futures.

It is evening... The three of us are sitting in the little garden outside the living room, looking out at the blue lights of the schoolyard and the splendor of the sky overhead. Sunset stained the western horizon an hour ago. We listen to our host, an unusually amiable and interesting conversationalist and narrator. He possesses the great Greek gift of harmless irony and good humor which, somehow, has been transmitted to the French, the gift of pleasant and gracious entertainment, what the Greeks called *terpsis* (gladness, delight).

We talked well into the night of deep purple, under a heaven of innumerable stars. And as we walked home a sense of melancholy came over us. We spoke softly, well aware that tomorrow we would be separated again, two brothers, united not by the flesh but by the bonds of friendship. We talked of the war and our troubled times, uncertain about when we would meet again. But graciously, God limits man's vision of things within a narrow consciousness, and draws the veil over an unknown future.

August 24, Sunday. Armentières is a textile town and also, to a lesser extent, a beer brewing town of about 20,000 people. It was totally destroyed in the Great War, patiently rebuilt including the church of Saint-Vaast and its Belfry, symbol of Flanders' municipal freedoms. In Roman times, it was a busy crossroads on the Roman Way from Boulogne, on the coast, to the Imperial city of Cologne, in the Rhineland. Armentières is also the point where the river Lys begins to be navigable and was a very important cattle market, hence the name Armentarius (cattle in Latin).

Rosa received me with great joy. She and her little son Charles, about two years old, live now with the grandparents Wille. They own a house big enough for the four of them, in the western part of town. The advantages for Rosa, the wife of a prisoner of war, are twofold: she has no rent to pay and, as she has to work for a living, the old couple can take care of the toddler.

The grandparents are delightful people. However my sister wishes her husband would come back soon so that she may have at last a house of her own. She lives here as a welcome guest but she cannot rearrange the furniture the way she wants to and everything seems to be of pre-1914 vintage. That was the year when the grandfather went to war and suffered a grave head wound at Salonika (or Thessaloniki) in Greece. The year was 1916, in the month of September. His son Charles volunteered in 1915 and was killed the same year. Grandfather, now entirely bald, shows a big gash where part of his cranium was sliced off by shrapnel. How he survived this wound is a mystery to me, so deep is the indentation.

The injury healed all right but the psychological wound caused by the death of his only son, never did. He and his wife nurture a deep and secret resentment against the world, against those invisible powers who sent their son to his death The government gave him, posthumously, a medal, called him a defender of the fatherland who will live for ever in the hearts of the French people and then promptly forgot all about him. There were so many like him you see, 1,700,000, more or less. Their grandson, the little Charles, is a consolation, but it is too late.

The grandmother, toothless, fusses around all day long, constantly cleaning or cooking. She is a sinewy, indestructible old woman, with tawny hide, leaning on her stick, squinting in the sunlight, and like most grandmothers, displaying a certain austere dignity.

August 25, Monday. Grandma is up early and has prepared breakfast, a meal worthy of the gods! She must have ransacked the whole town for we had real coffee (with chicory), white bread, raisin bread, croissants and the ultimate of luxury in these troubled times: butter!

She is surprised and pleased by my enthusiasm. Her eyes sparkle in the soft light, half mocking, half smiling, green-gray and shining. She eats with us out of a big bowl of coffee wherein she drops pieces of bread that, when sufficiently soaked, are scooped up with a large spoon: she has no teeth, remember?

Grandpa comes in from the garden in the back of the house, carrying the vegetables for the noonday soup and invites me to visit his Garden of Eden, as he calls it. He certainly works hard at it. Here are patches of various sizes showing a wonderful assortment of vegetables: peas, French beans, leek, white and red cabbage, salads, and a big area planted with potatoes, a good reserve of food for the winter. And over there, in a little corner an assortment of herbs, the indispensable complement to any French cuisine. Way in the back are a series of hutches where a dozen of serious looking rabbits, with twitchy noses, meditate, I am sure upon the brevity of a rabbit's life.

Rosa, Charles and I are on our way to Jules' mother. The latter is one of the numerous Great War widows, 610,000 of them. After more than 20 years of widowhood, she is remarried to the owner of a Hotel-Restaurant on the Grand'Place.

We arrived just before noon to find the place with very few customers. I meet Monsieur Ladou, the owner, a gray-haired gentleman, ravaged at fifty, with puffy drinker's lips and haunted eyes, a face thin and deeply lined. He wears his spare hair brushed forward which reminds me of the busts of Julius Caesar.

The place has the advantages of an old-fashioned hostelry in that everything is on an ample scale; the beds are large, the room is vast, the bathtub has not been designed for a dwarf, neither is the bath towel a miserable yard of cotton but a robe of imperial proportions.

Monsieur et Madame Ladou are unhappy, however. Because of travel restrictions businessmen stay away and the ones who do show up are black market people who steal the imperial bath towels and everything that is not nailed down. Furthermore the restaurant has to close at night because of rationing and the erratic food distribution system. They plan to close down both restaurant and hotel, keeping only the bar which is still popular. Wine and beer are not too difficult to get; spirits are another matter and champagne has disappeared entirely. The story is that it is easier to find the bubbly in Berlin than in occupied Paris. The Nazis buy it, like everything else, with the war indemnity the country is compelled to pay to the tune of twenty million Reichsmarks per day.

After a light lunch, we stroll around the Grand'Place, past the church of St Vaast, where I was confirmed by Bishop Liénart of Lille, on to the Belfry and Town Hall, where stands the War Memorial 1914-18. Most existing monuments to memorialize the Dead of the Great War are horrible piles of stone and metal, many of them of an antiquated ugliness of which a certain quaintness is the only attraction. In many towns and cities they obstruct traffic. In others, like Armentières, their actual removal would benefit the general appearance of the community.

August 26, Tuesday. There has been an attack on a German soldier in the Metro of Paris. We discuss this event because the Paris Kommandatur has threatened brutal reprisals. The Nazis will take hostages among the notables as well as those caught in anti-German activities, and shoot them if the culprits are not found. My position is simple. I am against terrorist acts that cannot, in any way, help in our battle for liberation. I keep believing that for the time being only civil disobedience is the order of the day. The thousands upon thousands pinpricks which will sap the strength of the Leviathan, such as a multiplicity of personal reactions reflected in improvised deeds – secret networks specialized in obtaining military and economic information, assisting in the escape and evacuation of war prisoners and Allied pilots who have parachuted from crippled planes, massing reserve of arms, printing anti-German leaflets and small newspapers and engaging in almost undedectable acts of sabotage.

In the afternoon Robert joins us and we go into town for a walk. There has been desultory fighting here in May, 1940 and there is some damage to be seen. But nothing like the disaster of the Great War which left the town a pile of ruins. We cross into Belgium less than half a mile away and push toward Ploegsteert with its huge military Memorial cemetery, the wall of which is inscribed, so I am told, with the names of 28,000 British soldiers whose bodies have never be found.

The front stabilized from here to Ypres, in September, 1914. Huge battles were fought all during the war for a few square kilometers of ground and at the cost of hundred thousands of lives. In four years of war, the British Empire suffered one million dead, most killed on the front extending from Flanders to the Somme; the bodies of over 150,000 were never to be found or if found, never identified. The names of Messines Ridge, Mount Kemmel, Ploegsteert Wood, Gheluvelt, Ypres, Passchendaele are all in the War history books. Mr. Churchill fought briefly in Ploegsteert and Hitler in Messines, only two miles away. The latter sketched the ruins of the village and it is here that he won the Iron Cross, Second Class, for saving the life of his commander in November, 1914. It is rumored in this part of the country, that in June of 1940, Hitler toured the area where he fought, from Loos (near Lille), to Ploegsteert, Messines, Ypres, Beselare, Passchendaele and Langemark.

We returned to find dinner almost ready and in time to get the real news from "La Poste" in other words the BBC, French program.

Grandma, great-grandma that is, has decided to serve dinner outside. It is a serene place, this courtyard. Under the waning sun, still warm and mellow, there is no movement except the flutter of a white pigeon over our heads and no sound except the soft echo of our voices. Then follows what to me seems the largest meal since the war began. Sumptuous hors-d'oeuvres of a variety one never sees in any restaurant, followed by a "lapin en moutarde", salad and then cheese and fruit. The main dishes are served with a wonderful wine of pre-war vintage. No, not this war, the previous one. It is part of the twelve bottles which were set aside back in 1915, to celebrate the return of son Charles from the war. It never happened and the distraught parents never found the courage to drink them. Until now. We consume three bottles, the rest will wait the return of Jules, the grandson, from captivity.

While we are eating, the moon slowly inches up over the landscape. Huge and golden-orange when it breasted the horizon, it changed its hue as it climbed the sky. By the time supper is over, it is its silvery self, presiding in glory over a magical night.

It is a grand feast offered to me as a going-away present, for I am leaving tomorrow. I will never forget my hosts' gentle and quiet hospitality that must have dug deeply into their food reserves. Robert returns home before curfew and promises to see me off at the station tomorrow morning.

August 27, Wednesday. After a tearful leave taking of the grandparents, Sister Rosa accompanies me to the station where Robert, leaning on his bicycle, is waiting for us.

The news is not good: the train to Belgium has been cancelled. Rosa is upset. I tell her not to worry, Robert and I have already planned an alternative. After a lot of hugging and kissing she departs for work a little anxious to leave her "little" brother marooned at the station.

Robert and I have decided to pedal to the nearest Belgian railroad station, Le Touquet, with the hope of finding a train to Courtrai and on to Brussels. We attach my bag to the handlebars and I sit on the rickety luggage rack behind my friend, holding on to the saddle, legs dangling. After several false starts, we are on our way. We take shortcuts by uncertain paths which force us to walk a good deal of the way. We cross the border at the railroad bridge over the Lys river. It is an illegal crossing but no official is around to stop us and the customs house is empty.

We now follow the path along the railroad track. A few minutes later, we hear the train, my train, consisting of only two passenger- and one freight cars, chugging along on its way to Armentières. With sign language we ask the machinist, the train has slowed down considerably to cross the hastily repaired bridge, whether he will return. The answer is an energetic affirmative shaking of the head; at the same time the rascal seizes the opportunity to throw a pail of water in our direction, howling like a laughing hyena. It's a miss however.

We at last reach the station. The news is that the train was delayed and later canceled, because of an air raid warning. As no RAF planes appeared, it was decided to respect the timetable, two hours late, which in wartime can be considered an inconsequential delay and just a little inconvenience. I made it to Kortrijk after expressing my thanks to Robert, hugging him like a brother, with promises to meet soon again. With a war going on, however, *Chi lo sa?* Who knows? At Wevelgem, the railroad line runs along the Luftwaffe air base. I can distinguish a few camouflaged single-engine fighters which look like Messerschmidts 110. At Courtrai, I was lucky enough to hop on a rather crowded train to Brussels, and by late afternoon, I was back home, ready to dispense all the news to an expectant family.

September 2, Tuesday. This Sunday, at our Troop meeting, our chaplain tells us about the address Cardinal Van Roey held two weeks ago to his seminarians. It was a patriotic and forceful speech. The Cardinal reminded his listeners that five centuries ago France was occupied by the English and everybody "collaborated" with the occupant: the notables, the University, the nobility, the bishops. But a young girl, Joan of Arc, inspired by God, took up arms, challenged the "collaborators" and won the battle. We don't have a Joan of Arc, the Cardinal went on, and we should not expect one. We ought to keep the faith however and resist because we are certain that our country will one day be free again.

The Cardinal is our best Resistance fighter. The Rexists, the followers of Léon Degrelle who are the Walloon collaborators, have attacked the Cardinal and the clergy very violently in the Nazi press. They have talked in ominous tones about the "loathsome" and "disgusting" clergy and the fact that the Roman red hat was "getting mixed up with the Freemason filth; the totalitarian State will keep this in mind."

September 5, Friday. I have, in the last month, somewhat neglected to note the main events of the war, especially in Russia. After a period of great progress, the Wehrmacht had to consolidate its gains and prepare for the new push forward. It seems now that the offensive has resumed at least on two fronts: in the direction of Leningrad and in the Ukraine, toward Kiev. It is difficult, however, to know what is happening. I hear the musical fanfares that precede a special bulletin: "Führer's headquarters: The High Command of the Wehrmacht announces... Der Oberkommando der Wehrmacht gibt bekannt..." assuring us that the final victory, heralded by the decisive battles in the east, is at hand!

The other day, I happened to talk to the father of Jean Van Eck, my sister Marguerite's husband. He (the father) is a retired major who fought in the Belgian army on the Yzer front in 1914-18. With my map of Russia in front of us, he explains to me the huge logistic problems facing the German army. Hitler and his generals after a first successful push forward have to reassess the situation. *First*, they have underestimated the strength of the Red Army. The Soviets are fighting ferociously and to the death, despite poor morale in some areas. *Second*, the logistic problems to supply such a huge army are staggering and the longer the supply line, the bigger the nightmare. To this we have to add the fact that, for weeks, the Wehrmacht could not use the Russian rail system which is of a different gauge than the standard European one of 1m44. All supplies therefore have to be transported by long columns of trucks on primitive roads which turn into liquid rivers of mud after every downpour; and these roads, when dry, produce an engine-destroying dust that stops trucks, armored cars and tanks. *Third*, because of the impossibility of advancing on a broad front, in such huge country and, to reduce the logistic problem, the OKW will have to privilege only a few lines of advance. According to my expert, the Nazis should target Leningrad, Moscow and Kiev. Reaching these goals would strike a deadly blow to the communist regime.

September 10, Wednesday. Well, Major Van Eck might be the best strategist I know. The OKW has announced the capture of Schlüsselburg, the "key" (hence the name), to Leningrad. My map doesn't show this location, but I find it in my atlas spelled "Shlisselburg", about 30 miles south of that town. According to the Nazis, Leningrad is practically encircled and the blockade of the town has started.

September 17, Wednesday. Back to school. I am in class 3A headed by Fr. E. Van Mulders, a great teacher, a distinguished scholar and a deeply religious man. He has an extraordinary talent for communicating to his students a great enthusiasm for learning and his love of Letters. He is known to be so carried away with his subject that draping himself in an imaginary toga and lifting his right hand with the first three fingers extended above his head, the solemn gesture of ancient orators, he would launch into a passionate rendition of a Demosthenes address or a Cicero discourse, leaving his listeners awestruck.

I certainly welcome the opportunity to spend a year with such a *rara avis* of a professor. On the negative side, we get a new History teacher quite competent but more than a little dull and unable to control a class of unruly adolescents. We call him, behind his back of course, Paillasson or doormat. The story is that, one day in a fit of exasperation before a particularly difficult class, he exclaimed: "I am not your paillasson." The name stuck and is now passed along to younger generations.

This year we will study with him the end of the Middle Ages, the Age of Discovery and the Renaissance up to the religious upheavals of the sixteenth and seventeenth centuries.

September 20, Saturday. A tremendous battle is raging in the Ukraine. According to the Nazi radio, a Panzer army corps in a pincer movement, has reached Kiev, and operated a junction with another army group coming from Tcherkassy after crossing the Dniepr river. This is how I see it after putting together the bits of information we are given and upon consulting the map, unfortunately not detailed enough for all the city names they are throwing at us.

September 25, Thursday. On the Ukraine front, several Soviet armies are encircled. With great fanfare, the Germans announce the bagging of 600,000 Red Army soldiers, together with huge supplies and equipment. Kiev has been occupied and the Wehrmacht is now beyond the Dniepr River on its way to Kharkov and, we are told, Rostov-on-Don, an important port on the Azov Sea.
Is the Soviet Union on the verge of collapse?

September 29, Monday. A footnote. The British announce the end of Italian resistance in Abyssinia.

October 4, Saturday. Hitler made a speech yesterday, at the Sportpalast in Berlin supposedly to make an appeal in support of the "Winterhilfe", a Nazi social program. But he has come to issue a major proclamation. "On the morning of June 22", he said, "the greatest battle of the history of the world has begun. Everything has gone according to plan and the enemy is already beaten and will never rise again."

Then he gave the list of victory's spoils: 2,500,000 prisoners, 22,000 artillery pieces destroyed or captured, 18,000 tanks out of action as well 14,500 planes. The German armies have advanced up to 600 miles and over 15,000 miles of Russian railroads are again in operation, most of them converted to the international gauge. "But" added the Führer, "the war in the East is not over; only when the German people become a single community of sacrifice can the nation hope and expect that Providence will stand by us in the future."

I don't know which providence Hitler is talking about but it is certainly not my Providence. Furthermore, I would like to challenge the statistics enumerated by Adolf: 22,000 artillery pieces? 18,000 tanks?? 15,000 miles of railroad tracks??? He must have added a zero somewhere.

October 12, Sunday. It has rained all night and the sky is dark and wild where the storm has gone; but now, overhead, little salmon streaks of color show through where the clouds are thinning and beginning to break up. We can expect to have sunshine before long and this is great because we have planned a Scout outing to the castle of Beersel. This castle can be reached by the suburban tramway we take at the Place Rouppe terminal. After about 45 minutes we get to our destination, a medieval ruin 10 miles or so to the south-west of Brussels.

It is a dream of a castle, very romantic, something you can expect to see in the movies with the great difference that this one is not a fake. Built entirely of brick between 1300 and 1310, it is in very poor shape but in the process of renovation based on seventeenth century engravings. It is triangular in design and, at each angle, rises an imposing tower to an height I estimate of 20 meters or 60 feet. One tower has been completely rebuilt, the other two will have to wait until the end of the war before restoration can resume.

We draw sketches, build a few fires in preparation for lunch and form a circle around the main camp fire. The Troop leader has asked me, the "historian", to prepare a brief review of the "life and times" at the beginning of the 14th century, the period which saw the construction of the castle.

In the world of that century, politics revolved around the triangle of rivalries between the Papacy, the Holy Roman Empire and the Kingdom of France. It is the latter which is of interest here because of the intervention of Philip the Fair (fair in face, unfair by nature) into the great and rich County of Flanders. In 1300, Philip annexes Flanders to his kingdom but this move incenses the burghers of Ypres, Bruges and Ghent. Hence a war that results in victory for the "Communes" at the Battle of the Golden Spurs, on the plain before Courtrai in 1302.

These commotions were a source of worry for the Emperor who was holding Brabant, Luxemburg, Hainault, Holland and many other provinces. To protect his territory and as a defense against a possible French invasion, he resolved to build the castle of Beersel.

It was a twenty-five minute speech, with interruptions and questions, rich cultural fare for the average boy scout. The Troop Leader is delighted. He is convinced that, from time to time, his little group should be exposed to our rich local and national history as well as the cultural heritage we share with the rest of Europe. I couldn't agree more.

October 14, Wednesday. I was given, today, a copy of Die Brüsseler Zeitung, the newspaper for the occupation forces in Belgium. It tells me of a great victory in Russia. (Didn't I hear that before?) Two Soviet Army groups have been encircled. (Yes, I know!) The Red Army "can essentially be considered as defeated" and the conquest of Moscow is just around the corner. (Wait and see.)

October 20, Tuesday. The Nazis must be approaching Moscow. The Soviet government and the diplomatic corps have fled to a town called Kuybichev, in the east. I find it on the map after some search, under the name of Samara. Like the French revolutionaries of 1789, the Bolsheviks have renamed quite a few of their towns after their revolutionary heroes. This makes it difficult at times to find out what is what in the list of localities. Stalin it seems has not left Moscow and will direct its defense.

October 23, Friday. From France comes more news about attacks on members of the Wehrmacht. The first German soldier killed in France after the armistice was shot in the Metro in Paris, at the end of August. This was followed by the gunning down of a sergeant at the Gare de l'Est, a major and a civilian in Bordeaux and on October 20th, of the Feld-Kommandant in Nantes.

The Nazis have reacted with ferocity. They have taken hostages, 600 of them, and they threaten to kill them in large batches if the assassins are not denounced or captured.

This is very bad. It could lead to a bloodbath in which innocent people will be the victims. I agree that we should resist the occupant but assassination is not the way. It should be clear that the enemy is all-powerful; he controls the field with his arms, communications and transportation. We can resist, through the daily pinpricks of civil disobedience. There is no need to explain further.

October 26, Monday. That which I feared would happen, happened. In France, the Nazis have shot 50 hostages in Bordeaux, 48 in Nantes and an unknown number in Chateaubriant, Brittany. Facing this horror, what can we do?

On the Eastern front, Berlin announces the occupation of the peninsula of Kertch, in the Crimea on the Black Sea, and the investing of the important naval base of Sebastopol.

I consult with Major Van Eck who conveys to me his perplexity. On the one hand, he is very impressed by the progress made and the victories achieved; on the other, he wonders whether the Germans are not trying to reach too many goals at once. It seems in his words, that "as in 1914, during the advance on Paris, the German Army is reacting to events, following the line of least resistance rather than dominating and determining the outcome."

5

November 3, 1941 - May 15, 1942

November 3, Monday. In history class we are studying the end of the Middle Ages and the efflorescence of Italian Renaissance. Prof. Hermans asks us to prepare a paper on a subject of our choice within the limits of that period. I choose Petrarch (Petrarca) for, although still quite medieval, he is also the harbinger of the Rinascento. The paper has to be ready by December 1st and will be graded as part of the first term history exam.

November 8, Saturday. In a speech at the occasion of the 24th anniversary of the Bolshevik Revolution, Stalin, talking to the peoples of the Soviet Union, has asked for a second front on the European continent, which would considerably lighten the nation's burden.

I don't have the full text but I noted the following.

1. The enemy is throwing ever-new forces into the front, making every effort to seize Leningrad and Moscow for he knows that winter will be bad for him.

2. The Germans assumed that the Soviets were disorganized behind their lines and disturbances would occur. They were mistaken.

November 10, Monday. Finland is leaving the war. They had joined the Wehrmacht in attacking the Soviets. The Finnish radio has announced that its military operations are drawing to a close. The Finns have recuperated the territory lost in 1939-40, and that's all they want.

November 11, Tuesday. Armistice Day and (surprise?) all patriotic ceremonies and display of the national flag are forbidden. I meet, by chance, Major Van Eck with whom I discuss Stalin's speech. He also noticed the reference to the winter, but he is not sure that the mention of "disturbances" is significant. I do, for the simple reason that a dictator has to be ever watchful for any dissent, especially in times of crisis.

Major Van Eck, who knows about my interest in studying the various nationalities involved in the war, wants to add a new one which might play a role in the conflict: the Japanese. He draws my attention to the mission of Saburo Kurusu as special envoy to the United States. He is convinced that this move is to keep the Americans occupied and happy while Japan gets ready for the next aggression.

This attack, says the Major, might take place in Indochina, where the French have allowed them to establish bases, toward invading the Chinese province of Yunnan. They want to capture Kunming the capital, thereby cutting the Burma road, which is the sole line of supply at present for the beleaguered Chinese.

Major Van Eck talked also about the heroism of the Belgian Army during the 18 days campaign May 10 through 28. The army fought several very hard battles against an overwhelming force with, unfortunately, little help from the Allies, who were thrown into confusion. The Belgian losses were heavy, around 7,000 dead plus, let us not forget it, more than 12,000 civilians killed mostly by the Luftwaffe's bombing and strafing.

November 13, Thursday. I just found out that the U.S. Navy, very quietly, has established a naval base in Iceland. With the occupation of Greenland, the U.S. now controls the Denmark Straits. This move will render it difficult for the Nazis to use the straits, which are free of ice all year round, for their attacks on British supply ships.

Nearer to home, the BBC makes mention of a heavy RAF raid on Berlin. The German Air Command has confirmed the raid as well as two others on Cologne and Mannheim. It is worth noting that the British sent out more than five hundred bombers! Of course air war is the only way for Great Britain to help the Russians.

November 15, Saturday. The German newspapers carry articles by their correspondents on the Russian front. They report "unimaginable oceans of mud" in the Ukraine. Men sink into these swamps up to their knees, losing their boots; and vehicles sink up to their axles. They also mention that, because of these conditions, the Luftwaffe is unable to build advanced military airfields.

Another journalist (read: propagandist) complains about

"enormous distances, smashed roads and scorched earth destruction." There is also an admission that the Red Army is the most stubborn and best-equipped force the Germans have yet faced.

Amidst all their victories, I notice that Hitler and the Propaganda Abteilung of Goebbels always, after their boasting of victory, call for further sacrifice to destroy Bolshevism and ward off the destruction of Grossdeutschland. From time to time, they use a journalist or a military commentator to instill a note of pessimism and remind their readers that the war in the East is not over.

November 18, Tuesday. The British Ministry of Information has announced that the aircraft carrier, the 22,000-ton Ark Royal, which the Germans often have reported sunk, has now really been lost, victim of a German U-boat. We don't hear much about the submarine war. The Kriegsmarine however seems to be very active in this field. It is their only way to counteract the supremacy of the Royal Navy. The German admirals can rely on the experience acquired during the Great War.

Very heavy attack and great victories around Leningrad, announced by both sides. To me this means only one thing: stalemate, at least for the time being.

November 23, Sunday. An extremely strong British offensive has started in North Africa. So far it seems to be successful. It started at the Egyptian frontier and even Berlin acknowledges its seriousness. The Imperial forces seem to be very close to Tobruk. This is the port remaining in British hands after the retreat seven months ago, which the Axis forces have tried unsuccessfully to take over ever since. This is very good news and in these dark, rainy, cold days we need a victory or two to sustain a very sagging morale.

Latest news. The German High Command announces a breakthrough in Tula which is just south of Moscow, perhaps 200 km away. The Russians have acknowledged this by mentioning heavy fighting in the Tula area, on what they call the "Moscow front"!

November 24, Monday. The offensive in Libya is going well and the Afrika Korps of General Rommel is fighting fiercely west of Tobruk. The garrison of this town is battling toward the south in order to link up with the advancing British forces. The communiqué mentions that these forces are using American-made tanks. It is the first time that such tanks are used in battle and proof that America "not neutral but co-belligerent" is becoming more involved in this war.

Big news also on the "Ostfront". The Nazis, with thundering fanfare, claim the capture of Rostov-on-Don, with no confirmation from Moscow. The Soviet communiqué talks about "the defenders of Rostov fighting courageously but being forced to retreat".

I am amazed by this German feat. How can they do it, far from their bases, in a sea of mud? The answer is: they can't. Except for the essential spare parts, they must live off the land, despite the scorched earth policy.

November 26, Wednesday. The Imperial forces have recaptured Bardia, a town on the Egyptian border they had taken in January and subsequently lost to the Italo-German army in April.

Good news like this will make people feel better in the midst of the gloom of this wretched winter which, according to the calendar, has not even started yet!

December 2, Tuesday. The Russians have retaken Rostov. This is probably the first setback suffered by the Wehrmacht since the start of their invasion of Russia. A setback only and not a defeat? Is General Winter helping the Red Army?

December 6, Saturday. The Germans have started a new great offensive on the Moscow front. The Russians have announced it while Berlin keeps silent. They are waiting perhaps until they can proclaim the long-awaited victory: the occupation of Moscow

December 8, Monday. Japanese airplanes have attacked American bases at Hawaii and Manila, in the Philippines. This took place on the morning of December 7th.

President Roosevelt has replied to Japan's undeclared war on the United States by decreeing general mobilization. People I have talked to are all quite excited. Now that Powerhouse America is in the war can the Axis countries possibly win? Someone tells me; "On the 826th day of this European conflict, war has spread right around the world"!

I am overwhelmed by these incredible events and reflect that:

1. The U.S. will take a long time before becoming an important factor in this war.

2, The British will probably have to fight in the Far East and that will stretch their forces to the limit.

3. Japan's move should help Hitler by bottling up anti-Axis armed forces far from Europe.

December 9, Tuesday. Three bits of news.

* Singapore has been bombed by Japanese planes.

* Imperial Headquarters in Tokyo have announced that Japan consider itself at war with America and Great Britain in the "Western Pacific".

* In France, two more German soldiers were attacked in Paris during the weekend and a bomb has badly damaged a Montparnasse restaurant taken over by the Occupant. There were no casualties at this restaurant but you can be sure that more hostages will be taken and shot.

December 12, Monday. There is a ton of news, some good, some quite bad.

1. Japan has announced that it has landed troops in the Philippines, that it has occupied an important strategic point in Northern Malaya (in Kota Bharu, to be exact; see map) and that her naval planes have bombed British destroyers in Hong-Kong.

2. It seems that in the first hours of the Japanese attack, the United States has lost more big ships than Great Britain has lost in the whole war, so far. If this proves to be true it will be the greatest reverse suffered by the U.S. in her 165 years of history.

3. The good news is that in Libya the British are still progressing albeit more slowly against the Afrika Korps. They have now occupied El Aden, near Tobruk. On the Russian front, the Soviets claim to have retaken Tikhvin on the railroad to Vologda, east of Leningrad, way up north!

4. Another piece of news is the statement by a military spokesman in Berlin that large-scale operations in the Soviet Union are finished for the winter. Is then Moscow out of reach until further notice? Are the Caucasian oilfields off limits until next spring? The Führer's only hope now is that General Winter and the losses the Soviets have suffered will prevent them from organizing dangerous counterattacks in the near future.

December 13, Tuesday. Hitler declared war against the United

States on December 11th and Musso obediently "goose-stepped" after him. The U.S. has about 150 million people and is highly industrialized. Russia's population is around 170 million. The two countries together can align an impressive number of divisions, if this can be achieved relatively fast. I am told that each of these countries can create armies of 10 million soldiers. But how many men does the U.S. have under arms now? Nobody can tell me but it is not a big number. And how about their training?

On the Eastern front, the Soviets announce that the Germans have retreated in the direction of Volokolamsk a town very near Moscow, on its west side.

December 19, Friday. We are in the middle of our first term exams. Not much time for anything else. I feel tired and am cold and hungry! Add the fact that the RAF bombers fly above us on their way to Germany and keep us awake. So far, we have been spared. Sometimes the ferocious barking of the FLAK guns shakes us out of our beds. We shouldn't complain, however, for the situation is a lot worse in many other countries.

December 22, Monday. Our history teacher is very pleased with my paper on Francesco Petrarca. "Well researched and written in very elegant French." I am delighted! The exams are almost over.

December 24, Wednesday. Last day of class. I have done well in this first term and find myself at the head of the class with a "special mention" for my paper on Petrarch.

Here is, in English translation, the last paragraph of the essay.

The Last days of Francesco Petrarca

"It was at the height of his celebrity and power, in 1369, that Petrarch came to dwell at Padua and shortly thereafter, tired of the life of court and city, retired to the hospitable house of the Augustinian friars at Arquà, in the Eugenean hills. He was so charmed with the beauty of the place that he got his friend, Lombardo da Serico, to negotiate for the purchase of a lot of ground comprising a vineyard, an orchard of olives and other fruit trees. Here he built a house, which still stands, structurally unaltered, and bears witness to the simplicity of his domestic habits and his appreciation of beautiful scenery...

...On July 18, 1374, on his seventieth birthday, they found him in his study his head bowed over a book. At first they did not know he was gone. They clothed him in a flame-colored cassock, garb of the Canons of Padua, and sixteen learned scholars carried him on a bier that was covered with ermine-lined cloth of gold, to the parish church of the village, and laid him down. Later they raised a marble monument, carving on it the epitaph written by the poet for himself:

This stone covers the chilled bones of Francesco Petrarca
Virgin Mother, receive his spirit
O Virgin's Son, be Thou indulgent
And may his soul, now so long wearied of this earth
find rest in the retreats of Heaven
Requiescat in Pace

December 25, Thursday. CHRISTMAS. The "midnight" Mass at the La Madeleine church is held at 7:00 p.m. on Christmas'Eve, because of the curfew. The church is freezing cold, the lights are dimmed. All you can see is the high altar illuminated with a great number of flickering candles which make me think of a medieval church. The nave, dark, is invaded by the pervasive clouds of incense, filled with mysterious figures moving about; all in all an awesome, godly place. The sacristan, whom I know, approaches says a few words that escape me and disappears in the shadows.

The church is jammed for in difficult times people get a little more religion and, moreover, it is Christmas. The choir is exceptionally good and the solemn liturgy must be a balm and solace for many unhappy and worried souls.

Today, Mother has performed miracles with her scanty reserves and prepared a delectable dinner served in the kitchen, a large and most pleasant room, the only heated place in the house. It was a real feast, considering the times we live in. We had soup followed by a delicious ham, potatoes and green vegetables. Besides these, there was a multiplicity of smaller dishes such as pickled eggs, asparagus and apple tart. Not to forget a good Bordeaux (where does that come from?), a real delight.

December 29, Monday. I just found out that Hitler has fired Field

Marshal von Brauschitsch, the head of the Oberkommando des Heeres (OKH), and designated himself as his successor. This means, some of my advisors tell me, that the OKH is "kaputt" and for all practical purposes eliminated in favor of the Oberkommando der Wehrmacht (OKW), which is already completely submissive to Hitler.

I wonder how the Führer can handle the heavy load of dictator and warlord. It seems he wants to control everything, which no one can do, not even a genius.

1 9 4 2

January 2, Friday. When I ask people, I find that for many of them the war is little more than a distant noise in their ears. They have no radio; they never read a newspaper, controlled by the Nazis and full of lies anyhow; the words: Leningrad, Benghazi, Tobruk, Malaya, Singapore are names casually heard, signifying nothing. Their lives are hard and they are absorbed by them, by the daily problems of work, scrounging for food, keeping warm and fighting despair. Life is out of control; it has to be taken in small increments, without a thought for the future. There have been too many disappointments and setbacks, too many hopes crushed.

I can now detect the symptoms of an approaching defeat and this diagnostic is valid for both sides. At first, there is mention of a reverse. Oh! a small one, mind you, nothing to worry about, everything is under control. Then there is great optimism in the communiqués. We are regrouping, the enemy is in bad shape. Also, we shot down three enemy airplanes, blew up seven tanks and bagged 92 prisoners. Finally, more communiqués, more important news, another reverse and then another. Our troops are now fighting around the town of X which, to everybody's surprise is twenty miles behind the original line of defense.

January 7, Wednesday. Back to school on a very dismal, frigid day. The classrooms, unheated for more than two weeks, are literally iceboxes. It seems warmer outside than inside. Not a very good start! However Prof. Van Mulders is not affected by January weather. He is as enthusiastic as ever. I notice that over his cassock he wears a nice, thick, black sweater.

January 12, Monday. There is utter confusion in the Far East. The Japanese seem to be winning on all fronts. There is very little hard news. Kuala Lumpur, the capital of Malaya, is threatened. What then will happen to Singapore, the big British naval base perched at the tip of the very long peninsula?

January 23, Friday. From Berlin: A comprehensive ban on dancing is in effect over all of Germany including the teaching of dancing. This is done, it is stated, at the express wish of members of the Wehrmacht "in view of the difficult operations on the Eastern Front".

The news seems to confirm the reports of a strong Russian offensive started last December and still in progress. The Soviets have announced great German losses especially on the Moscow front but is difficult to get to the truth and distinguish between propaganda and reality. My adviser tells me of heavy German equipment and transportation losses. "This," he says, "is reflected in Hitler's appointment of an Inspector General of Motorized Traffic." The chosen general is authorized to investigate all motor traffic in Germany, the Occupied Countries, including the war zones, whether in military, civil, party or private hands.

One thing is sure as far as we are concerned: less and less cars and trucks in the streets of our capital city and even stricter controls of motor transportation.

More depressing news from the Far East. The Japanese have occupied part of the Philippines, most of Malaya and they are closing in on Singapore.

This war is, among other things, a lesson in geography.

January 25, Sunday. Our Troop leader asks me if I am interested in attending the next Training Session for Assistant Troop Leader to take place in the Summer. I sign up right away.

He also requests me to plan a "cultural" outing to either Bruges or Antwerp. He expects a detailed outline in one week. This being a one-day trip, we will reduce the visit to two or three places (Cathedral, Museum...), at the most.

February 2, Monday. Let's start with a footnote. The first

American infantry division has arrived in Great Britain, in Northern Ireland to be precise, at the end of January. A good sign.

I also find out that there has been a big naval battle between the Japanese Imperial Navy and U.S. and Dutch naval and air forces in the Straits of Macassar. After some search I find these straits to be south of the Celebes. It means the Japanese are on their way to Java, part of the Netherlands East Indies! There is, in the eastern part of that island, an important Dutch naval base, Soerabaya, less than 500 km from the Straits! Can the Dutch and the Americans resist successfully or shall we get more bad news soon?

February 8, Sunday. I present a plan for a trip to Brugge (Bruges) that could take place on May 14, Ascension Day. Leaving early, we would go by train from Brussels, via Ghent, a journey of about sixty miles.

Ascension is a very special occasion because, on that day, Bruges celebrates the possession of a holy relic of the Holy Blood brought back from the Crusades by Dierick of Alsace, Count of Flanders. A great Procession of the Holy Blood has been held every year since 1150, except for brief interruptions during the stormy times of the French Revolution, the Great War and the present one. We will visit the Town Hall, the Oude Griffie, the Belfry, the Church of Notre-Dame, the Hospital St. Jean and the Minnewater.

This is a lot and will result, I am afraid, in quite a few sore feet.

February 13, Friday. The German radio claims that street fighting in Singapore City has ended and the defenders overcome. The British say Singapore is holding on. Singapore is fighting back and counterattacks on the Japanese left flank have been declared successful.

And I say: tomorrow, according to the theory I explained earlier, the BBC will announce that Singapore has fallen.

The Scharnhorst and Gneisenau, the German battle-cruiser Prinz Eugen, the survivor of the Bismarck encounter, all ships that were hiding in Brest, have successfully steamed through the Dover Straits and escaped to Heligoland, their base in Germany.

February 14, Saturday. In France, the Nazis have ordered the execution of forty-five Frenchmen who are held held as hostages, unless the perpetrators of two recent attacks against Germans in occupied France are discovered or denounced in the next few days.

Furthermore, twenty men are to be executed at Tours unless the person who attacked a German sentry is arrested. Twenty-five other hostages will be shot in Rouen if the people who threw a bomb at Germans in that town are not found before this Sunday.

These innocent people will pay for the culprits who are probably communists. The latter couldn't care less about their compatriots as long as their ideology triumphs. They are as totalitarian as the Nazis.

February 16, Monday. Hitler has decorated General Rommel with the Oak leaves and Swords of the Iron Cross, for his "defensive victory" in Libya. Sometimes nice things happen to you even when you are a defeated general.

This General Rommel is very, very popular in Germany for his past victories in North Africa, his recent skillful retreat in Libya and also for his gallantry.

February 18, Wednesday. The Imperial forces in Singapore surrendered unconditionally to the Japanese on Sunday. This was confirmed by Mr. Churchill in a broadcast to the British people. Here is a fragment of his speech, all I could get because of the jamming.

"It is a British and Imperial defeat. Singapore has fallen. All the Malay peninsula has been overrun. This is one of the moments when the British nation can show its quality and its genius. This is one of these moments when it can draw on the heart of misfortune the vital impulse of victory."

February 21, Saturday. Here are a few profiles of some of our teachers.

Mr. Van der Linden. Excellent math teacher. Severe as a Doric column, very strict and therefore not popular. Good flow of language, speaks in a somewhat high-pitched voice. Neat and clipped like his moustache, precise like the crease of his pants.

Mr. Michiels. Flemish (Dutch) language teacher. Vast bulk in a baggy suit. Voice deep and pitched for open air work. Speaks perfect Flemish, of course, but has little use for syntax as generally understood when he speaks French; nevertheless makes himself mighty clear.

Father Goris. Our religious education professor. Short, bald and dapper, with quick bird-like movements. Speaks rapidly in a clear but not too strong a voice without emphasis or exaggerations. A good man and a good priest.

Father Van Dongen. Assistant Director of the St. Pierre High School, in charge of Organization and Discipline. Not a pillar but a tower, square-set, built of solid masonry. Enunciates with the gravity of ancient Rome. Sharp-eyed, he is feared by the students.

March 3, Tuesday. Musso the Benito has announced total civilian mobilization in his country. I am thinking of Signor "Gastella" whom I met with his wife, in August 1940. He cannot be very happy. He had almost made his niche in his adopted country of France and now I can visualize him in uniform somewhere in Dalmatia or Albania or, God forbid! in Libya or Russia.

As far as the mobilization is concerned, it will not make a bit of difference. In a dictatorship the civilians are at the beck and call of the satraps who rule them They shut up and do what they are told.

March 7, Saturday. To get news from America is rare indeed. Here it is: American car manufacturers have ceased all civilian production of automobiles. They will instead switch over to the production of tanks and military vehicles of all kinds. It is a sign that the United States is taking this war very seriously.

March 9, Monday. A sad day for the Dutch in the East Indies. Batavia, the capital, has been occupied, and Java, the island, has capitulated. The Japanese seem to be everywhere victorious. I don't understand how they can be in so many places all at once. I remember my conversations with Major Van Eck on the subject of logistics and I still cannot see how they can supply so many widely separated areas of battle with men and equipment. It must be a logistics nightmare.

Wednesday March 11. It had to happen also in Brussels. Yesterday, on the Boulevard Anspach, the main North-South artery of the capital, a bomb was thrown into a crowd assembled to celebrate the departure of Belgian SS volunteers to the Russian front. Only a few people were injured, none fatally.

I have not paid much attention to this agitation created to lure young men to join the Crusade against Bolshevism, as the Nazis

101

call it. At the head of the movement in French-speaking Belgium is Léon Degrelle, the leader of the Rexist party, now openly in favor of a Nazi regime. At first, Degrelle joined the Wehrmacht, then enrolled as a major in the Waffen SS and now will lead the 28th "Wallonien" Freiwilligen Panzergrenadier Division to fight the Soviets. These volunteers have signed up with the "Waffen" (armed) SS under the German army command, although they are trained separately under SS supervision. The sleeve flash is a badge with the Belgian colors vertically disposed: black, yellow, red, and at the top the word WALLONIE. The Waffen SS cuff title is WALLONIEN, the collar emblem on the right side show the SS runes and on the left the Burgundian knotted sticks in the form of a St. Andrew cross.

I intend to research this SS organization which is so often talked about and has gained such an evil and fearful reputation.

March 16, Monday. The following information cannot be found in the Nazi newspapers.

Mr. Eden, the Foreign Minister, in the House of Commons, has disclosed Japanese atrocities in Hong-Kong. Two of the worst revelations he made:

1 Fifty British officers and men were bound hand and foot and then bayoneted to death.

2. Women, both European and Asiatic, were raped and murdered.

The Japanese will of course deny these accusations. Radio Tokyo has mockingly proclaimed: "Peace and order are being rapidly restored in all occupied areas."

Yes, the peace of the cemeteries and the order of well-aligned tombs.

March 17, Thursday. The Japanese have occupied three towns in New Guinea and are now only about 400 km from Port Moresby that· if taken would be a perfect staging area for an attack on Australia.

Another footnote. The Commander of the Canadian Forces in Britain has warned that a German invasion of England may be attempted this spring; this would be "one of the most dangerous things that could happen to us. It must be a great temptation for Hitler to try to knock England out of the war!"

This general is a joker, for there is no way Hitler will attack this spring. There would be, in Western Belgium and Northern France, heavy concentrations of troops and equipment as well as ships, barges etc., as in the summer of 1940. And although in matters military I am a nobody, I can assure him that there is no trace of build-up in Flanders or any other part of Belgium. Hitler is much too busy dealing with the Russians and preparing for a new push toward Moscow and the Caucasus.

Monday, March 23. I learn that the Minister for War Production in the USA has said that America's output of military supplies could be doubled if all existing machinery were used 24 hours a day, seven days a week.

Yes, but do they have the trained manpower to man this equipment?

April 3, Good Friday. There has been a commando raid against St. Nazaire in France, apparently very successful. The raiders used an old American destroyer with her bow specially reinforced and the ship filled with high explosives.

The destroyer made it through the defenses at the entrance, crashed against the gate of the largest dry dock on the Atlantic Coast and demolished it entirely. The pumping station and dock operating gear have also been destroyed. This action will deprive Hitler of the only dry dock that can lodge a battleship. Good Show!

April 5, Easter Sunday. Easter this year is not early, yet winter tenaciously refuses to loosen its grip. The day is howlingly windy, with what appears to be a promise of snow in the air. A sullen roiling sky hangs in angry motion over the city giving it the look of an El Greco painting.

And the war meanwhile thunders on.

On the Russian front, after a long and difficult winter the Wehrmacht has gone on the offensive along the Kalinin front, midway between Leningrad and Moscow. Further to the south fierce battles are reported in the Kharkov area.

I am surprised to find out that American troops are still fighting in the Philippines. They are resisting in the Bataan peninsula, around the fortress of Corregidor, on the island of Luzon.

April 7, Tuesday. In Burma, the Japanese are trying very hard to cut the "Burma Road", the lone supply road to China. They are also aiming at the oilfields of northwest Burma and the gateway to India, the town of Chittatong.

Do you know Prome? Well, until today I had never heard of it either. It is a town north of Rangoon, menaced by the Japanese. The city is strategically important as a barrier to the rich Yenang-Young oilfields and guards the road to Mandalay.

April 10, Monday. Marshal Pétain has asked the French farmers to collect all possible stocks of wheat to ensure the daily bread ration of the French nation.

We have the same problem, if not worse, here in Belgium. It is increasingly difficult to get enough food to get going. I don't think anyone is starving today in our country. For the housewife however and certainly for Mother who has to feed eight people, it is a daily struggle where connections with the right farmer and imagination in the preparation of palatable dishes play an important role.

The official daily rations being insufficient, everybody has to look for a complementary source of calories. So one turns to the black market. I would guess that one Belgian in six is today involved in this kind of unlawful activity, mostly on a very modest scale. There are in my opinion not many big time "smokkelaars" around. The country is small, only 12,000 square miles; internal controls are strict. It is therefore difficult to get anything organized on a large scale. Every family relies on its own small supplier for a particular type of food: flour, ham, bacon, fats, perhaps eggs. Prices vary widely according to availability and season. It is a different matter for very rare items such as butter and cigarettes.

Father deals directly with a few farmers and comes home at regular intervals with bread and less often, bacon. Everything unfortunately disappears into our stomachs in no time at all. It is the problem of the Danaides, the 49 daughters of Danaus who, according to the ancient Greek tale, were condemned to pour water forever into a leaky vessel. It's never enough!

April 14, Tuesday. British negotiations to mobilize India's 300 million people as a fighting force on the side of the Allies have met with serious difficulties. It appears that the dominant Indian party will reject the British plan for self-rule. I wonder: will the

Japanese cut them a better deal?

April 18, Saturday. Pierre Laval is now in control of the internal and external affairs of France under the authority of Marshal Pétain. This means that Laval has become the virtual dictator of France, with the Nazis supporting him. How will he implement his undoubted intentions of closer collaboration with Hitler and his henchmen?

There has been a bombing raid on Tokyo by American planes. No information so far as to number of planes and where they came from. Mention was made of heavy damage. How do they know? Tokyo for sure will not divulge any details. It is nevertheless quite an accomplishment and must make the Japanese somewhat nervous.

April 26, Sunday. Scouting activities are increasingly frowned upon by the Occupant.

Almost every month there is a new regulation often at odds with former ones. The Nazis know of course that any youth organization in Belgium, except for a very small minority of collaborators, is anti-German and a source of opposition to the regime. Belgium is under military control and the Wehrmacht is a little more lenient than civilian Nazi authorities who are dominated by the SS and the SD or Sicherheitsdienst. This is the case in Holland, Norway and other occupied countries.

April 28, Tuesday. Goebbels announces that the Führer has assumed full discretionary powers in terms of justice. This means that he can be as ruthless and murderous as he wants without having to bother with the legalities.

On this day, in Belgium, France and Holland, all Jews have to wear the "Star of David" the yellow star with, in black, the word "Juif", in French or "Jòod" in Flemish/Dutch.

May 2, Saturday. Radio Bruxelles (French) and Radio Brussel (Flemish) have both announced that a chemical plant at Tessenderloo, in the Limburg province, was destroyed by a powerful explosion that killed two hundred fifty and injured more than a thousand people.

Later in the day, both radio networks informed us that a Technical School and a number of nearby houses were also destroyed or gravely damaged by the blast. No cause was given.

May 4, Monday. Lots of talk in town about the Tessenderloo catastrophe. The factory is a unit of the S.A. Produits Chimiques which manufactured sulfuric acid, synthetic ammonia and nitric acid, all raw materials used for the production of explosives. It also produced fertilizers of different kinds as well as detergents.

Nobody believes the official denial that the plant was manufacturing chemicals for war purposes. It was an hybrid operation like most important factories nowadays in Belgium.They all have to work for the enemy or else be taken over or shut down with their workers deported to Germany as forced labor under the fallacious name of "Arbeitsfreiwillige" (volunteer worker).

A heated discussion is going on as to whether the explosion was due to an accident or sabotage. It is known that the "Witte Brigade" (White Brigade) is active in the Antwerp/Limburg area. My hunch is that they are not involved because the reaction of the German authorities has been so very subdued. This might be, however, because no Germans were killed.

May 6, Wednesday. In the Far East, there is a lull in the fighting. The Japanese have now to decide between invading India or Australia as they probably don't have the strength to tackle both objectives. After the huge successes of the past few months, they may be overextended.

Nazi-controlled radio Brussels announces bombing raids by the RAF on air bases in the provinces of East- and West-Flanders. The RAF is getting more aggressive in attacking military targets, not only in our country, but to a much bigger extent in Germany. The Nazis don't seem able to stop them.

May 8, Friday. Events are happening so fast and all over the world. It is time for an overall review.

* The Red Army has struck at three German military concentrations where Hitler is believed planning his Spring Drive, attacking Kharkov, Kursk and Taganrog.
* Corregidor has fallen. It was the last American stronghold in the Philippines. The now famous fortress, along with others in Manila Bay, was forced to yield after a prolonged siege.
* In Burma, a general withdrawal by the British and the Chinese

armies is said to be underway with the Japanese advancing over the Burma border into China at Wanding. A second Japanese column is trying to encircle the British along the India border in preparation for a march into India!

* The British have landed in Madagascar two days ago, and fighting has taken place between the Vichy French and the invaders. The latter are interested in the capture of the big naval base of Diego Suarez. The British move is to forestall possible attempts by the Japanese to seize the island and to cut off the supply routes around the southern tip of Africa to ports in the Middle East and India.

May 11, Monday. For Belgium, the war is now two years old and there is not much we can look forward to in the immediate future. The liberation we yearn for cannot be achieved until America has geared up for a total war in all sectors of their industry to provide tanks, planes, guns, trucks, airplanes - everything that is necessary to achieve victory.

Footnote. I just learned about a naval engagement in the Solomon Islands that was highly successful. This is the first American victory against the Japanese Navy since the attack on the American naval base of Pearl Harbor, last December.

May 15, Friday. Yesterday, Feast of the Ascension, our Troop went to Bruges on a "cultural" trip. In order not to attract undue attention from our "protectors" we went in civilian clothes, no uniform! traveling in small groups.

We left early and although the train was very crowded we didn't encounter any major difficulties like bombing, strafing or lengthy delays. They happen often and nowadays they are part of daily life.

We arrived in good time for the High Mass at the Basilica of the Holy Blood. Due to the war, sadly, there is no Procession. It was at first simply a religious ceremony but gradually the procession took on the spectacular features the Flemish love so much, including representations of the Apostles, the Nativity, King Herod and so on.

The lower chapel of the Basilica, the crypt, has been restored and is now just as it was in 1150, when it was built. In the opinion of many critics, it is "the most beautiful and perfect specimen of

Romanesque architecture in Europe",

Facing the Grote Markt (Main Market) and towering three hundred and fifty-three feet into the air, the famous Belfry cannot be overlooked while its chimes can be heard for many blocks around. The original structure, dating from the very early Counts of Flanders in the ninth century, was destroyed by fire in 1280 and rebuilt.

To reach the bells, one mounts a steep dark staircase said to have three hundred and sixty-six steps, although we did not count them. The chimes are claimed to be the finest in Europe, and comprise forty-seven bells, weighing in the aggregate fifty-six thousand one hundred and sixty-six pounds. They were cast by Georges Dumery in 1743, and are noted for their soft tone.

The view from the summit of the Belfry is one of the most superb in Flanders, especially if the visitor is so fortunate as to have come on one of those days when the clouds roll in great fleecy masses of dazzling white, forming a wondrous background for the grim, gray tower of St. Salvator and the tapering red spire of the cathedral.

For close to seven hundred years this belfry has watched over the city of Bruges. It has beheld her triumphs and failures, her glory and her shame, her prosperity and gradual decline. In spite of so many vicissitudes it is still standing to bear witness to the genius of the Flemish people, to awaken both memories of old times and admiration for one of the most splendid monuments of civic architecture the Middle Ages produced.

Our next stop was the Church of Notre-Dame erected during the fourteenth and fifteenth centuries. In this church there is an interesting "Adoration of the Magi" by Daniel Seghers, a painter of the late Antwerp school. Another notable treasure is the statue of the Virgin and Child by Michelangelo, executed in 1503, but is hidden at present.

The most famous of the possessions of Notre-Dame, however, are the superb tombs of Charles the Bold and his daughter, Marie of Burgundy. The tomb of Marie is older and by far the finer of the two. It consists of a sarcophagus of black marble upon which rests a life-size recumbent figure of the princess who died of an injury in 1482, at age twenty-five. This was less than five years after her marriage to Maximilian, who later became Emperor. At the command of her son, Philip the Handsome, this masterpiece of stone and bronze was designed by Jan Borman, begun by Pieter De Becker in 1495, and completed in 1502. The figure of the princess reclines above all this, with her hands folded as if in prayer, a crown upon her head and two hounds lying at her feet.

The body of Charles the Bold was brought from Nancy in 1550 at the command of Charles the Fifth (Charles-Quint), his grandson, and eight years later the funeral monument was begun by order of Philip II, and completed in 1562. The figure of the "terrible Duke" is shown clad in armor, with his helmet at one side and a lion crouching at his feet.

At Bruges, for the admirer of the painter Memling, the first place to visit is the St. John's Hospital. There, the first thing to see is the world-famous shrine of St. Ursula. Little it is, yet beyond price in value. It was built as a casket to contain the relics of the saint and was completed in 1489.

The St. John's Hospital possesses three of the master's greatest works: two triptychs entitled "The Marriage of St Catherine", the "Adoration of the Magi" and the diptych representing "The Madonna and Martin van Nieuwenhove."

On our way back to the station, we went by the Minnewater or Love Lake, which, apart from its exquisite beauty, is another memento of the city's former commerce. This was the chief harbor for shipping: and it was, no doubt, thronged with sailing craft, while its banks swarmed with merchants checking their cargoes, stevedores carrying boxes to and fro, with all the varied noise and bustle of a great seaport. It is strangely silent and deserted now. The grass grows tall about the round tower, built in 1398 by Jan van Oudenaerde, and the white swans float serenely and majestically beneath the black arches of the adjoining bridge. It is said that he who stands on the central arch of this bridge at midnight and expresses a wish will have it fulfilled.

Before leaving, we went along the banks of the little lake to a point wherefrom, looking back, we had the round tower and the bridge in the middle distance, the lake in the foreground and the towers of the city on the horizon. This view is, without doubt, the finest the old town can offer to its visitors.

6

May 16 - September 7, 1942

May 16, Saturday. The period of Ascension/Pentecost is a mini-vacation for us at school. It is the last breathing spell before the last seven weeks leading us to the end of the school year. Classes will resume on May 19.

On the war front, I note Mr. Churchill's speech to the Empire made about a week ago in which he warns Germany that any use of poison gas by the Nazi military machine would result in the RAF carrying gas warfare "on the largest possible scale far and wide against military objectives in Germany".

Regarding a possible second front, Mr. Churchill said that the "militant spirit" demanded one but "naturally I shall not disclose what our intentions are". This to me means just one thing: Don't count on a second front this year!

May 17, Sunday. The weather today: fine; light cool SW breeze; the sun is just showing now. The air is clouded with the mist of a fine morning.

May 19, Tuesday. New types of tanks (where do they come from?) are leading the Red Army advance into the outskirts of Kharkov in one of the greatest battles of the war. This is not confirmed by the Germans.

May 20, Wednesday. In Paris, ten days ago, an SS squad, at dawn, executed fifty Frenchmen, "communists and Jews", the name given by the Germans to all who resist Nazi rule. They died for an attack on a lone German soldier.

May 28, Thursday. Reinhard Heydrich, Deputy Gestapo chief and Reich Deputy Protector of Bohemia-Moravia, was critically wounded during an attack on his automobile by Czech "terrorists" at a town near Prague. All Nazi-controlled radio networks announced the news. No details were given.

May 29, Friday. Anyone who has read Mein Kampf (I read it, in French, and found it abysmally boring) is aware that Hitler is an anti-semitic rascal. I don't know when it started in our country but virulent attacks on the radio and in the papers have been conducted against Jews. Later, steps were taken by the Nazi administration to "reduce the plutocratic Jewish influence in all aspects of Belgian life" especially in the commercial- industrial- and liberal professions.

As mentioned earlier, as of April 28, all Jews living in Belgium are required to wear a yellow star on the left breast of all outside clothing worn in public. This is awful and ominous. For the Jews, it must be the rock bottom of humiliation and degradation.

June 1, Monday. In Libya, General Rommel is attacking in force and pushing the Imperial forces back toward Egypt. It looks serious.

June 2, Wednesday. No wonder there were so many planes way, way up there humming all night long. Two days ago a huge air raid was conducted by the RAF against Cologne, the fifth-largest city in Germany. More than 1250 planes took part in the attack and dropped 3,000 tons of bombs. It is said that the town is now in ruins.

June 6, Saturday. Reinhard Heydrich died two days ago in a Prague hospital, one week and one day after the attack on his automobile by Czech patriots. A blackout of information over the Nazi radios was lifted yesterday with the news that the total of executed persons has reached the official figure of 176 for a crime none of them committed.

In North Africa, the situation has changed for the worst. The Imperials have been pushed back from their front at El Agheila to Ain el Gazala and Bir Hakeim, 500 km to the east.

For his outstanding victories and generalship Hitler has promoted Rommel, Beloved of the Nation, to the high rank of Field Marshal, the youngest ever in the history of the German army. His full name is Erwin Johannes Eugen Rommel born,

November 15, 1891, at Heidenheim in Württemberg. He is not yet 51 years old.

The RAF air offensive against Germany intensifies. After Cologne, Essen and Bremen have been attacked, as well as air bases in occupied France, Belgium and Holland. More than 1,000 planes were involved in these raids.

June 15, Monday. The town of Lidice in Czechoslovakia has been wiped out. This was announced by General Kurt Deluege who has replaced Heydrich as the "protector" of the Czechs. Deluege added that the entire male population of the village has been executed.

The Nazi statement says further: "In the course of the search for the murderers of the SS leader Heydrich it has been definitely proven that the inhabitants of the village of Lidice near Kladno, in the Czech coalmining district, have offered assistance and help to the perpetrators of the crime.

"Their hostility against the State has furthermore been established by the fact that pamphlets hostile to the State, as well as arms, and an illegal radio set have been found.

"Since therefore, the inhabitants, by their activities and the assistance rendered to the murderers have proven their hostility, all male adults of the village have been shot, and the female inhabitants have been taken to a concentration camp and the children sent to a more appropriate institution.

"All the buildings of the village have been razed to the ground and the name of the place has been abolished."

It is obvious that there was no trial, just torture, summary executions and deportation. A perfect example of Nazi terrorism and murder.

The town of Lidice is gone
but its name will live forever.

June 16, Tuesday. From America, via London comes the news of a big naval and aerial battle and a great victory in the mid-Pacific, but no further details are available. Is it pure propaganda? I hope not. We need some very positive news for a change to cheer us up.

June 26, Thursday. A German offensive is in full swing on the Kharkov front as Field Marshal Fedor von Bock has thrown in 400,000 men to gain control of the vital Kharkov-Rostov railway and other objectives.

On the Sebastopol front, the Russians themselves acknowledge that the situation is serious.

In North Africa, Tobruk has fallen to the Germans; Rommel and his Afrika Korps have penetrated Egypt!

July 1st, Wednesday. As the sun rose this morning, a thin streamer of pink light lay across the east. The gray clouds that have so recently played with the stars now caught fire and became gold arrows in the heavens. The light grew minute by minute, the pink turned a dull red, then to mauve, a veritable furnace of light blazed up above it. In the midst of this, the sun came up over the Flemish plain.

Despite war and calamities, eternal nature displays its summer beauty.

July 3, Friday. As exam for French composition, Prof. Van Mulders requests from us an essay imitating a passage of a famous author, ancient or modern, from Homer to Victor Hugo. We have only ten days to produce a masterpiece. Easily said; and there is a long list of other exams! I will have to skip this Sunday's Troop meeting and perhaps the next one too.

July 4, Saturday. For my essay, I have chosen to imitate "The Bore" by Horace, the Latin poet (65 - 8 B.C.). And I will change the title to: "The Adhesive Bore"!

No time for war news but brother Lucien tells me that the eastward drive by Rommel and his German-Italian forces have been halted at El Alamein, in Egypt, only 70 miles from Alexandria. In 11 days, Rommel and his troops have advanced 340 miles from fallen Tobruk, in Cyrenaica.

July 5, Sunday. I take some time off from study to check on the war situation and find that in Russia the battle for Sebastopol is almost over and the Germans are the victors!

In England, a few days ago, Mr. Churchill delivered another one of his realistic speeches before the House of Commons. The Prime Minister disclosed that 50,000 men have been lost in Libya and he warned gravely that instead of ending in 1942, as many wishful thinkers hope, the war will be a long one.

He declared that the present situation is the most critical since the fall of France and at any moment we may receive news of grave importance. He asserted, however, that the Battle of Egypt is not yet decided and that brilliant offensive activities by the United States Navy and Air Force had definitely swung the balance of power in the Pacific from Japan to the U.S.

To the "blood, sweat and tears," which were all he could promise at the outset of his regime, Churchill frankly admitted he had to add "muddle and mismanagement."

He offered to take full responsibility and in heartfelt tribute to the prodigious war effort of the United States, he hopes that better times will come.

July 8, Wednesday. No time for the diary. Working hard at preparing a slew of exams plus the Essay "Le Fâcheux" (The Bore.) It is getting longer and longer.

July 13, Monday. Finished and remitted "The Bore". I think it is good. Other exams, all right.

July 16, Thursday. Last exams of the school year. Tomorrow we get the results and start Summer vacation. Prof. Van Mulders is very pleased with "The Adhesive Bore".

July 17, Friday. Very good results. I get the "Prize of Excellence" which means top of the class. My family will be proud. I am exhausted.

July 20, Monday. I slept, slept, slept... and now feel better. Two weeks ago, or thereabouts I received excerpts of a speech made in Washington by Oliver Lyttleton, the British War Production Minister. Here are some of his comments.

Britain's manpower. Out of a population of 33 million between age 14 and 65, 22 million are working full time in industry, the armed forces or civil defense. This is equivalent to the mobilization of 60 million people in the United States.

Britain's womanpower. The country has mustered five and one half million women in industry and of this number one and one half million did not work in peacetime. They work up to 55 hours a week and do jobs which two years ago would have been described as impossible for women to handle.

Britain's war production. The country produces tanks, jeeps and other mechanical vehicles at the rate of 257,000 a year. It is manufacturing 40,000 big guns a year, supplying them with 25 million rounds of ammunition. (I calculate that this represents 625 rounds per gun, on average.) Aircraft production has increased by 100% above the last quarter of 1940 and merchant ships by 57%.

The numbers are impressive but are they accurate? Why have they been divulged to the world, especially to the United States? I have a suspicion that Mr. Lyttleton is telling America: "This is what we have done; we can go no further. It is up to you to now assume the burden of war."

July 25, Saturday. Father Pierre Capart, whom I have known for about three years now, has asked me to join his group of leaders to help run the Youth camps he has organized recently. These camps welcome and shelter undernourished boys age 11 to 15, from the poorest part of Brussels and its suburbs, who are in great need of physical, mental and spiritual guidance, in these times of want. His organization is supported by the "Oeuvre Nationale de l'Enfance" a branch of the Health Ministry, which provides help, mostly in the form of special rations, unavailable otherwise.

I agree to help at the Youth camp set up for the summer at the Collège Cardinal Mercier, on the outskirts of Braine l'Alleud, a town about 15 miles south of Brussels, near the famous site of Waterloo. I will report on Saturday, August 1st, for a stay of three weeks. Brother Lucien will accompany me.

July 28, Tuesday. Rumors have it that the Nazi "authorities" have plans to send Belgian workers as forced labor to Germany. Nothing definite and nothing official yet. This affects our family directly as brother Michel falls within the age bracket of potential "Fremdarbeiter in Deutschland."

August 1st, Saturday. On our way to Braine L'Alleud, we have to catch a connection at the North Station of the Belgian Railroad System. Upon arrival at the station, we notice a huge banner at the top of the building which says: "V" is the symbol of German Victory" in French and in Flemish. The "V" is partly surrounded by two crossed laurel branches.

This is the Nazi response to the immensely successful "V for Victory" campaign launched by the BBC Belgian program, designed to encourage resistance to the Nazis and it has been an instant hit in our country. Almost overnight, a rash of "V"s, chalked or painted, have appeared on almost every available flat surface in the kingdom. The Germans at first tried to stop the movement by painting over or washing off the seditious sign but this proved more than futile. In no. time at all there were hundred of thousands of "V"s to daub over: an impossible task. At present, the Occupant tries to counter this national defiance by unfolding, here and there, a banner carrying his own impotent slogan.

We reached the College just in time for the noonday meal in the midst of the deafening din of shrill, youthful voices, and the clatter of crockery, forks and knives.

I sit at the head table and make acquaintance with the team of leaders, six of them, myself included, for a group of sixty very noisy young people. I am immediately put in charge of "planning". Why people always assume I am a planner beats me. I am not. I don't like the stuff at all. I am more of a fast improviser. Anyhow, I am also in charge of morning gymnastics, refectory supervision and afternoon outings. At night, I am in charge of the juniors dormitory and will sleep in an adjacent alcove for purposes such as tummy aches, bad dreams and, yes, sleepwalkers. The seniors have their own room and brother Lucien got a very nice one. The college is a boarding school, giving us all the amenities of a well organized institution including showers (hot water is rationed), tennis courts, football (soccer) fields, a swimming pool and a beautiful gym. This is real luxury.

There is only one problem, I am told. We are not alone! Half of the buildings and grounds have been requisitioned by the Wehrmacht as a rest and refit station. They occupy all premises outside our central building, which in itself is quite impressive and self-sufficient. The station seems to be the headquarters of an important unit disseminated around Braine l'Alleud. We civilians, potential spies and saboteurs, are not supposed to get too curious but we find out anyway. It is impossible to hide troop movements and there is always some loose talk.

August 6, Thursday. Comfortably settled in my new "job", I have rapidly established my authority over the boys. They are a good group, ready to listen, eager to learn; at times a little wild but boys will be boys. They learn a lot: proper table manners, good hygienic habits plus readily accepted discipline, firm but not harsh. They get good food, regular sleep and participate in a host of activities that take care of their spiritual and physical needs.

August 8, Saturday. Brother Michel called me this morning. It is official: Belgian men, age 18 to 45 can be called up for forced labor in Germany. Exceptions are foreseen for those who can prove they hold an "essential" job in this country; that is if they collaborate directly with the occupants or hold a job in a firm producing goods for the Nazi war effort.

August 11, Tuesday. From the window of my room, I have a grand view of the plain of Waterloo, the "morne plaine" of Victor Hugo, where the great battle was fought on June 18, 1815, which ended the Napoléon era. And quite near, less than a mile away is the "Butte du Lion", the Lion's Mound, erected in commemoration of one of the famous battles in world history. The view gives me the idea of organizing a tour of the battlefield, including the Mound, with our group of adolescents. It will be an excellent lesson in European history and a reminder that our country has been forever a battleground where the Great Powers came to settle their silly dreams of conquest and glory.

August 13, Thursday. Every morning, around 11 o'clock, I lead the flock to the swimming pool for the daily romp in somewhat frigid water. The weather has been fine but the cool nights have kept the pool temperature on the low side. This doesn't trouble the kids. I am amazed at their resistance to cold. They can swim and splash around for forty-five minutes without showing any sign of being chilled or numb, symptoms we are always watching for.

We share the pool with the Germans. We have it in the morning and they come in the afternoon, usually in groups of thirty led by their Gefreiter (sergeant) singing their marching songs in perfect unison. After two years of occupation I recognize a few tunes, like Valderi-Valdera, Veronika and the inevitable "Wir fahren gegen England". At times, they take up the rousing battle songs of 1813, the German war of Liberation against Napoléon:

> "Der Gott der Eisen wachsen liess
> Der wollte keine Knechten."
> The God who made iron / Had no use for lackeys.

Another song I pick up is:
Ins Feld / In die Freiheit Wohlauf Kameraden,
aufs Pferd, aufs Pferd gezogen".
Stand up, comrades, on your horse, on your horse/
To the battlefield and to freedom to come

Except for "Wir fahren nach England" these are all Army songs. I have been told that within the confines of the Wehrmacht, the military brass doesn't want too much interference from the Nazi party.

August 17, Monday. Almost daily, weather permitting, we have short afternoon outings. Today however we get ready for a tour of the Waterloo battlefield. We start with the Butte du Lion, close by. It was raised in 1823-27 by the then government of the Low Countries (Belgium plus present Netherlands). A truncated cone, it is 150 ft. high and 530 ft. in diameter at the base, surmounted by a colossal molded lion looking towards France.

At the foot of the Lion is a circular building which houses an immense panorama, 330 ft. long, depicting the entire battle, the last effort in a four-day campaign.
Napoléon led 130,000 men into Belgium in June of 1815. He fought the Prussians at Ligny and Fleurus then headed toward the English. He attacked them on the Plateau of Mont-St-Jean, near the village of Waterloo.

The Emperor was unable to begin the battle until about noon; the sun was hidden, the weather rainy (what else!) and he could not maneuver his artillery. The Farm of Haie-Sainte and the Plateau were attacked. Marshal Ney courageously led his cavalry in repeated charges. The Emperor prepared to support these charges with the infantry, hoping for victory before the Prussians arrived.

Once again, Ney directed his cavalry to the Plateau of St. Jean and charged fiercely against the English battalions disposed in square formations. It was seven o'clock in the evening and the English were falling back. Napoléon attacked with a column of the Garde to break the center of the English lines. It had hardly started when Blücher appeared on the right wing and Grouchy with his 30,000 French troop was nowhere to be seen.

At that moment, Wellington attacked with his reserve battalions waiting in the adjacent wheat fields. Their deadly fire spread disorder through the ranks of the Garde, and they scattered. It was eight o'clock. All that was left to the Old Garde was to endeavor to cover the rout of the fleeing French army which was being hotly pursued into the night.

The battle of Waterloo in which a total of 49,000 soldiers on both sides lost their lives, soon entered history as legend.

We rejoined the road to Braine l'Alleud and reached the College, tired and hungry but the possessors of a little more knowledge. At supper the amosphere is very subdued as some of the younger ones hardly can keep their eyes open. We sent them to bed early and didn't hear a peep all night.

August 18, Tuesday. Because I speak German, sort of, I have been designated as the spokesman for our group with the Occupiers on all matters involving the use of common facilities such a the swimming pool, the sporting complex, which includes the football (soccer) fields, tennis and basketball courts.

In order to make me feel better, the big chiefs give me, jokingly, an official and fancy title: "Minister Plenipotentiary Extraordinary" or MIPLEX, in imitation of military acronyms.

My interlocutor on the other side is an Oberleutnant; I therefore outrank him by a big mile! The first time I met him, I stumped him somewhat because of my greeting in a half-mock military manner.

"Melde gehorsamst, Herr Oberleutnant."

Curious, he wants to know where I learned the proper way of addressing an officer, how I know he is a first lieutenant and how come I speak German?

I don't quite answer these questions but I get his attention and, hopefully, respect, which should make my job as MIPLEX a lot easier.

August 19, Wednesday. I am asked to stay until August 24, instead of the 22nd because my replacement is not available earlier. No problem.

August 20, Thursday. My Oberleutnant came to see me this morning, after breakfast, with a request from his colonel: Could they use the Paradeplatz this Saturday morning? The Paradeplatz is the big courtyard in front of the central building a perfect place for a parade, a military parade that is. It is not for me or the leaders of the Youth camp to give such authorization and I refer him to the college administrator. He has that approval, he answers, but his commanding officer wants to be sure we have no plans to use the courtyard that morning. We have no objection except that we use it for our daily gymnastics early in the morning. No problem, the mustering before the parade will not start until ten o'clock.

He clicks his heels, a short bow, a perfect military salute and leaves.

August 22, Saturday. After breakfast I rush through the front doors and find myself in the courtyard almost bumping into a group of officers. I notice my oberleutnant who bows very slightly in my direction and, curious, I survey the scene. Our esplanade has truly become a Paradeplatz. There must be at least eight hundred soldiers arranged in squares of company size, all rigidly arrayed for the parade.

I look at the officers and get another surprise. Among the forest green of uniforms, with the rimmed collars, the silver epaulettes and hobnail-style rank stars, I notice a touch of red. Yes, indeed, the red of the collar patches of the first German general I have ever seen.

He is tall and slim, not at all my idea of a Wehrmacht general officer; I expect him to look rather like an arrogant Prussian Junker. He is more like a professor, except that he is perfectly groomed. I am attracted by the uniform, the excellence of cut and cloth, the riding breeches with the red stripes and the gleaming riding boots.

As is well known, no uniform is fun without medals; my general wears, on his left breast, a row of ribbons plus the Iron Cross First Class and the wound badge. More important, around his neck, the Ritterkreuz or Knight's Cross awarded only for activities having a decisive influence on the course of the war. It is suspended from a ribbon of the same color as the Iron Cross Second Class, black, white and red, but slighly broader. A Ritterkreuzträger, I am told, wears his award at all times, even when in shirt sleeves. The general wears a peaked cap with visor, of high quality as it should be for a person of his rank, with reddish piping around the top and a chinstrap of pink-colored cord.

August 25, Tuesday. Yesterday, after lunch we left Braine l'Alleud and the youth camp.

We had a little going-away dessert, an excellent cherry pie, my favorite. I enjoyed the experience with the leadership and the boys who greatly need the exercise, the discipline and the better food.The members of the leadership were great and of a quality which makes me wonder. I will have to discuss this with Fr. Capart next time.

I am now preparing for a four-day training program for future Troop leaders which will take place on private property in Godinne, near Namur. The choice of the place was made to minimize any problems we might encounter with the Occupant, always suspicious of any assembly of young people, especially in isolated areas. They fear the constitution of guerilla bands or the "maquis", and keep sharp eyes on such groups.

August 26, Wednesday. A week ago, at Dieppe, on the Normandy coast, the Allied forces made a large Commando landing and after a nine-hour battle re-embarked for England after suffering heavy casualties and great loss of equipment.

At this occasion, the OKW made a special announcement:

" A large-scale landing made by Britain, U.S., Canadian and de Gaulle troops, about one division strong, in the early hours of today on the French Channel coast near Dieppe, under strong protection of naval and air forces, and including tanks, was repelled by the German coastal defense troops with heavy losses to the enemy...

"More than 1,500 prisoners are in German hands, including sixty Canadian officers. The enemy casualties are very high."

The other side has not much to say and is not a little embarrassed: "Apart from the losses inflicted on the enemy, vital experience has been gained in the employment of substantial number of troops in an assault and in the transport and use of heavy equipment during combined operations...".

The Allied Headquarters mention further: "In addition to the destruction of the six-gun battery and an ammunition dump... a radio-location station and a flak battery were destroyed..."

All right, but do you need to send out a full division to achieve these results? There is something fishy in the whole enterprise.

What were the objectives? Have they been achieved? Apparently not.

August 27, Thursday. On the Russian front, the Germans have massed possibly 800,000 men on a 60-mile front at the Don river elbow in an attempt to smash through to Stalingrad. I gather from the communiqués that a battle is raging throughout the entire Don elbow at the point where it is closest to the Volga river, 40 miles west of Stalingrad.

In the Caucasus, units of the Wehrmacht are pressing hard around Krasnodar, and the Soviets are again forced to retreat. If the Germans reach the petroleum fields of Baku, the Russians will be in big trouble indeed.

It is strange that the Nazis are not making much progress around Stalingrad or on the Moscow front: a case of not being able to push into several directions all at once?

August 28, Friday. American troops have invaded some islands of the Solomons and a big battle is underway. From the scanty information we get, one of the island is called Guadalcanal, which I found easily on the map. Another one is Tulagi, an island I cannot find but seems to be important.

The "experts" tell me that the future of the entire Solomons' campaign hangs on the success of this battle.

August 29, Saturday. In town, I notice a few Afrika Korps men who are here on leave. They are dressed in sand-color tropical tunics made of what seems to be lightweight cotton and matching field caps with visors. They wear combat boot shoes with short leggings and not the heavy regular jackboots.

August 31, Monday. It is not easy nowadays for a young man to travel by train in this country. If you look 16 or over you can be sure to attract the attention of the "Grüne Polizei" which, as far as I know, is the uniformed branch of the German police in occupied countries.

They will stop you, scrutinize your ID card and ask all kind of questions such as: is this your current address; where are you going; what is the purpose of your trip; where will you be staying; when do you plan to be back; do you transport any contraband (black market goods); where do you work?

The last question is a dangerous one for they might be looking for "volunteers" for the great Paradise of Grossdeutschland and recruit you, without further ado, on your way to that paradise.

Furthermore, you shouldn't travel with too many pieces of luggage, for even if the Grüne Polizei is blessedly too busy somewhere else, you can still fall into the clutches of the "inspectors". Their job is to curb the universal black market system and stop the small "smokkelaar" a slang word for black marketeer, who travels from town to town with his precious and illegal wares: butter, real coffee, ham and bacon, or cigarettes.

If then, you should carry a heavy knapsack or voluminous suit cases you can be assured to have your luggage thoroughly searched. Should you be caught with forbidden goods, you are fined on the spot and the precious cargo confiscated. If you don't have the money or refuse to pay, you will be carted off to jail and the judge will impose a heavier fine.

As to the big and important traffickers, their merchandise travels through much safer channels, thanks to "protectors" who allow them to carry on, their business unhindered. I have even heard that these protectors are often high placed officers of the Wehrmacht or Nazi big shots who will exchange plundered goods, mostly food, for stolen works of art, those they cannot snatch without an intermediary.

September 1, Tuesday. The above explains why our group of eighteen trainees has to be very watchful. To avoid unhappy encounters we have switched to civilian clothes, carrying our scout uniforms in our luggage; we travel as light as possible using a medium-sized suitcase and a satchel containing our lunch and our dinner for tonight. We have been told to be careful and sit in separate compartments.

We meet at the Luxembourg station left of the ticket counters at precisely 10 o'clock. There are eleven of us (the rest will join us in Namur), energetic, assertive and right away discipline breaks down and all caution is thrown to the winds. We make acquaintance, talk loudly, pace the departing hall and finally stride towards platform 2, when our train is announced.

We pile into one compartment and soon the air is thick with

cigarette smoke. In our Troop smoking is frowned upon and practically non-existent but that doesn't seem to be the case in other troops. In protest, two members of the group take refuge on the rickety-rickety platform joining the railroad cars. They call it taking "a bit of fresh air".

Ensconced in a corner, I watch them talk animatedly with expressive gestures as the train rattles on. The young man facing me is of average height and slim built with good features and light hair; the other one is a tall, muscular fellow with a friendly face and slate-gray eyes. He has the largest hands I have ever seen. They seem to have a life of their town constantly in motion, twisting and turning, as though eager to have something to express.

As I intend to live a little bit longer, I resignedly leave the group to its fate when an irate conductor, appearing from nowhere, orders them back to the compartment. They comply and right away proceed to open the window, creating a draft strong enough to blow away a bewigged passenger's hairpiece. I discreetly switch to a quieter place in order to gather my thoughts about the days ahead.

After Gembloux, the train suddenly slows down to a crawl and finally halts on a sidetrack at a little empty station. Nobody bothers to tell us the reason for this unexpected stop. But we know. It is either an air raid in the making or a bottleneck the result of a previous bombing run or, perhaps, we have to leave the passage free for more important traffic.

Everybody alights while some anxious faces scrutinize the empty skies. About five minutes later a German-built locomotive chugs along pulling a military convoy. It is unusual because this type of convoy travels at night for fear of being blown to kingdom come. It must be a hurried operation or someone high up is a great optimist.

First comes a flatbed car, half of it occupied by a four-barreled anti-aircraft gun, the 20mm Flakvierling 38; the other half carries two German armored cars. This tells me that a Panzer division is under way since this type of armored car is its forward screen in battle.

More flatbeds roll by carrying tanks with a skeleton crew, needed I guess for loading and unloading the rather impressive monsters. I make out two types: the smaller ones must be the 20-ton Mark III and the bigger 27-ton Mark IV with its 75mm elongated barrel. From time to time, bunched in groups of two or three, appear regular freight cars, some hermetically closed, and others with doors half-opened, showing black-clad soldiers in a leisurely pose. I notice that both flat and regular freight cars are from different countries, the majority with the distinctive "B" of the Belgian National Railroad, as well as German and French units. I even find a car with the identification "B.B. Oesterreich" neatly crossed over by a white bar and carrying underneath the new stenciled sign: DR or Deutsche Reichsbahn.

As the train moves along, I am wondering how many pair of eyes count and discreetly note the number of cars and the load it carries. How long will it take, I muse, for this information to reach the proper channels for transmission, if important enough, to the appropriate offices in England.

The last car has disappeared behind a curve and for another twenty minutes nothing happens. In the meantime the "tall muscular young man with the friendly face" is pacing the grass overgrown platform no doubt to release a surfeit of impatience. Not yet knowing his name I have privately nicknamed him "porte-avion" because he is sporting a crew cut with a particular peak above his brow that reminds me of the flat top of an aircraft carrier.

All of a sudden, the train engineer releases two short steam hoots punctuated a few seconds later by the conductor's shrill whistle. At that point, in a burst of nervous energy, "Porte-Avion" starts to impersonate a Nazi official, marching to and fro shouting: "Allen einsteigen, hinein... schnell! schnell!" to the astonishment of the passengers wondering about the apparition of a non-uniformed Nazi, in a train of no importance, not going any further than the provincial town of Namur. Then turning on his heels, he spots an older lady clutching a huge handbag not proceeding fast enough to his taste, at whom he yells in his best SS accent: "Was denken Sie meine Dame, schnell einsteigen, los! los!"

Startled, she miraculously recovers her long-passed youthful nimbleness and, the handbag notwithstanding, disappears in the steaming train. I can almost hear her comments when, reunited with her friends and gasping for breath, she whispers: "Tout de même, ces Boches, ils ne respectent rien." (Truly, these Huns, they respect nothing.)

Meanwhile, "porte-avion" is proceeding towards the end of the train, surefooted and shouting at the top of his lungs with the majesty of an aircraft carrier slicing through the immense ocean and leaving a wake which gleams in the starlit night.

The train is now well on his way and we think we have lost our SS impersonator when he appears, out of breath, at the other end of the passenger car having, immersed in his teutonic agitation, almost missed the train.

The action has made porte-avion hungry; his name is Jean-Marie Lagae, by the way. He now proceeds to unwrap a magnificent sausage which he endeavors to cut into thin slices. They soon become common property and are put in a very safe place, our stomachs, with the now current remark; "Encore un que les Boches n'auront pas," best translated as "Another national treasure the Hun will not get."

At the Namur station, because of the delay, we are prepared to rush in order to catch the connection for Dinant, when we spot a squad of German police. We disband at once and proceed to melt away into the crowd. Only two of us are stopped, checked and released.

One by one we reach the platform for Dinant acting as nonchalantly as we can. We have nothing to hide, of course, but with the Nazis you never know.

All is well. A group coming from Liège has joined us; it helps to increase the decibels in the train which delivers us in the little town of Yvoir. There we meet the two Scout Masters who will be our leaders in the leadership program.

With our luggage safely stowed into a little cart pulled by a pony, we walk to Godinne in small groups of three or four again not to attract too much attention. But by now we have become an uncontrollable bunch. We end up in a tight group talking, shouting, smoking and behaving like school kids that of course we are. It is fortunate that we did not, once underway, encounter an inviting café or we might have reached our destination very late indeed.

As it is, we get to the Collège of Godinne as night falls. The building lies along the river Meuse on the side of a gently sloping valley, surrounded by low hills and spread out toward a higher hill further away, where the sacred forests, it seems, have grown almost undisturbed since the beginning of time, concealing whispers of the gods and the howling of the wolves.

September 2 and 3. Wednesday-Thursday. A leadership program, like the one we are now attending, normally requires camping under canvas. The war circumstances do not allow it. We therefore use two small dormitories at the College, the equivalent of the ones at Braine l'Alleud, and we can sleep in relative comfort. The rest of the program, however, follows the regular tough schedule: Réveille at 6:15 a.m., cold shower, PT drill followed by Mass when available and breakfast. Then follows a series of lectures on the history and the basic tenets of the Scouting movement, how to develop organization skills, adolescent psychology, the human qualities required from a leader and many other topics, some boring and some of great interest.

On Thursday, after breakfast, we are told to get ready for a 24-hour solitary hike which includes a night under the stars. We are to leave at ten o'clock to return before noon on Friday. The rules are simple: a hike of at least 40km (25 miles) alone; no contact is allowed with any of the participants except, in case of a fortuitous encounter, greetings and a little chat. The trip has to take place under cover of the woods; the use of paved roads is forbidden. As equipment we take with us a blanket, raincoat and a satchel or knapsack containing knife, canteen, mess kit and compass plus a few provisions consisting of three medium-size potatoes, half a bread, and also oh luxury! a slice of ham and two pears. That's it. We have to survive on this diet and anything else we can find. Stealing of course, is a no-no; buying is allowed to an amount of ten francs.

It has rained most of the morning and as we leave, the sky is dark and wild where the storm has gone. Overhead little salmon streaks of color show through where the clouds are thinning and begin to break up. I suspect we'll have sunshine before long.

After a look at the map we are not to take with us, I decide to walk east towards the village of Crupet and then further to the outskirts of the town of Spontin. I will then veer south for a few miles and plan to spend the night in the forest nearby.

I take a path through the woods along the Bock river which I follow until it is joined by the Crupet. I walk up that river to the village of same name which, as an inveterate tourist-historian, I proceed to visit. I find that it contains a small castle of the 14th century, surrounded by a moat. It is still private property and cannot be visited. I then turn to the dark little church of the same period. In the shadowy light, I spot a small rack of votive candles and light one; the light shines on a marble man in armor and a marble woman, sleeping side by side: the Sire d'Autricourt who died in 1485, and his lady. Over those two is a gracious peace that confounds the cynic. "Till death do us part" I whisper and dedicate the candle and my prayer to the memory of these long-forgotten souls.

So, feeling a thousand years old I walk slowly through the village. A fresh breeze comes over the wooded hills and bustled small clouds out of the sun's way. The earth is spongy under the graveled road and the morning rain has left the grass and trees with a share of summer's greenness. Life is not bad despite the storms of war and the faraway past.

I meet an elderly man who doesn't respond to my greeting. He is gaping vacantly around, gazing into the sky as though he had never seen it before. I am about to take a path into the leafy shade, when I spot a neat-looking farm and its sight turns my thoughts to an ever existing concern: food. I have been thinking that my potatoes, bread and the slice of ham will not be sufficient to sustain me during this hike. I have to find a supplement somewhere and this farm might do.

The barking of two ferocious-looking dogs prompts the appearance of an inquiring lady whom I assume to be the farmer's wife. "Bonjour", she says, projecting an enthusiasm for life I thought had been lost in the modern world, "What can I do for you?" I show my two five-franc pieces and ask her what I can buy for that amount. She laughs and without a word disappears in the backroom. I am standing in the entrance hall that reeks of sour milk but is as clean as a whistle.

Ten minutes pass, and not a sound; did she forget about me? At long last there she is with a bowl of milk. "Drink" she says and without another word she is gone. A few minutes later she reappears and my eyes pop. She is carrying two thick slices of white bread, the kind I have not seen in a long time, a boiled egg, a nice slice of bacon and an apple. She took five francs: "that's enough."

A few moments later she asks: "Are you a maquisard or a réfractaire?" (a member of the Resistance or a forced-labor dodger?) "Neither" is the answer "I am a boy scout, an Assistant Troop Leader in training." She doesn't know what I mean. "We are always ready to help." I thank her heartily, and leave. I walk a few steps and then turn around to rapidly sketch the farm which I intend to include in my report.

My next stop is Spontin, a nice little town known all over the country for its mineral waters. I first turn my attention to the beautiful castle dating from the 12th century and restored in the 16th, in Renaissance style, with rose bricks and pepper pot towers. Later I retrace my steps towards Crupet to visit the plant that bottles the Spontin waters. I take advantage of the free sampling and in addition fill my canteen.

It is time now to think about dinner and find a place for the night. I am soon back in the forest walking in a southerly direction until I find a satisfactory site. Our instructions require that we sleep under the open sky or in a little hut of our own making. As there is no way I can trust the Belgian weather, I choose a little mound (for good drainage) surrounded by five magnificent fir trees. Right away I proceed to light a small fire to get coals for baking the potatoes, followed by a search for sturdy sticks to build the frame of my abode for the night. These I cover with fir branches with the needles placed downwards so that the rain or moisture will drain away towards the exterior.

Supper is a delight as I am so hungry. I devour the potatoes, bread, ham and a small piece of the bacon as well as the fruit except the apple. What's left is for breakfast.

Later on I walked to the edge of the woods to enjoy that softness of the evening, a fineness so magical with light, with fragile glory, with the luminous glance of the sky. The last rays of the sun were fading away into the night going from rose color to violet and deep purple under a heaven of innumerable stars.

September 4, Friday. The night was peaceful, with no darkness-loving animal pushing its snout into my shelter to lick my face or steal my food. It is an ideal morning, the rain having washed the air. Not a cloud, the sun has the sky to itself. After a great

129

breakfast and having cleared all traces of my overnight stay, I am soon on my way to the castle of Poilvache in an easterly direction.

I pass the ruins of the Géronsart Tower and just before reaching the Meuse River, at the village of Houx, I proceed north to the château of Poilvache. It is in a sad state of repair having been destroyed by an armed band from the town of Liège, in the year 1450, and was never rebuilt. When erected as a fortress, 450 feet above the Meuse, around the year 920, it was called the Emerald Castle and got its name of Poilvache in the 14th century, after a successful attempt by the people of Dinant to take it over.

I was tempted to make a detour to visit the Abbey of Leffe where the monks make one of the best and strongest beer in Belgium. However at the Spontin mineral water plant I was told that, due to the lack of the prime ingredient of hops, the Carthusian Fathers have to be content to produce "small beer", just like any other brewer. As I am not interested in that kind of beverage I decide to continue north, pacing myself to arrive at 11:30 a.m. ready for an early lunch and the "debriefing" in the afternoon.

September 7, Monday. We had a final review and critique of our four-day activities. I didn't do too badly and got my confirmation as Assistant Troop Master. I also received my assignment as Troop Master designate for the new Troop at the parish of St John the Baptist in Molenbeek St. Jean. This fast promotion is due to the dearth of older leaders who are POWs in Germany; or have been arrested for "activities prejudicial to the interests of the German forces and the Reich"; or have disappeared for some other reason. I will have to build up this Troop from scratch and it is quite a responsibility.

7

September 8 - December 27, 1942

September 8, Tuesday. Back to reality? and gray normality? Vacation is almost over and time has come to prepare for another school year. I have applied for a transfer to a more demanding school and have been accepted at the *Institut Ste. Marie* which is located in Schaerbeek, a northern suburb. I have to meet with the Director tomorrow for a final interview, a mere formality for he has my most recent school reports and warm recommendations from three of my former teachers.

September 9, Wednesday. The interview went well and I am definitely accepted in Class 2A, Sciences. The premises are much smaller than at St. Pierre's. The reason is simple: no Flemish section, and this cuts its size by more than half. The school was built around the turn of the century but the front office and a good deal of the classrooms are new, airy and quite modern. Unfortunately, my class is located in the old building. The new school year starts September 15, at 8:30 a.m.

September 11, Friday. I have a little time for catching up on world events. I note that on August 25, the Nazis ordered the mobilization of all young men in the former provinces of Alsace-Lorraine. These men will certainly be reluctant soldiers. The Wehrmacht needs every able body it can get for the Russian front. Furthermore these new conscripts will be parceled out among different units to avoid any concerted resistance.

I note also the annexation of the Grand-Duchy of Luxemburg into the Reich, a tiny country of 990 square miles. Poor Letzerburgers! They are few, around 300,000 of them, but it is a proud and very independent people. They speak a Germanic tongue and, with the outside world, the inhabitants speak German or French.

Further, since the end of August, a formidable German offensive is underway with the Volga and the oilfields of the Caucasus as objectives. The Germans have made substantial progress toward the town of Stalingrad but the Russians are fighting resolutely and seem to never run out of reserves. This must be a great surprise to Hitler and company..

Also at the end of August, Rommel started a new offensive in Egypt with Alexandria as the ultimate goal, 60 miles away. He got nowhere, and by September 7 the offensive was called off. Another defeat for the Axis. Good!!

September 16, Wednesday. My second day at my new school. A bit disoriented but getting to know my schoolmates. Most interesting is the fact that I have to spend time using public transportation, that is the streetcar or "tram" as it is called in Brussels. From home to school is about a 35-minute ride, whereas earlier it was less than a ten-minute walk.

I take tram 35 or 14 to the top of the Boulevard du Jardin Botanique, at the Porte de Schaarbeek. I can then catch a connection along the rue Royale toward the St. Mary's church - the one with the dome - and then a short walk to school. To reduce the cost of transportation, a special pass is offered to students. It is white with half an inch red vertical stripe in the middle with name and address, etc. It allows me to make unlimited rides at any time of the day, including Sundays. The pass is valid for the full year from September 1 to August 31. It is quite handy and I find the streetcars clean and rather fast but very crowded. There is one problem: the trams are not heated; furthermore the platforms, front and aft, have no doors with the result that, in winter, you freeze. Body heat helps but not much.

September 18, Friday. I have made the acquaintance of Wolfgang Weil who speaks French with an accent. At first I thought he was a refugee from the German-speaking region of Belgium, Eupen-Malmedy, which has now been re-incorporated in the Reich. To my astonishment however I find out that he is German and half-Jew. And he is not in hiding!

He tells me his story. His father, an "Aryan," is a veteran of the Great War, gravely wounded in Flanders in 1918. For this reason, the Wehrmacht is protecting him and his family. To make sure that his wife is not importuned by the Jew-baiting Nazis, some general-officer had the family removed to Brussels where they are free, within limits, to move around as normal civilians.

I am astonished, I never dreamed that the Wehrmacht could act so independently of the Nazi regime. And, upon reflection, I feel that after all we are lucky, here in Belgium, to be under a harsh military administration rather than a criminal Nazi rule, under a Gauleiter, like in Holland and in Norway.

September 25, Friday. Now that I go back and forth to the city center, I have come to notice more than before the presence of the occupation forces. I guess it is for their benefit that the "V" sign in French and Flemish displayed at the North Station has been replaced by a new banner proclaiming: "V"- Deutschland siegt an allen Fronten! (Germany is victorious on all fronts.) Great consolation for the soldier on leave here from the Ostfront; or for the German civilian freshly debarked from a destroyed city in the Reich.

Yes, there seem to be all kinds of Germans in Brussels, mostly of course military personnel.

We have the ordinary soldiers but very few young ones. They are middle-aged, part of the occupying forces guarding high officials such as the Militärbefehlshaber General Baron von Falkenhausen; also the army and air force headquarters, strategic points such as airfields, military depots, railroad centers and bridges. These are static units with their horses and carriages, leftovers it seems of the Great War and put back into service. Their fastest means of transportation is the railroad that often is pre-empted for the first-line combat divisions. Here in town they use our streetcars and have the second compartment of the first car (the former first-class) reserved entirely for them, its access strictly forbidden to Belgian civilians.

One can see them walking in pairs or alone. On the right breast, above the pocket they all wear the Nazi symbol of sovereignty: the stylized eagle clutching a wreathed swastika. I don't know when it started but, for the last few months, undoubtedly for fear of terrorist attacks, they carry at all times a Mauser carbine, usually on the left shoulder, rarely slung across the shoulder. Also, attached to the belt, on the left, is a short bayonet, in a metal sheath, as well as a field-gray cylinder containing a gas mask. I don't know why they have to trundle this contraption around; its need must be remote indeed.

I do not fail to note that the "Landsers" often carry an army-issue canvas bag, like an outsized briefcase, always bulging and rather heavy. I wonder what it might contain. Their own lunch plus ten other ones stolen from the Belgians? Articles in short supply in Germany that can still be found here and bought with their over-evaluated Reichsmark?

I encounter also a few officers, Wehrmacht or Luftwaffe, whom I can identify as to their rank, perfectly groomed, with boots shining. They behave correctly, keep their distance; a few of them, the Prussian types, are quite arrogant. What can you expect from the Uebermensch?

Going up the Boulevard Botanique, on the right, is a Kriegslazarett, or military hospital, which means that from time to time one encounters Army nurses with their stiff headgear and white/blue-lined uniform. They look uniformly pale, tired and not too happy. There are also women enrolled in non-combat auxiliary forces, dressed in a mouse-gray uniform who were promptly nicknamed *souris* or mice.

Finally, we have Nazi civilians active in the political and economic spheres. They are either party hacks or members of the secret police apparatus or the specialists who supervise the systematic plunder of the country. Two-thirds of the national production, I am told, is siphoned off into the German war effort. But there is no way to come up with hard numbers. Everything is hidden behind smoke and mirrors. However, almost every day, Father witnesses the departure for Germany of long freight trains loaded with foodstuffs and industrial products.

September 26, Saturday. Looking at the map and perusing the German communiqués as well as the learned comments of some older friends, I come to the conclusion that the Nazi offensive is developing on four fronts: in the north, from Rzhev toward Kalinin; south of Moscow, an attack in the direction of Voronezh; in the center the goal, Stalingrad, has been reached and a huge battle is underway; in the south, the Germans have launched a two-pronged attempt to take Krasnodar and Tuapse and another to take possession of the badly needed oilfields of the Caucasus.

The "Schwerpunkt" (the main effort), as the OKW calls it, is definitely Stalingrad.

Some bad news from France. In Paris, some five thousand people were arrested during the past weekend. Some of these arrests were made for violation of the 36-hour curfew imposed by the Nazis after the execution of 116 Frenchmen following repeated attacks on German soldiers. "C'est l'escalade" as they say in French, the escalation of violence.

September 29, Tuesday. I have struck a friendship with Wolfgang Weil. I use every opportunity to improve my German, he speaks it so beautifully. We have constituted a team of "balle pelote," a simple game played against a smooth wall with a small stuffed hard ball, the size of a golf ball. It is not, by any means a Basque pelote but is nevertheless a fast game exercising the entire body and requiring quick reflexes.

I am very curious about his family's status but he is very elusive about it and gives no sign of being ready for more information. I have to respect his secret, which in this day and age, can be a matter of life or death.

October 2, Friday. After about a year of silence, Hitler made an interesting speech at the Sportpalast in Berlin, at the occasion of the Winter Relief Fund drive. He admits that last winter was a dreadful one for the German people and mentions that the captured provinces of the Soviet Union are being organized into a big food-producing territory.

He also reveals the objectives of the advance in Russia. These are: the conquest of the area between the Don valley and the Volga, including the city of Stalingrad "which certainly will fall into our hands".

Then "Little Mustache" proceeds with an attack on Churchill and Roosevelt. Of course, he sneers, these two have time to travel for weeks round the world with a sombrero on their heads and wearing silk shirts. They can give more time to talk "while I in recent months, I took more time to act".

"To concoct an Atlantic charter is simple, but it is also nonsense. This nonsense will last but a very few years. It will be wiped out by hard facts. Of course it is difficult to argue with people who think, for instance, that Namsos [in Norway] was a victory, that Dunkirk was the greatest victory in history, that an expeditionary force that lands for nine hours is a success not comparable to ours.

"When we advance 600 miles, that is nothing. If in the course of the past few months we have penetrated to the Don and the Volga, and now besiege Stalingrad and shall also take it, "Sie können darauf rechnen" (you can count on it), that is nothing! If we advance to the Caucasus and occupy the Ukraine, the Donets Basin, with their corn and iron ore and oil, that is nothing!

"But if a troop of Canadians with a small appendix of Englishmen comes to Dieppe and remains for nine hours only to be wiped out finally, then this is a sure sign of the eternal power of the British Empire. What against this is our Luftwaffe? What of our U-boats? They are nothing!

"And now they have promises for the future. They speak of a second front. They tell us a second front is coming. They tell to be careful and look around. We have not been careful and we have not looked around. We have gone steadily on.

"I say to Herr Churchill (Shoorshill): 'You have never frightened me!' It is true, we must give some attention to this. If we had an opponent of some military size one could guess where he could start a second front, but if you have to deal with military idiots you cannot know where they will attack. But wherever those madmen, those eternal drunkards, may attack, I can tell them they will not stay longer than nine hours.

"Behind us lie the winters of 1941 and 1942 in which the German people have been tried by the "Vorsehung" (Providence). Nothing worse than this trial can happen again. That we have beaten General Winter, that we could resume our attacks in the early summer is proof that Providence means well for the German people.

"The aim of the German offensive," Hitler pursued, "is to deprive the Russians of their remaining grain areas, take from them their coal mines, and get as near as possible to their oil wells, and finally cut their main transport lines, especially the Volga. The occupation of Stalingrad, which will also be completed, will further increase the cut-off process".

We now know Hitler's aims. I detect, however, a certain

hesitation as to whether he can reach the Caucasus oilfields ("get as near as possible to their oil wells") and his uncertainty about the second front. How can you deal with "military idiots?" Furthermore, nowhere in his speech does the Führer promise "final victory". I failed to mention it, but he also assured his people that Germany will answer the British bombing, but he didn't elaborate. After a full year of waiting, this speech doesn't offer much hope to the German people.

This is further underlined by the terse communiqué, issued the same day by the OKW:

"In the northwest Caucasus and south of the Terek, German and our Allied troops advanced further after hard fighting.

In Stalingrad more sectors in the northern part of the city were taken by storm. The enemy lost 34 tanks during unsuccessful relief attacks.

On the Don front, German and Italian troops repelled several Russian attempts to cross the river."

October 5, Monday. I still attend the 26th Troop meetings on Sundays where I am now officially Assistant Troop Master. I also started planning for the new St. John the Baptist 66th Troop in my quality of Troop Master designate. Fortunately I have a few months to get ready.

October 9, Friday. I am almost settled at my new school and quite at ease with my new schoolmates. Their family names reflect the mixture of French and Flemish stock in the Brussels area. French sounding ones like Lebeau, Dachy, Poissonnier, Fallon, Doutrelepont, Winandy; and Flemish such as Callewaert, Van den Weghe, Devos, De Meester, de Gheldere, Van der Straeten. Plus a few Spanish names, relics of the times of the Spanish Netherlands (16th and 17th century): Ortega, Pacheco, de Villegas, del Marmol and Annez de Taboada. The Spanish influence is more profound than many realize. It all started with Charles, son of Philip the Fair, of the House of Habsburg and Juana of Castille (the Mad Queen). He was born in Ghent in February, 1500 and, as Count of Flanders, became the heir to the Holy Empire of the German Nation as Charles V; at the same time from his mother side, he inherited the Kingdom of Castille and Aragon, as "El Rey don Carlos".

October 17, Saturday. Like Horace in Rome, I was walking to school this morning along the Rue Royale, *totus in illis,* (absorbed in my thoughts), when my attention was drawn to two posters freshly plastered upon a wooden fence. I copied them down as they are propaganda inviting young men, if they are stupid enough, to join the Waffen SS.

The first one in French is for the "Légion Wallonie" under the command of Léon Degrelle, the leader of the Rexist Movement, turned pro-Nazi and collaborator.

TU DEFENDS LA BELGIQUE
En luttant au front de l'Est!
Viens à la SS division blindée "Wallonie."

In the background, is a view of famous towers of Wallonia where I recognize the Belfry of the town of Mons as well as the cupola of the Palais de Justice in Brussels. In the foreground a group of soldiers in battle array.

YOU DEFEND BELGIUM
in fighting on the Eastern Front
Join the SS Panzer Division "Wallonia."

The next poster is in Flemish, sponsored by tiny pro-Nazi organizations.

TREEDT AAN IN SS STANDARD "WESTLAND"
SS Vrijwilligers Legioen "Flandern."
Meldt U aan bij "Flandern der Waffen SS"
Antwerpen, Koningin Elisabethlaan,22
VNV - Zwarte Brigade
NSJV - De Vlag

In translation, we have:

Join the SS Standard "Westland."
SS volunteers Legion "Flandern"
Contact the Waffen SS "Flandern"
Antwerp, Queen Elisabeth Lane, 22
VNV (National Flemish Union)
The Black Brigade
NSJV(National Socialist Youth Movement)- The Flag

I have noted earlier that the Resistance Movement in Flanders, in response to the "Black Brigade" has taken the name of "Witte (White) Brigade."

October 20, Tuesday. My habits have undergone a few changes since the beginning of the school year. In years past, I could easily go home for lunch and enjoy my meal even it was sometimes a bit hurried. At present, I can still go back home but I have only 15 to 20 minutes to partake with lunch before rushing back to the tram, hoping there will be no delay.

I therefore often take a sandwich with me and eat either at school or in a canteen. No ration coupons are needed, the price is low, the food wholesome but bland and unappetizing. Beggars can't be choosers!

On Tuesdays and Thursdays there is no school in the afternoon. Instead of going home, I stop at a few bookshops, in the rue Neuve, and look for new arrivals. Sad to say, because of the paper shortage, Nazi censorship and the disruption of war, fewer and fewer books are being published, to my great disappointment. The latest book I looked at is the one written by Henri De Man under the title: *Après Coup* (After the Event). Although a socialist, De Man is flirting with the Nazis, attracted perhaps by their program of "socialized redistribution of wealth." This, however, is reaching for Utopia, with its totalitarian undertones.

What I cannot get into a bookstore I try to find at the bookstalls of the famous Flea Market. With a little patience, I can build up my small library at bargain prices.

October 21, Wednesday. On October 18, the Wehrmacht Bulletin announced that the "last pockets of resistance" by the Soviets in Leningrad have been wiped out. In the Caucasus the enemy is still putting up "embittered resistance" and German positions in the north, outside Leningrad, and to the east of Orel have been further extended. No word about Stalingrad.

The Afrika Korps under the command of Field Marshal Rommel have, as we know, advanced to within 100km (60 miles) of Cairo and are preparing for the last leg of the march on the Suez Canal.

November 1st, Sunday. There is a big battle underway in North

Africa. The Imperial forces have launched an offensive against Rommel and his Afrika Korps.

November 3, Tuesday. From time to time, on the radio, the Nazi propaganda machine plays the "Horst Wessel Lied." This is the battle song of the SA (Sturm Abteilung) the storm troops of the party.

Horst Wessel was a young Nazi thug (the radio doesn't mention this of course), a platoon leader in the SA, who was killed in 1932 by Communists, in a street brawl in Berlin.

The "Horst Wessel Lied" is a rousing song set to the tune of an old German student ditty, with the title: "Fahnen hoch!"

The banners high, the unit in close order
The S.A. marches with quiet solemn tread
With comrades killed by the Red Front and reaction...

November 6, Friday. The German communiqué about the Afrika Korps: "There is little to report about the battle. The British are continually attacking with a superiority in artillery and tank forces, supported by aircraft. There is fierce fighting going on and the German-Italian troops threw back the British onslaught."

And now a summary of the British report: Rommel's Afrika Korps and his Italian Allies are in full and disorderly retreat. General Ritter von Thoma, Commander of the Afrika Korps (under Rommel), has been taken prisoner. Rommel's second in command, General von Stumme, has been killed in action. The German losses are high: 260 tanks have been destroyed, 270 guns captured and 9,000 prisoners taken.

November 7, Saturday. The British talk about utter defeat for the Axis troops in North Africa. The German communiqué is brief: "The bitter fighting in Egypt is continuing. Thanks to the strategic skills of Field Marshal Rommel the enemy has not yet been able to break through decisively. The enemy is continuing his attacks despite heavy losses."

My comment: What do they mean by "not yet"?

November 8, Sunday. In Egypt, the British 8th Army has retaken Mersa-Matruh, captured or destroyed 500 tanks, taken an impressive number of guns as well as around 40,000 combatants, most of them Italians.

The Afrika Korps, what's left of it, is fleeing toward the Libyan border. They seem to be in a panic. If true, this is the first time in this war that German troops have cracked and fled in great disorder. As to the Italians, they are finished.

November 9, Monday. STOP EVERYTHING!
American forces have invaded North Africa, simultaneously on the Mediteranean and Atlantic coasts.

A later bulletin from London mentions landings in Casablanca, Algiers and Oran. This is big and serious; perhaps the Second Front?

At long last the Star of Hope has appeared on the low horizon; it is our fervent wish to see it rise gradually into the firmament, every month shining brighter and brighter...

November 10, Tuesday. The Vichy-French did fight against the Americans in Morocco and Algeria but Oran has fallen, the French fleet has been wiped out; Casablanca and Algiers are about to fall.

The Commander in Chief of the Allied forces engaged in these operations is Lieutenant-General Eisenhower. Never heard of him. If this is the Second Front, it will take a long time to reach us and therefore the Star of Hope will be very, very slow at reaching its zenith.

First, the Allies will have to take over all of North Africa and deal with Rommel in Libya. This will take time. Then what? Invading the Balkans? No, too mountainous. Italy? No, too narrow. Southern France? Too far. Conclusion? The invasion is purely defensive: to deny the Southern Mediterranean Sea to the Axis forces, keep the Suez Canal open and neutralize the Italians by bombing their industrial centers.

Next time and before they make a move, the Allies should consult me!

November 11, Wednesday. Laval who for all practical purposes has supplanted Pétain as top man in Vichy-France is, we are told, in Berchtesgaden for important talks with Hitler.

November 12, Thursday. This is quite a month! And never a dull moment!!
The Nazis have taken the unoccupied part of France, that is Vichy-France. The news was announced to the French people by

Radio Paris (under German control) quoting letters from Hitler to the French people, and from Pétain.

November 13, Friday. Berlin has announced that German and Italian troops have reached all their objectives in the formerly Unoccupied Zone and have taken up positions on the French Mediterranean coast.

There is no news about the French Fleet based in Toulon. In North Africa, Admiral Darlan, who is representing Vichy in Algiers, has ordered all French resistance to cease.

Meanwhile, the Germans have landed airborne troops in Tunis and Bizerta. Looking at the map, I discover that Tunisia occupies a vital position on the southern shore of the Mediterranean. It juts out within 150 miles from Sicily and commands the narrow waist of water through which all shipping must pass.

As to Bizerta, it is a naval base of first importance situated 700 miles from Gibraltar, 1100 from Alexandria, 240 from Malta and 450 miles from Marseilles. If the Germans can get a solid foothold in Tunisia, it will be mighty hard for the Allies to dislodge them.

November 14, Saturday. In studying the map a little more closely, I discover that Sardinia is closer to Bizerta than Sicily is. The reason is that Italy and Sicily are oriented on a northwest/southeast axis, whereas Sardinia (and Corsica) are on a north/south line.

November 17, Tuesday. The Imperial forces are well underway to Benghazi that is, if I am not mistaken, 440 miles from Mersa-Matruh! It seems that they will not stop there as the Nazis and the Macaronis have lost most of their equipment and cannot get new supplies by sea because of the presence of the Royal Navy.

If our information came from purely German sources we would, like the German people, still be kept in ignorance of the full extent of the Axis defeat in Egypt and Libya and even be under the impression that the tide is turning.

The whole African battle is described as a struggle for transport routes and the Germans claim that Allied shipping resources cannot last much longer in face of the losses inflicted on them.This last statement is undoubtedly true if you replace "Allied" by "German" shipping resources.

November 18, Wednesday. What a busy week for this diary.
This time I hear about the so-called battle of the Solomon Islands where the Americans slug it out with the Japanese Navy and Army.

For quite some time now, the Americans have been fighting for the islands of Gualdacanal and Tulagi and they are still at it. But the Japanese have sent an important fleet to oust the Americans from the islands. It appears that after a three-day sea- and air battle this Japanese Fleet has suffered heavy losses and could not relieve their forces still on Gualdacanal.

November 20, Friday. Berlin can no longer hide Rommel's rout in North Africa. An amazing admission of the German defeat was made by Major-General Ramcke, of the Afrika Korps, over Berlin radio about two days ago. Ramcke was in charge of the 2nd Fallschirm (Parachute) brigade near the Qattara Depression southwest of El Alamein. He spoke in a tired, halting voice.

"When the British broke through at El Alamein, I received the order to retreat northwest. We were not motorized; the only vehicles we had were for heavy equipment and ammunition.

"We marched through the night under great difficulties. Next day the English renewed their attack and it became clear that they had not only torn right through the German lines to the west but they had also encircled us from the north and the south.

"The next night we went on and then came the third night's march, the worst I have ever experienced in my life. Just before dawn we saw the enemy coming, columns of Tommies from the left and the right. Our men were terribly hungry having been without regular food for two days, they were dead tired but fortunately we then found food and water".

As far as I know, this is the first time a high-ranking general is describing a grave setback on the Nazi radio that usually tells us about the great battles and the glorious victories of the German armies everywhere. What is going on? Who decided to air this pessimistic piece of news? Isn't it because, through many other sources, it is already known and it has become impossible to hide the sorry facts?

November 21, Saturday. Big news everywhere. In Libya, Benghazi has been evacuated by the Afrika Korps. Rommel is in big trouble. The Allies have reached Tunisia but the Germans seem to be well entrenched. The situation is very confused and the communiqués don't help at all.

On the Russian front, Berlin says that heavy attacks have been launched against the Rumanians in the Don bend. The Nazi radio adds that this attack is an attempt to loosen the Wehrmacht grip on the Volga. At Stalingrad, the Soviets are still holding on; will this battle go on forever?

I lay down my pen, turn off the light, and stand relaxing my fingers by the deep-set window, looking out on a pale blue, darkening sky. The evening star hangs above the afterglow, so soft, so brilliant that it seems to bathe in her own silver light. War is far away, invisible, for a few blessed moments.

November 23, Monday. There is a lot of talk about Stalingrad but not much is said about what is going on in the Caucasus which has long been an elusive goal for the Germans. It was very hard work for them to fight along the Caucasus Mountains from Maikop to Tcherkassy, Piatigorsk and Naltchik. Then, finally they were close to Ordjonikidze, their real goal.

Ordjonikidze is a town of great strategic importance at the northern end of the Georgia military road that winds over the Caucasus Mountains to Tiflis and oil, 100 miles to the south. The town used to be called Vladikavkaz: "The Key to the Caucasus". The Nazis want and need it very much to provide good winter quarters for a considerable force. Its possession will give the Wehrmacht a good starting point for an offensive up the road into the mountains when time and weather become suitable. It would at the same time break the deadlock that has long blocked their eastward drive towards the Grozny oilfields.

In their thrust forward to Ordjonikidze, the Germans used two armored divisions plus one motorized division. Two weeks ago they reached the outskirts of the town. They could get no further. Now the Russian counterattack has apparently set them in retreat.

November 28, Saturday. The Germans didn't arrive in time and Hitler has lost the French Mediterranean Fleet. Every battleship, cruiser, destroyer and submarine in Toulon, except for two which escaped, has been scuttled. Among them the great battleships Dunkerque and Strasbourg, both of 26,000 tons.

By sinking itself the French Fleet has secured the greatest naval victory of the war (for the Allies!)

December 9, Wednesday. Everybody knows that all is not well in Italy. Benito has decreed the mobilization of all industries in the country. I don't know what it means. Probably create a bureaucratic nightmare and nothing "positive" will come out of it.

December 11, Friday. The Russians have launched an offensive in the Don-Volga region earlier this month. And it looks like the Nazis are in trouble at Stalingrad.

The Afrika Korps is still retreating, but more slowly, into Libya. The British forces are regrouping for the final onslaught towards Tripoli. Incredible!

I just found out that the general at the head of the British Eighth Army is someone called Bernard Montgomery.

December 13, Sunday. In the coming week, we will start the first term (1942 / 43) exams. I have started to study hard. No time for anything else. Last exam: December 22. We will get the results on Christmas' Eve and then: blessed Vacation!

December 24, Thursday. I didn't do too badly with my exams despite the handicap of a new school. I am first overall, which surprises me. First in math, trigonometry, geography, history, French, Flemish and English. I am number two in German but there is no way I can beat Wolfgang Weil.

December 25, Friday. Third Christmas under Nazi occupation!

The whole family went to High Mass in a church full to the rafters. In times of war, religion experiences a comeback for very good personal reasons. Furthermore, in our country, the Church is a veritable bastion of resistance to the Nazis, a fact which attracts even the lukewarm believers. They come to hear the preacher express bold statements about the Occupant and its minions, the collaborators. Statements frowned upon by the Cardinal who doesn't want to lose his priests to a concentration camp. They come also to listen to the latest pastoral Letter of Cardinal Van Roey in which, against his own advice, but with great diplomacy, he castigates the latest atrocity such as the treatment of hostages or the roundup of young men deported as forced laborers to

Germany.

The church was not heated but after a while the body heat of such a crowd rendered the temperature supportable if somewhat graveolent.

For the occasion all lights were blazing, all candles were lit and the beautiful pageantry of the Catholic Liturgy of Christmas Day unfolded solemnly, assisted by the full choir, reinforced for the occasion by two professional singers.

The sermon was very good and non-political. It was given by one of the best preachers in the district. In our time of want, of pain and suffering, it is easier to convey to the faithful the message of Christ, the Anointed, the Messiah, who came to save the world from persecution, injustice and despair.

As we were jostling through the throng towards the exit, I noticed a beggar in the narthex close to the imposing portal. He looked like the sexton of Notre-Dame, small, entirely bald and I could see that he limped. His face had a corpselike pallor and he suffered from a nervous twitching of the lips. He was not one of our local beggars (most of them have disappeared) but, moved by the Christmas spirit, I gave him some change; he received it with lusterless eyes rendered dim and melancholy, it seemed, from despair and sickness..

A feast, a banquet, was waiting for us at home. For weeks, Father and Mother had accumulated hard-to-get provisions to make this Christmas an almost perfect holiday. And in Belgium, especially in Flanders (see the famous Breughel paintings), a holy day is not perfect unless accompanied by a substantial meal. Well, in this case it was not that substantial but it was succulent and it lasted until early evening slowly darkened the cloudy sky.

We had vol-au-vent followed by braised rabbit, one of those we raise in the back of the garden, served with Belgian endive sautéed in butter, as well as potatoes; then came salad with vinaigrette and a small piece of Maredsous cheese. After a long pause, a delicious cake was served with ersatz coffee, nothing more than roasted barley tasting of nothing, the only reminder of war on this beautiful day.

Later on, I stepped outside into the frozen garden and stared up into the gathering darkness. The graying sky was tinged with the dying rays of the setting sun and a faint breeze carried the fading sounds of the city towards me.

December 27, Sunday. Important news from the Russian front. First, the German Sixth Army is encircled and under heavy attack at Stalingrad. A Wehrmacht counteroffensive is underway to extricate them. Second, the Russians, after heavy battles, have succeeded in lifting the siege of Leningrad that lasted for almost three years.

In North Africa, Admiral Darlan has been assassinated. He was the successor-designate of Maréchal Pétain at Vichy and was sent to Algeria to conduct the armed resistance against the Allies. He quickly changed sides however and was more or less recognized by the Allied commanders as the "valid negotiator" in North Africa.

How far Darlan was considered an asset for the establishment of a quiet and orderly administration in North Africa is very puzzling. General de Gaulle in London repudiated him at once, and Darlan was equally determined to dismiss the Fighting French. It was concocted by the Allied military authorities with the best of intentions, but it clearly shows insufficient knowledge of French politics and politicians.

But who ordered the assassination?

8

January 3 - May 29, 1943

January 3, Sunday. A review of the latest war events shows that the war is at a turning point in favor of the Allies. The great battle of El Alamein has turned back Rommel's deepest advance in North Africa. Then, on November 8th, the Americans landed in Morocco and Algeria. Rommel is now threatened from behind and the dream of Mussolini making the Mediterranean a *Mare Nostrum* is at an end. Although the Nazis have quickly occupied the rest of France, Festung Europa (Fortress Europe) is now vulnerable from the south.

Furthermore on the eastern front, General von Paulus' Sixth Army 22 divisions appear to be cut off by a Soviet counterattack at Stalingrad. To the north, Leningrad has finally been relieved.

Does all this mean that the German high tide on the eastern front has passed? And can we look for our liberation this year?

January 9, Saturday. From time to time, I read SIGNAL, the propaganda magazine published in many languages, under the auspices of the Wehrmacht and probably under close supervision of Goebbels' Propaganda Ministry.

Technically it is well done, printed on better paper than other publications. As to the contents it is pure, unadulterated propaganda. This is why I don't read it very often and I never buy it. Nevertheless at times one can glean bits of interesting information not available elsewhere.

It is an army publication full of excellent pictures showing the victorious Wehrmacht in action on all fronts: lots of enemy dead but not a single wounded or dead German soldier.

The latter always shows up in battle in impeccable uniform, a shiny helmet, terribly clean weapons and a very big smile on his face or dead-serious in the task at hand. Truly, the conclusion must be: "All is well in Naziland!"

January 13, Wednesday. Back to school for the second term of the school year 42-43.

It is freezing cold and a damp wind is blowing. I have only a dark blue raincoat to protect me on the open platform of the tramway. Under the coat I wear a sweater, a jacket and a woolen scarf. No headgear and I have to stamp my feet to keep the circulation going and keep warm.

The RAF has been active recently, especially along the coast and up to Ghent. Their favorite targets are the Ghent-Terneuzen, as well as the Ghent-Ostend Canals.

January 17, Sunday. The British refuse to recognize the annexation of Tangiers by Spain, at the tip of Morocco. I didn't know Spain had done such a thing.

I attended the scout meeting and noticed that a few of our "senior" leaders (above 21) are gone. They are réfractaires or forced labor evaders who have "disappeared". But what happens to them? There are a few options.

1. Change of identity and continue to live as before under an assumed name. A genuine new ID card is not too difficult to secure thanks to courageous civil servants in many towns and villages who, at great risk to themselves, issue such documents.

2. Change of identity and reduction of social life to the family circle; never use public transportation in order to avoid a German police raid; exercise only at night, sticking to the neighborhood.

3. Change of identity and join the Resistance movement if steps 1 or 2 are not possible. This would mean leaving for the Ardennes region, the only area in Belgium where one can hide with a good chance of survival. This however would necessitate a total break with the family and great physical hardship.

Most réfractaires choose number two. It is not a sure thing but, except for a direct denunciation, it is the safest of all three options. With 99% of the Belgian population solidly anti-Nazi, the Gestapo simply doesn't have enough manpower to pursue those who say "no" to work in Grossdeutschland.

January 25, Monday. Even junior officers have to take the streetcar to travel around town. One of them steps in with me on the way to school. I check his shoulder boards and identify him as a major.

The German army prides itself on the appearance of its uniforms and this officer is a good example of impeccability.

First, the cap with leather peak and silver-colored chinstrap of high quality. It has silver piping around the top and the branch-of service color just above the chin strap, it is green, indicating infantry.

The major wears the informal dress tunic, perfectly cut, with pleated pockets, the lower ones with scalloped edges. The standing collar used to be dark green now it is forest green like the rest of the uniform, with collar tabs. He wears one row of ribbon decorations I cannot identify. He also wears the Iron Cross First Class, and the wound medal.

His legs are stuck in shiny black riding boots and, around the waist, a dark brown leather belt with double pin buckle to which a ceremonial dagger is attached.

He is not a general, I observe, only a major, but you feel he is very conscious of being a part of the officers' caste trying hard to make an impression.

January 27, Tuesday. Tripoli, in Libya, has fallen. This has been acknowledged by the Germans. What is left of Rommel's army is now fleeing without a fight towards Tunisia. Real resistance to the Allies' advance is not expected until Rommel can make a stand on the so-called "Mareth Line" which, consulting my map, I find situated in southern Tunisia on a southwest line running from Gabès, to Mareth to Madenino.

Not much news from the fight in the rest of North Africa. I think the Americans are stuck. The German soldier, with almost four years of fighting experience, is a tough nut to crack; resourceful, disciplined, tenacious, not at all the kind of robot he is sometimes described to be.

On the Russian front, the Soviets announce the recapture of the town of Salsk, a key railroad center and one of the vital points in the ring of German defenses around its pivot at Rostov-on-Don. If Stalingrad cannot be saved, Rostov is next and the oil of the Caucasus is forever lost to the Nazis.

January 28, Thursday. Total mobilization of men (15 to 65 years of age) and women (17 to 45 years) has been ordered in the Reich. I don't quite know what it means. I guess it allows the Nazis to do what they want with their people. But they are pushed to the limit already.

February 1, Monday. The German Army in Stalingrad has been wiped out. Field Marshal von Paulus, Commander in Chief of the Sixth and Fourth Panzer Armies, was captured yesterday a few hours after he had been promoted to the highest rank, by special proclamation from Hitler's headquarters.

Furthermore, two powerful Russian offensives are nearing their climax. West of Voronezh, the Germans are retreating at full speed towards Kursk, a place Hitler must hold if he wants to retain a link between the central and the southern front.

In the Caucasus, the situation is not much better. Twenty divisions are threatened with envelopment and annihilation following the capture of Tikhoretsk and Maikop.

Little Mustache must be suffering from a terrible Ostfront headache.

The OKW has decided to admit the seriousness of the war situation with the following statement: "Between Voronezh and the Donetz estuary, a very big chunk of the Ostfront, the enemy continued his attacks with increased pressure. Between the Kuban and the lower Don, the Caucasus front, the enemy attempted to break through the German lines."

February 3, Wednesday. A special Radio Bulletin from the OKW, the Supreme Command of the Armed Forces, announces: (Der Oberkommando der Wehrmacht gibt bekannt) "The battle for Stalingrad is over. True to their oath, to the last breath, the Sixth Army, under the exemplary leadership of Field Marshal von Paulus, succumbed to superior strength of the enemy and adverse conditions."

Then the second movement from Beethoven's Fifth Symphony was played. A four-day national mourning has been declared during which all movie houses, theaters and places of amusement will remain closed.

February 6, Saturday. Cold - Cold - Cold! It is freezing and we have a hard time to get the coal to heat even a small part of the house, the kitchen, and whenever possible the living room.

We are "entitled" to a certain amount of coal but what we get is the so-called "Schlamm", a German word for "mud." Our Schlamm/coal is a combination of crushed coal mixed with water and clay. It burns and heats unevenly leaving a hard residue consisting of slag and hardened clay. You have to hit it very hard to break the clump into pieces for removal. Not good for the stove!

Fortunately, Father brings back almost every day, in his oversize briefcase, between five and eight kilos of fine quality anthracite. How? As an employee of the Belgian railroads he has unimpeded access to all areas of any train station, including the freight depots where often, long lines of freight cars intended for Germany wait to be switched to their destination.

The depots are under guard but Father knows the soldiers, older men who are bored to death and want to go home. He talks to them, encourages their despondency and offers some strong home-grown tobacco. They don't mind when he slips behind the long lines of convoys and "samples" the merchandise be it potatoes, coal or any other commodity.

It is a godsend for us and keeps the family warm and on the positive side of undernourishment. But it doesn't always work, especially when the guards are reassigned. At that point father has to reaffirm his "rights".

Today I go on one of such "inspection" tours. I meet Father at the station in early evening. We proceed to the end of the long platform then follow a pebbled path until we reach a signal post where we find the guard. Next to the post, in the falling night, I notice a small cone-shaped air-raid shelter with a few narrow ventilation vents and a low steel door, enough for the protection of perhaps four people.

The post is dimly lit and stinks of harsh tobacco smoke, I recognize the smell of Father's brand. The bored soldier is delighted to see us and asks whether we have brought any special goodies for him. Father, who has his own plans for the evening, brings him indeed a present in the form of a small bottle of "schnapps" some kind of clear alcohol, indefinite in nature. The bottle is uncorked and two small glasses show up as I refuse to share in the event. Father, a nondrinker except for an occasional glass of wine, accepts a few drops all the while making conversation of a non-political nature, mainly about the inclement weather, the soldier's family and his fear that they could be bombed to kingdom come.

After ten minutes or so we leave with the promise to check back after completion of the job at hand.

Our goal this evening is a shipment of potatoes for the troops stationed on the Belgian and Channel coasts. It is very dark and very still in the marshalling yard as we approach, with halting steps, the black line of railroad cars, stumbling over unforeseen obstacles.

We stop. Father projects a ray of light from his railroad-issue flashlight on the lead seal of one of the railroad cars and, promptly cuts it with a small pincer. The bolt is lifted carefully and the heavy door pushed slowly to the right, just wide enough to allow access inside. Here are tons of potatoes, our potatoes, intended for the enemy. We want a small share of it in the form of one sack of the precious tubers that will help us and, at the same time, defeat the Hun in a small way.

Because I am much thinner and nimbler, I slide through the opening. With the help of the flashlight dimmed with a handkerchief, I find a sack and push it into the strong hands of Father and I am down in a moment. The door is closed and Father proceeds to install his own unmarked lead seal. It is not quite the same as the destroyed original but only a railroad employee can spot the fraud. Furthermore, the railroad car will be unloaded by soldiers or untrained workers. The Gefreiter (sergeant) or the foreman will cut the seal without a thought as long as it looks untouched. They may count the bags but will not bother if they come up one short. Miscount is not unusual in this business.

So says Father, as we look for a very dark place to transfer the potatoes to two smaller bags. "About a 60-pound bag," he conveys to me in a murmur, "that makes thirty pounds each." The burlap bag is folded and placed under a pile of railroad ties seemingly thrown down here and then forgotten.

Now comes the tricky part. From official "inspectors" we have become "thieves". I am nervous and tense. My heart is beating wildly but Father's voice remains calm. He has done this many times before, albeit on a smaller scale.

Father walks ten meters ahead of me. If challenged, I have to leave the bag and disappear in the shadows toward the cemetery, climb its crumbling wall and go straight home. No talking, no running, that's an order.

Nothing happens but the going is hard in pitch-dark. At long last we reach the end of the platform until, near the fence surmounted by barbed wire, we stop at a strong door with a solid lock and no handle. We deposit our bags in a corner and retrace our steps to pay a second visit to the guard. He is half asleep and pays very little attention to us. We want, however, to be seen with no baggage in the guardhouse and none outside, if he cares to watch us.

Father goes straight to the station to fetch his bicycle and I return to the fence and sit down, shivering from fear and cold.

A rustle, a click, the grating of a bolt, the door opens haltingly and my father edges his way in. We are out in thirty seconds, door locked, one bag on the handlebars of the bike the other behind on the narrow luggage rack. We push our precious cargo along the misty, poorly lit streets with hardly a soul in sight, past the dark mass of the Town Hall, down Church street then left on Wemmel Lane and home!

The adrelanine kept me going but now the reaction sets in, leaving me drained of all feeling and very weak. I will get over it but I tell Father I have no wish to repeat the performance. It is not worth the risk. Brother Michel, who has gone through the same ordeal earlier, strongly concurs. Father agrees it is perhaps a little too much for us, but he doesn't seem particularly affected by the event. Of course he knows the actors and the scene but the script keeps changing according to the whim of the mustachioed playwriter, in Berlin, who happens to be a manipulator and a murderous lunatic.

Father then bows to our opinion. There will be no more expeditions. Although sixty pounds of potatoes, together with other provisions, will keep us fed for a few weeks, he will stick to the much safer routine of a little at a time, several times a week. And we heave a great sigh of relief.

February 9, Tuesday. Radio Berlin announces the withdrawal of Japanese forces from Gualdacanal, that island in the Solomon archipelago, "mission accomplished." The Americans have been fighting there since last August. They now control the most important island in the Solomons and are in a position to launch assaults on the Japanese base of Munda (New Georgia Islands), as well as the Shortland Islands with the important base of Bougainville.

February 10, Wednesday. On the Eastern front, the Soviets have recaptured Kursk and are now attacking towards Rostov. The fall of Kursk, I am told, endangers the entire southern front based on Kharkov. General Winter has not stopped the Russians from repeated attacks. The Nazis are in big trouble.

February 14, Sunday. The Soviets recaptured Rostov and Voroshilovgrad. And the offensives continue, unabated. Where do they get the troops and the equipment? How come they are beating the all-powerful, invincible Wehrmacht?

February 16, Tuesday. The advance continues. The Russians have retaken Kharkov and the news is confirmed by the OKW. The extent of the defeat cannot be hidden from the German people any longer. All is doom and gloom in Berlin.

February 19, Friday. Yesterday, Reichspropaganda Minister Joseph Goebbels, at the Sportpalast in Berlin, in a hysterical speech to a selected audience of party members, has proclaimed the advent of "total war" and has called for "the supreme effort". He is quoted as saying: "Do you want this total war to be, if necessary, more total and radical than can even be imagined today? Do you accept the fact that anyone who detracts from the war effort will lose his head?"

This is pure madness and the result of ten years of unbridled dictatorship. This Nazi regime has to be destroyed and uprooted.

February 23, Tuesday. This morning as usual I take tramway No. 13, around 8 o'clock, on my way to school. We go down the Avenue de Jette and just before the Place Simonis, the driver applies the brakes as if to avoid a pedestrian or a cyclist and stops abruptly, shaking up quite a few unwary passengers.

Shortly thereafter, we hear hoarse German voices: Allen aussteigen! Raus! Los!... Los!! We are surrounded by a dozen men from the Grüne Polizei armed with Mauser carbines and a MP-40 submachine gun. This is a two-lane very wide avenue, separated by two rows of majestic chestnut trees. At present, the right lane is closed to traffic. I help a flustered old lady down the steps, who mumbles a few incomprehensible words while stroking her gloved left hand with jerky moves.

We are herded against a brick wall amidst screams of "Schnell! Schnell!" We must be at least sixty, lined up, facing the wall.

I try to look round to see what's going on; we are surrounded by guards aiming their weapons ay us. A rifle butt in my right kidney tells me I shouldn't be too curious. "Nicht umwenden" (don't look around) is the shout.

Now we are ordered: "Ausweis fertig machen, Taschen öffnen", (prepare I.D. papers, open bags). Everyone is checked. I have nothing to hide, just school stuff and note books. For some reason our inspectors are suddenly no longer in a hurry and go about their duty in a perfunctory way. It is all done in about fifteen minutes. As far as I can ascertain nobody has been detained. In the same boorish way we are told to reembark and with a nervous cling-clang of its warning bell, the streetcar is on its way.

There is tension among the passengers. Not a word is uttered. The Nazis have made their point: to instill fear and terror among the civilian population, to better control it. A show of force, a display of weapons is sufficient as a warning not to try anything like sabotage or spying or distributing anti-nazi leaflets.

March 2, Tuesday. As I was holding on for dear life in an overfull streetcar going up the Boulevard Botanique, we passed a truck crawling uphill, huffing and puffing. There are not many of them left for civilian use. Those who manage to keep their cars on the road run them on energy provided by burning charcoal in bolted-on devices called gazogènes. They are a sight to behold as they chug along looking like a diminutive smelting furnace.

March 8, Monday. Now that I travel back and forth to the city center almost every day, I cannot fail to notice the numerous signs posted by the military authorities to guide their people to the right destination. They read as follows, black on white or, more often, black on yellow.

Ortslazarett - City military hospital
Zentral Ersatzteillager - Central Depot for spare parts.
Hauptwerkdirektion - Brüssel.- Central Operations -Brussels.
Feldzeuglager - Equipment Depot.
Sanitätspark 632 - Sanitary Station 632.
WH Zahnstation - Wehrmacht Dentistry Station.
NSKK Gruppe Todt - National Socialist truck drivers
Organization Todt. (This organization is responsible for capital

construction projects such as the "Atlantic Wall").
OKW - Zell 33 - Oberkommando der Wehrmacht - Unit 33.
Der Militärbefehlshaber in Belgien und Nord-Frankreich. - The
Military Commandant in Belgium and Northern France.(This is
the highest authority in the region.)

I notice a Deutsches Kino or German movie theater "Nur für
Angehörigen der Wehrmacht", that is restricted to members of the
German Army. It is a requisitioned movie theater with two huge
red Nazi banners with a white circle and black swastika, hanging
on each side of the entrance.

March 15, Monday. Now that the winter is almost over in
Russia, the Germans seem in a better position to stem the Soviet
onslaught. The German News Agency claims that German troops
have recaptured Kharkov "after three weeks of Soviet
occupation".

But the Russians have taken Viazma, and Smolensk, and Hitler's
main base in Central Russia is now directly threatened. It is said
that two Soviet armies are converging in that direction after the
capture of the Viazma stronghold.

The strength of the German counter-attacks, in which big tank
forces are being used shows to me that the OKW is now making a
large-scale attempt to stop the Soviet offensive, once and for all.
But will they succeed? The whole front from Leningrad to
Kharkov is in a state of flux and it is impossible to say where the
line will harden, if it ever does.

March 21, Sunday. It is now official. I am confirmed as the
Acting Troop Master of the 66th/Brussels Scout Troop at the St.
John the Baptist parish, in Molenbeek-St-Jean. The first meeting
will take place at the elementary school on Easter Sunday April,
25th. We already recruited 12 "tenderfeet" but we are building up
this troop from scratch and have no settled meeting place. The
school will do for the time being, but this state of affairs cannot
last too long.

To top it all I don't have a good Assistant Troop Master. He is
no other than Henri Martin, who has not improved much since
1941, being still a bit too erratic in his behavior. Furthermore, he
is my senior in everything except that I am the boss now. He has
some good qualities, being friendly and endowed with a good

voice, which is an asset. Fortunately, I have the support of the parish priest, himself a former Troop Master, and I can count on him for guidance and advice.

March 25, Thursday. The German people have at long last heard from Little Mustache/Adolf last Sunday. He has not talked to them since the Russian offensive started in the Fall and it was his first public appearance in well over four months.

Contrary to what we might have expected, Hitler did not work himself into a frenzy. Instead he talked for only eleven minutes in a high pitched and monotonous voice.

March 26, Friday. Meanwhile Mr. Churchill, in London, speaking in sober and confident tones makes it clear that he doesn't share the belief of many that the war will be over soon.

"I can imagine that sometime next year - but it may be the year after - we might beat Hitler and his powers of evil into death, dust and ashes. Then we will immediately transport all the necessary additional forces and apparatus to the other side of the world to punish the greedy and cruel Empire of Japan."

Mr. Churchill also expressed the hope that the United Nations, headed by the great powers of the British Commonwealth of Nations, the United States of America and Soviet Russia, will begin to confer upon the future world organization which should be the safeguard against war.

He finished his speech by announcing that General Montgomery's Eighth Army is on the move in South Tunisia.

They are indeed. The latest information is very good. The British have smashed through the Mareth Line and have captured Gabès. Farther north, the Americans have taken Gafsa (twice as a matter of fact), and are advancing northeast to cut off what's left of the Afrika Korps.

March 31, Wednesday. Thanks to Benito, women in Italy are now subject to mobilization whether they like it or not. But it is probably too late to save the country.

April 3, Saturday. There is a very popular song which is played on all radio stations, all over Germany and the occupied countries. Its title is Lili Marleen.

According to *Signal* the words were taken from the volume of poetry "The Little Harbor Organ" by a Hamburg poet with the name of Hans Leip, music by Norbert Schulte. The year was 1938.

In the summer of 1941, the German soldiers' station in Belgrade broadcasted the song to the troops. It was an instant hit. Suddenly, all over Europe, people whistled or hummed the song interpreted by Lale Andersen:

> Vor der Kaserne, vor dem grossen Tor
> Stand eine Laterne, und steht Sie noch davor
> So woll'n wir uns da wiedersehen
> Bei der Laterne woll'n wir stehn
> Wie einst Lili Marleen!"

Which was translated (sort of):

> "Underneath the lantern by the barrack's gate
> Darling, I remember how you used to wait
> 't was here you whispered tenderly,
> That you lov'd me; you always be,
> My Lili of the lamplight, my own Lili Marlene."

April 6, Tuesday. Father learns from colleagues that Belgian- and refugee Jews are rounded up and sent to East Germany and Poland by freight trains in very primitive conditions. This is part of the "resettlement" program which, according to the Nazi propaganda, will move the Jews to model camps with spartan but clean and healthy accommodations. One such camp is often mentioned: Theresienstadt, but no others. This is puzzling. Just one camp?

In the meantime, for more than a year now, the Jews in this country as well as in France and in the Netherlands, have been subjected to harassment and humiliation. Every month or so, there is a new regulation further limiting what is left of their freedom of action.

Examples: Jewish men are called to work as forced labor in Germany or in work camps in Eastern Europe. All Jews above the age of six years must register with the authorities in their place of habitation. Quite a few professions are now closed to Jews: most businesses and all scientific and liberal professions. Access to any university is severely limited and, in many cases, entirely forbidden.

I have not in the past paid enough attention to this persecution of the Jews in this country because it was done so secretly, but I

159

intend to stay informed in the future.

April 8, Thursday. Great news from North Africa: The British Eighth Army and the U.S. First Army have linked up in Tunisia. It is now only a question of time before the Axis forces are thrown out of Africa.

April 9, Saturday. To stand in a long queue outside the grocery store is a very boring chore. Today is sister Léona's turn and to alleviate the boredom I decide to keep her company. Easter is not far away, but even in its death throes winter tenaciously refuses to loosen its grip and the day is howlingly windy, with what appears to be a promise of snow in the air. A sullen roiling sky hungs in angry motion over the neighborhood, giving it the look of an El Greco painting.

Léona doesn't seem to mind the cold. She talks and talks. Her eyes smile in the soft light, half mocking, half friendly, greenish-gray and shining. There is nothing wrong with the design of her eyebrows. Her nose is short and straight, her mouth curved up at the corners, and her cheeks have faint hollows in the right places. Her face doesn't add up to a standard type of beauty but it has character and vitality. No anxiety, no confusion: a good deal of self assurance, knowing she looks attractive.

April 12, Monday. Fritz Sauckel, the German Minister of Labor, and Pierre Laval, the French Prime Minister, have signed a pact that makes French prisoners of war free laborers in Germany. This is of interest to me because the pact could affect the situation of my brother-in-law, Jules Wille, who has been a POW in Germany for almost three years now.

Sister Rosa has written to us with the news that Jules is ailing and if it is serious enough there is a possibility of repatriation. The Germans do not want sick POWs.

April 13, Tuesday. This is my birthday and what better present can you give in these times of privation but a magnificent bar of soap from before the war? This is exactly what I got. My brothers and sisters are rather jealous but they shouldn't worry: I intend to share this treasure with the whole family and this means that it will not last very long.

April 17, Saturday. The Nazis claim to have discovered a mass grave containing the bodies of about 4,500 Polish officers, in the village of Katyn, near Smolensk, in the Soviet Union. Preliminary medical examination has established that the executions in the Katyn forest took place in the spring of 1940, a fact immediately publicized by the propaganda machine of Joseph Goebbels.

If the date is correct, it is the Soviets who committed the crime. If later, then the Nazis could be the perpetrators as both sides are perfectly capable of such atrocity.

April 18, Sunday. The brother of Léon Malfait, Henri, has been arrested by the Gestapo and is probably now at the fort of Breendonck which is the transit camp for further transport to a concentration camp in Germany. Léon is a good friend; we attend the same school and we are active in the same Scout Troop. His brother Henri is older, but I know him because he is always ready to help when I need him, especially in math. He is a student at the University of Louvain and has apparently been involved in the Resistance movement that must have led to his arrest.

Nobody, least of all his parents, knew about his underground activities. The whole family is in a state of shock but friends and relatives are trying to find out where he is being detained in order to bring him, if possible, food and some clothing.

April 20, Tuesday. Between two exams, I pass a medical examination in school under the auspices of the Health Ministry. Like all young Belgians I am: 1) underweight; 2) underfed (no great news to me); 3) I have, like most of my co-students, latent TB, but no need to worry the doctor tells me; 4) I have some skin problems due to a vitamin deficiency and bad hygiene for lack of soap. Otherwise, I am all right but my teeth need attention except that dentists cannot exercise their profession properly, for lack of adequate equipment (most of it requisitioned by the Germans) as well as medicines and drugs.

April 22, Thursday. No news of Henri Malfait. His parents have gone to Breendonck, the concentration camp situated between Brussels and Antwerp. This is the "reception" camp for all political prisoners in Belgium. They found out nothing. Under the Hitler decree of *Nacht und Nebel* (Night and Fog), no information is to be given about arrested persons and no contact between them and the people outside is permitted. Once detained, you disappear without a trace in the secrecy of the Nazi concentration nightmare.

In late afternoon I pay a visit at the Malfait house. The parents are desperate. The father tries to keep his composure but it is hard and he is not succeeding very well. The mother is in a state of deep depression staring in the void, not responding or reacting to the visitors' words of sympathy. Léon is a pillar of strength in the house, full of attention for his parents, receiving the friends who come to share the pain of the family, talking on the phone with "influential" people, hoping to get some news of the whereabouts of his brother, serving ersatz coffee or lime-blossom tea.

My thoughts are that at this very moment, all over Europe, other families are grieving for fallen soldiers or for the victims of Nazi brutality and oppression. Where is the hope of finally getting rid of this scourge and live again in a world more or less at peace?

April 25, Sunday. As planned, we started the new 66th Troop at Molenbeek-St-Jean. It was a great success. We have seventeen boys age twelve to fifteen, full of energy and enthusiasm. We are not without problems however. The premises are cramped; due to textile rationing, the uniforms do not meet the minimum regulations and they look quite shabby. But "c'est la guerre" and nobody really minds.

The weather is fine and in the afternoon, instead of staying in the confining space of the schoolyard, I decide to bring a little culture into my very novice Troop and soon we are on our way, as a rather disorderly group, toward the House of Erasmus, in the nearby suburb of Anderlecht.

The House built in 1488 and enlarged in 1515, called "The Swan", was the property of the church of Anderlecht and lodged the Canons of the Chapter and their guests. One of the latter, in 1521, was no other than a Dutch scholar, theologian and humanist, by the name of Geert Geerts, better known as Erasmus.

On the ground floor we visit the "Chamber of Rhetoric", the Chapter Hall with their beautiful paintings of old Flemish masters, among them the splendid "Epiphany" of Hieronymus Bosch. We now enter Erasmus' study exhibiting a simple writing desk and a series of portraits of the scholar by Quentin Metsys, Dürer and a copy of the well-known portrait by Holbein the Younger.

The first floor shelters very precious original editions of the works of the great humanist, among others a very rare volume of the first edition of his In Praise of Folly (1511), as well as other precious editions of his other works: Adages, Colloquies, and the originals of some of his letters. It is interesting to note that "In Praise of Folly" went into thirty-nine editions before 1536!

Heavy stuff for my young friends? I don't think so. They are at an age when one can absorb a lot of cultural facts which will stay with them and form their taste for the rest of their lives. My father did it for me. With him I visited Bruges the Magnificent, the splendid cathedral at Tournai, as well some monuments and churches in Ghent and the great cathedral of Antwerp. It has helped me tremendously in the appreciation and enjoyment of truly beautiful works of art.

April 28, Wednesday. At home, brothers Michel and Lucien, as well as sisters Simone, Léona and Marie-Thérèse and myself, for some reason, talk about Joseph Goebbels and his propaganda machine. We find that the difference between propaganda and information is fundamental: propaganda aims at subjecting people; information aims at emancipating them.

May 3, Monday. During the Easter vacation I have reflected on Stalingrad. On the one hand we have the dogged resistance of the Russians on the Eastern front and the heroic fight of the Soviet guerillas behind the German lines. On the other we have a totalitarian State with the murderous Stalin at its head who, for all practical purposes, is as bad and despicable as the Nazi régime. Hitler has killed and is still killing thousands of people; Stalin has killed millions of his people (the famine in Ukraine). Hitler has thousands upon thousands of men and women in the KZ's (concentration camps). Stalin has ten of thousands of prisoners in labor camps.

Some of my friends who, by the way, are not communists, tell me I have it all wrong. I should not and cannot say that there is no difference between the two ˙ regimes. Yes, there have been atrocities committed in the Soviet Union; yes, it has been ruled by Stalin with an iron hand but this is nothing compared to the Nazi thugs. To this I respond: how come in the first stages of the war, in 1941, the Russian population did greet the advancing German troops with the traditional bread and salt of welcome? And what about the political assassinations and the Katyn massacre? But I agree that I don't know enough about the Soviet regime and I have decided to study these matters, starting today!

May 5, Wednesday. Well, I didn't start right away. But today, first day of class following our Easter vacation, I went to the school library and found nothing on the subject of Russia or the Soviet Union. So, in late afternoon, I visited our municipal library which has exactly six books on the subject but it is quite a disparate collection!

To get a good overview of the subject, I will have to study 1) the history of Russia and the Soviet Union. 2) its literature, 3) perhaps also the language. A tall order.

Furthermore it looks like I will have to look for more specialized libraries. This means the universities. But the University of Louvain's library is in a shambles after the fire of May, 1940. It is being reassembled in different places but there is no easy access. The Free University at Brussels has been closed by the Nazis because of its open opposition to the Occupation authorities.

It leaves me with the libraries of private organizations with a special interest in Russia/Soviet Union. There cannot be very many of them.

A friend gives me another idea. Why not try the Flea Market, Place du Jeu de Balle, in town? There are a few stalls selling used books of all kinds. By visiting them from time to time, I might be lucky and find what I am looking for, at low cost.

May 8, Saturday. The British Broadcasting Corporation (BBC) has announced that the Allied troops have liberated the towns of Bizerte and Tunis in Tunisia. It is now only a question of days before the Axis troops are kicked out of Africa.

We are a family of "radio criminals" because listening to the BBC is strictly forbidden by the Occupant. But except for a specific denunciation, there is no way the Nazis can enforce this ban. So they try to jam the airwaves and, depending on the weather conditions, it is often effective especially during the broadcasts in French or Flemish. I therefore listen to the BBC news service in English which is less often jammed.

May 11, Tuesday. Joseph Conings, my former Troop Master at the 26th Troop, unexpectedly showed up at our home last night with an almost incredible story.

A few days ago he received the order to present himself at the German Labor Office for a medical examination prior to be sent to Germany as forced laborer. He had asked for our opinion and we advised him not to show up. They might embark him on the spot. He went anyway because he was afraid of retaliation against his brothers.

And now he is at the door in great excitement, with a file under his arm.

He told his story. He presented himself at the appointed hour at the Labor Office and was given his file which he had to present at every stage of the thorough medical examination. At the end, after resuming his clothes, he was directed to another part of the building for an interview about his professional skills. Instead of going right, Joseph Conings went left and coolly walked out of the Office with his papers tucked under his shirt. We were incredulous at first, but the file under his arm is proof of his tale's veracity. The German Labor Office has lost a forced laborer-to-be and will never find him again. All trace of Joseph Conings has disappeared. He has to be careful and avoid being caught in one of those round ups the Germans conduct in Brussels and other towns. To that effect he must avoid public transportation and all gatherings of more than five persons. This certainly will put a crimp on his social activities, especially with the Troop. Here goes another leader...

This bleak outlook doesn't put a damper on his spirits and we celebrate this "victory" with war cookies made of brown flour and very weak beer.

May 14, Friday. It's all over in Tunisia. The Axis' bid to create an African empire has come to an inglorious end. General von Arnim, who replaced Rommel in Tunisia, has been taken prisoner together with about 150,000 of his troops. Quite a defeat for Hitler! He needs these soldiers in Russia; this is true also for Musso the Benito, who needs them in Italy. His popularity has dropped to about zero.

What's next? Surely the Anglo-Americans, to relieve the pressure on the Eastern front, will have to attack somewhere in Europe. In other words open the Second Front everybody talks about. Where will it happen?

May 17, Monday. Riding to school, at the Place Rogier downtown, I notice small groups of SS Panzer soldiers, easily recognizable by their death's head insignia on their black collar patches and on their field caps. People give them side glances and nobody comes close, such is their reputation of brutality and ruthlessness. According to the adage: "Know thy enemy," here is an overview of their organization.

The SS

The SS *or Schutzstaffel* is an independant unit of the NSDAP, the Nazi party, with at its head the Reichsführer SS Heinrich Himmler.

The first and foremost task of the SS is the protection of the Führer, Adolf Hitler. However, by order of the Führer, this task has been expanded to include Germany's internal security.

To accomplish these assignments the SS-man is selected among the best Germans of Aryan stock. Every member of the SS will be taught the values of the National Socialist ideology: Loyalty, honor, obedience and valor. Unconditional obedience is especially demanded from him. He will also be trained to mercilessly fight the German Reich's most dangerous enemies: The Jews, Freemasons, Jesuits and political clergy.

By his example,the SS-man will convince people of the truth of the National Socialist "Weltanschauung". He will fight for these Nazi lofty ideals and will try to accomplish at all times great feats both physical and mental. He will be sustained in these efforts by his companions in the SS fraternity and by reading Der Schwarze Korps (The Black Corps), the aggressive weekly paper of the SS, and he will do his utmost to see that it is distributed among and read by the entire German people.

The SS, as far as I can find out, is organized as follows:
1. The Allgemeine SS (General SS): This encompass all the voluntary part-time members.

2. The SS Verfügungstruppe later called The Waffen SS, the elite troops fighting with but distinct from the the Wehrmacht. They have their proper organization and ranks. For example, a SS Gruppenführer is a Lieutenant-General in the Wehrmacht and a Sturmmann is a Lance Corporal.

3. The SS Totenkopf Verbände, the Death's Head Formations who guard the concentration camps and provide the manpower for secret operations.

4. The Sicherheitsdienst or SD, the Party's Security office which is the Secret Police.

5. The SS Rasse und Siedlungsamt, the SS Race and Settlement Office, responsible for the resettlement (read: deportation) of entire segments of the population in the East, especially the Jews.

All in all, a powerful and fearsome tool to keep Germany and all occupied countries under tight control.

May 22, Saturday. In the last few months there has been a great increase in activity by the Allied air forces over Belgium. The RAF is active at night and the Americans in daylight. During the day one can hear an imposing number of bombers which can be seen when the sun reflects against their aluminum bodies. Fortunately they do not bomb us very frequently. Rather they are on their way to Germany where they inflict great damage. I hope this will hasten our liberation. The German FLAK, the anti-aircraft guns, is not as active as before. They now go into action only from time to time and mostly at night, and then they create quite a racket. I guess it is a plot to keep us awake.

May 23, Sunday. With my fledgling 66th Troop, we went to the Royal Park of Laeken where there is plenty of space and fresh air for instruction and games. Part of the park, not accessible to the public, surrounds the Royal Castle, where King Léopold is kept as a prisoner by the Germans. Atop the castle, floats the Wehrmacht flag, not the Nazi flag, although it now shows the swastika in the middle whereas, before 1933, it displayed the Iron Cross. At the castle's entrance in their sentry box, which is painted black, white and red, two soldiers mount guard, day and night.

The weather cooperated; it was sunny and dry. Our troop is slowly becoming a disciplined unit but it will take time to spot and train the young leaders. We are growing and gain at least two or three members at every meeting. Soon we will have three packs of eight scouts which, considering the fact that we are hardly one month old, is quite an accomplishment. Of course the recruitment started long before our first meeting.

May 25, Tuesday. Everywhere the Allies are busy on their respective fronts. The Americans keep moving up from island to island in the South Pacific. The Russians have reached the Donetz River along a 110-mile stretch and heavy fighting is underway in the Kuban, the region near the Black- and Azov seas. The American air force and the RAF are pounding German cities as well as Sardinia. Will the next Allied move be against Italy? And if so, where?

An interesting piece of news. Radio Tokyo has announced the death of Admiral Isoroku Yamamoto, the Japanese naval leader who masterminded the attack on Pearl Harbor and who had promised to write the final terms of American surrender in the White House! According to Tokyo, Yamamoto was killed by the Americans while directing a battle in the South Pacific. I wonder what he was doing there.

May 29, Saturday. I went to the Flea Market downtown, which looks to me like a semi-official black market place. To my surprise, I found quite a few bookstalls with old books, very old books and more recent ones. I browsed for more than two hours and was delighted to find what I was looking for: books on Russia and a few on the Soviet Union.

9

June 2 - August 29, 1943

June 2, Wednesday. My godfather, Joseph Devoldere, is with us, on a visit. He is returning to Germany after a two week vacation in Izegem.

He is an "Arbeitswillige", a volunteer for work in Germany. Actually he is a forced laborer. First, the Germans closed the shoe manufacturing company where he worked as a shoe machinery specialist. Then, as an unemployed person, they are sending him to work in Germany. At this point he chose to "volunteer" before being forced to go and that gives him a few advantages like better food, a room of his own and being employed in his field of specialization. He works now in a small town, thirty miles from Koblenz.

On his way to Belgium, he passed through the important city of Köln or Cologne. The spectacle of this town, he reports, is stupefying. The city has been bombed until it looks like it is nothing more than a huge pile of rubble. The Cathedral is still standing but badly damaged. Almost every street in the city center is blocked with huge chunks of brick and stone sometimes two stories high from buildings blasted to pieces on either side.

"If the Germans win this war, God forbid," says my godfather, "they will force all POWs and foreign laborers to work in the rebuilding of the destroyed German cities. They will also enslave the English population for that task, in retaliation for the 'terrorist' bombings."

As a specialist, my godfather doesn't live in a camp but has found a place to stay with an elderly couple, whose three sons are in the army. One has recently been killed on the Russian front. They live in daily terror of receiving some more bad news. The mother is inconsolable. Scheisekrieg!

They never discuss politics, keep mostly to themselves and have few contacts with friends and neighbors. They give to the

Winterhilfe because they have to, show their enthusiasm for the regime by having a portrait of Hitler in the house as well as a copy of "Mein Kampf" which lies on the coffee table, unread. Later on, I accompany my godfather to the North Station for the night train to Köln-Koblenz-Mainz-Frankfurt, and wish him Godspeed, hoping the Allies will spare him on his journey.

June 5, Saturday. I have finished reading Wasilewski's extremely interesting book *Littérature Russe* and I am very impressed by the fact that all the great Russian writers, with the exception of Pushkin, who came earlier, flourished within a sixty-year period starting around 1835.

From then on, and until 1900, the year of Wasilewski's book publication, Russia had produced beside Pushkin (d.1839), Lermontov, Gogol, Turgenev, Dostoevsky and Tolstoy: the great Six, plus Tchekov a late comer. Following Wasilewski's advice, I will concentrate on these great writers and prepare a plan of lecture covering their main works. I have, in the past year, read Tolstoy's Guerre et Paix (War and Peace) in the French translation of W.J. Bienstock published in 1921. It enchanted me and I intend to reread it at the next opportunity. I was surprised to discover that the original Russian contains a great number of phrases in French, a reminder that Russian high society in the eighteenth- and early nineteenth century spoke mostly French among themselves.

June 8, Tuesday. Fr. Capart got in touch with me inquiring whether I could help him during the summer vacation with his new youth camp, which is now permanently based in a beautiful building situated in the middle of a park in the little town of Tourneppe (in French) or Dworp (in Flemish).

I cannot give him a definite answer because I still have to plan a week's camping trip with the 66th Troop which is planned for the latter part of July. I suggest early August without any definitive commitment.

June 11, Friday. The first new potatoes!! And very early...How delicious they are, sautéed and served with a rash of bacon. The best meal I ever had. At least it seems so when for months one has to eat more or less edible foods with no taste such as rutabaga, a kind of turnip and other insipid comestibles. But now, for a few months, we will have fruit and vegetables from our garden that will help us forget the winter past and not to worry too much about the one to come. One thing is sure, we cannot often count on milk, eggs, cheese and meat, except that we keep rabbits, and from time to time father brings a chicken home.

June 14, Monday. Someone tells me that Stalin has decreed the dissolution of the Comintern. Since I am more and more interested in things Russian or Soviet, I have done some research on the subject.

The Comintern or *Kommunistcheskyi Internatsional* was founded in March, 1919, in Moscow, to replace the "Second International" which collapsed at the outbreak of the Great War. The Communist International was meant to help, control and also finance the new revolutionary (communist) parties being organized in the industrialized world.

The Comintern has tried, over the years, to influence these communist parties hoping to bring them in line with the policies of the Communist Party of the Soviet Union. But in its 24 years of existence the Comintern failed to win a single country anywhere in the world to communism.

June 15, Tuesday. The British have announced the occupation of the Italian islands of Pantelleria, Linosa and Lampedusa. Searching for them on the map, I find that they are situated between Sicily and Tunisia. The most important one is Pantelleria with an area of 72 km2. Its ancient appellation was Cosyra; it is not a Greek name, perhaps Phoenician?

But I digress. The news is significant because the islands can help as springboards for an offensive against Southern Italy. Will it happen? When and where?

June 19, Saturday. It was four o'clock and the sun was toppling over toward the west. I went to pay a visit to the Malfait family. No news from Henri. The father is pale and gaunt but he has gone back to work; he is a civil servant in one of the Ministries, downtown. Sadness and desolation marks Léon's face but he is very courageous and is greatly helping his family face their little world that has changed forever.

The mother is still in the throes of a deep depression but is reacting in a more positive way to the people around her. She acknowledged my presence by a brief flutter of the eyes and sunk back in her private misery. Relatives and neighbors are a great help in an unobtrusive way. They clean, they cook, they talk softly to elicit an unburdening of her thoughts that will smooth the path to recovery. An old priest, a very wise man, comes to see her often in an effort to rebuild an internal strength and acceptance without which no healing is possible.

June 26, Thursday. I get together with Henri Martin to plan our first camping trip with the brand-new 66th Troop. Camping is not the right word as there will be no living under the tent, as any Boy Scout would wish. For one thing, the Occupant will not permit it and furthermore the members of our Troop are too inexperienced to sustain the rigors of eight nights under canvas; even less so if the weather is not favorable.

We have also to find a place not too far from town so that we can organize a "Parents' Afternoon" always a great success, as parents are anxious to know how their child is faring and whether he is being taken care of properly.

We go over a few possibilities in the area and none seem to fit our needs until Henri, a little hesitantly, reminds me of the Castle of Humbeek. Yes, I remember our stay of August 1941, and Humbeek could be the best choice provided that a certain Marie-Françoise doesn't interfere too much with his duties as Troop Assistant. He is ready, he says wanly, to avoid the wily snares of the young woman; I assure him that I will not brook any breach of this promise, better take good note of it!

We agree on the dates of July 22 through 29; I will contact the Count and Countess for permission to use the grounds and the loft above the equipment building and make sure the dates are convenient.

There are many other details to attend to: finding pots and pans for about thirty people and, most important, planning the food supply. I will ask a Troop Assistant at the 26th to come and be our quartermaster. Every participant will have to provide in advance or bring with him a precise amount of food to insure we van offer wholesome and abundant meals.

This is quite a project and we should have started working on it several weeks ago. Potatoes, vegetables and fruit will not be a problem; bread or flour should be available with a little effort but meat, fats, milk, eggs and cheese are a big question mark. We will have to use all our contacts in the farm sector and perhaps secure some of it on the black market. Fortunately Fr. Ruys, our chaplain, who will be with us for part of the week, has promised to find at least two big hams, at his expense, among his farmer friends. Good!

And some parents might come up with some unhoped-for additional supplies...

June 30, Wednesday. I received an answer from the Count and Countess; they graciously agree to be our hosts on the proposed dates. They will however be away for part of that week but their head farmer will take care of us. A big sigh of relief: Marie-Françoise will not be there to create unwanted distractions for Henri.

In a post-script to their letter, our future hosts promise to supply us with 120 lbs of potatoes "for the kids." We are more than grateful.

July 3, Saturday. I write Fr. Capart to announce that I am available from Sunday August, 1st through August 29th, to help at the youth camp at Tourneppe. I guess the duties will be very similar to those of last year at Braine l'Alleud.

July 7, Wednesday. There is a further increase of the Allied air forces' activities over Germany, Northern France and Belgium. Day and night they fly over, in amazing numbers, to bomb German cities. Once, on a clear afternoon, I started counting the planes and stopped after passing number 600, suffering from a bad case of a stiff neck. So far Brussels has been spared, except for a few minor raids against airfields and the railroad center at Schaarbeek.

Sometimes at night, when the British fly lower than usual, the hated sirens modulate their mournful warning, the FLAK enter into violent action waking up dogs, cats and people. Cats go into hiding; dogs utter a long mournful bark and people, groggy with sleep, descend into inadequate basements or cellars. After an hour or two, most people have rejoined their bed and are sound asleep, their dreams interrupted briefly by the All Clear signal. Sometimes the warning is sounded twice a night and the loss of restful sleep makes people nervous and aggressive.

July 10, Saturday. Not much time for war news because of exams. In the southwest Pacific, the Americans are systematically retaking the series of islands lost to the Japanese in early 1942. After Guadalcanal, they have now announced a great naval victory in the vicinity of New Georgia. I check the map: it's still a long way to Tokyo.

Another piece of information leaves me perplexed. According to the BBC, Admiral Lützow, a German naval expert, in a broadcast to the German people, frankly told them that the U-boat war is now going in favor of the Allies and offered no hope or consolation. Is this true? I cannot believe Joseph Goebbels allowing this kind of negative news to slip through.

July 14, Wednesday. Last day of class. Everything went well. I keep my place at the head of the class, but barely. We resume classes in September, for my last year in high school.

I have now to concentrate on the camping trip. Fortunately, Henri Martin and Henri Loves (of the 26th) have already taken care of most of the preparation. There are still a great deal of details to attend to, however, and we still have to pay a courtesy visit to the owners of the manor and inspect the grounds.

July 15, Thursday. Five days ago, British, Canadian, American and Polish forces invaded the big island of Sicily. The Germans were the first to give any news about the invasion. The Italians were informed by Musso the Benito, in a brief communiqué.

The situation is still very confused but the Allies say they are making good progress. They seem to have landed, in Southern Sicily, between Licata and Portopalo. This is only a guess. The German bulletin also mentions parachutist troops.

July 23, Friday. We spent a whole week in frantic preparations and now we are in Humbeek as guests of the small but magnificent castle.

We were received by the farmer and his son, two men who look as if they are made of wood: cubical faces, broad cheekbones, square-shaped bodies; and shoulders that look like a high plateau.

But they are kind and ready to help. In no time at all we get the straw we need for our beds and put up a few shelves for our provisions. The food most attractive to some animals, our two hams, for example, is taken to the farm for safekeeping.

Meanwhile Ron-ron (yes, he is still here) sits on a beam, gazing out of the large window, superb, urbane and of a silvery blackness of tint. A timid little white dog peers in at the portal with a deprecating mien; and the cat tolerates such canine intrusion with the dignified affability of large natures. Ron-Ron's position in life is an assured one, while that of the little dog clearly is not. The dogs pass but the cat remains, gazing across the pasture where, among the trees, the cattle, chewing cud, pensively count the hours to milking time.

Later after the hustle and bustle of an installation day, and when the scouts are safely asleep in their rugged straw beds, the two Henri's and I sit outside on a rough bench. It is one of the most beautiful nights of the year. There are no clouds. The moon is rising, a thick orange-white sliver, like a slice of a cantaloupe, sitting cocked against the edge of the horizon. Above it hangs a brilliant infinity of stars, high and bright, in the deep blueness of the sky.

July 25, Sunday. Parents' Day is the most devilish happening ever invented by man. For the organizers, that is. The whole Troop starts preparing right after breakfast. The scouts, under the direction of their pack leaders, clean their areas thoroughly and decorate their corners.

Yesterday, a group of them went with Henri Loves around the neighboring farms to get some flour. They came back with enough of the brown stuff to bake delicious cookies (in their opinion) wherewith to receive the parents. We also prepared a kind of weak lemonade which was declared "almost first class" by the majority of the assembly. A long table has been put together with boards, beams and poles, with the solemn promise that all of it will be returned to the farmer... and not end up in the camp fire.

Our secret weapon is that half of the flour has been set aside to make very thin and delicious pancakes such as you can find only in Belgium. As it is still the cherry season, we have collected and pitted enough to prepare, with a generous amount of sugar, a jam which is out of this world.

We have also organized a very primitive musical ensemble together with two clowns chosen for their exuberance, and the

66th Troop is now ready for the greatest show on planet Earth.

It is indeed a great success. Every false note of the band is applauded as if it were a performance at the opera, the clowns would have cut a good figure at any great circus, but the star of the afternoon is the pancakes. They are a bargain at one franc apiece and we can't make them fast enough despite the fact that we have two cooks, plus one kitchen boy to grease the pans, and one jam spreader. Soon we run out of dough and the latecomers have to make do with the cookies which by no means are to be sniffed at.

By six o'clock, every visitor has departed and by seven fifteen all trace of the 66th Troop Summer Festival is gone. The basic elements of the long table are returned safely to the farmer. The pasture is clean, the courtyard in front of our imposing building has never looked so beautiful.

The boy scouts are fast asleep by nine o'clock. (We go to bed early as there is no electricity in our part of the building.) In the twilight, the three of us are sitting on a comfortable old bench found downstairs, our faces illuminated by the dying sun. As is our custom, we review the events of the day to learn about our failings and avoid them in the future.

The sun goes down at last, a circle of liquid fire, turning first to bronze and then to a deep blood orange as it slides toward the horizon, its rays refracted by an evening mist that promises further and greater heat tomorrow.

Suddenly, inspired by the moment, like a bard of old, Henri Loves, a great fan of Virgil, starts to recite, in Latin, an excerpt of the Immortal Poet:

> The night had come, and weary in every land
> Men's bodies took the boon of peaceful sleep
> The woods and the wild seas had quieted
> At that hour when the stars are in mid-course
> And every field is still; cattle and birds
> With vivid wings that haunt the limpid lakes
> Or nest in thickets in the country places
> All were asleep in the silent night.
>
> Aen. IV, 522-529 (transl. Fitzgerald.)

July 26, Monday. About mid-morning, I step out of our loft and look at the sky. I can smell a change in the weather, a strong scent of mid-summer in the air. The sky is light blue with only a few cloud banks to the west. There is increasing warmth mixed with moisture and those clouds are advancing fast.

An hour or so later, I find nature hushed, languid, and the very trees droop in the heat. The sun is hiding behind the jagged peaks of the high fir trees. Storm clouds have brooded over the village to the north; scudding mists swirl from the south to join the impending revels of the elements; the pall of heat on the flat land is pierced by lightning flashes, thunder reverberates menacingly over the landscape.

Then the storm bursts with crash of thunder, with lightning hissing and leaping from horizon to zenith, smiting the line of dark trees opposite the farm with rosy fire or, darting earthward, hovers mockingly around the little spires of the Renaissance manor. A dense cloud drifting from the direction of Humbeek appears to strike that village with a solid wall of water. Havoc of speedy disaster ensues. The flowers of the gardens are destroyed, the trees writhe in the tempest and shed their branches on the ground.

In half an hour, the countryside is flooded. Rivulets gush from every spout and pour down the erstwhile dusty road. Our chatter-prone boy scouts, huddling in any convenient shelter, are mute for a change.

Later, when the sun shines forth once more, and the balmy midday asserts tranquil supremacy, we prepare a soggy lunch and resume our games until the time comes for a campfire and a play in early evening.

July 27, Tuesday. Well, well. We are so busy with our camping activities that we fail to keep track of world events. This morning, the farmer brings us a Flemish newspaper conveying the news that Musso (the Benito) has been arrested on orders of the king of Italy, Vittorio-Emmanuele III. Marshal Pietro Badoglio has formed a new government. Hitler must be shaking in his boots or eating what is left of his office carpets.

Today in a short ceremony we inducted eight boys into the fraternity of the Boy Scout movement; we also confirmed two pro-temps as pack leaders in our Troop. In this way, we are strengthening our very young group and hope that, in a few years,

177

it will be as solid and as effective as the 26th that has "nurtured" me and which I try to emulate.

July 28, Wednesday. We break up camp after lunch. We invited the Count and Countess for lunch to express our gratitude for their hospitality. They graciously invited us back next year, hopefully, as the Count says, in a new and free Belgium.

Marie-Françoise is still on vacation with relatives, so that Henri Martin was not lost to us for an attractive young lady. We made sure everything we used is put back in its right place; we didn't break any windows because there are no windows in the loft! The straw is bundled and our brooms cleaned our quarters so thoroughly that the farmer wished we would come again soon, "just to keep the grounds clean".

Ron-ron, sensing a departure, peers at us with round yellow eyes in a silent goodbye and then vaults onto some projection of an adjacent wall and proceeds to taunt the farmer's dogs, to spice a little of an otherwise rather dull life. It is a diversion that never fails to incite the cat to execute varied stealthy descents into enemy territory. A frantic dash, a growl and scramble across the garden ensues, the brood of puppies whimpering with excitement in the rear, too young to join the sport. And Ron-ron is once more perched on the wall, with a mien of cool impertinence and abstraction, as who would say:
-Can you possibly be barking at me?
-Some day, the fierce dogs will catch you, I admonish, caressing the pet.
The cat replies in a conceited manner and as plainly as a cat can, while briskly purring thanks for any interest in the matter:
-Is that your opinion?
Adieu! Ron-ron. Till next year, maybe.

July 29, Thursday. Back home, I am trying to catch up on the news from Italy.

I discover that the Allies have made good progress in Sicily. The Americans in a big dash along the coast and across the island have taken Palermo and Termini Imerese; the British are in Syracuse and Augusta along the east coast and are closing on Catania.

These events had a profound effect on the governing authorities in Italy that brought about the defeat of Musso in the Fascist Grand Council on July 24, and then his arrest and the formation of a new government.

But the war goes on: the King and Badoglio made this clear.

The Story of Musso the Benito
The Little Caesar

Musso the Benito, the man whom Mr. Churchill describes as "the bloated bulldog of the Pontine Marshes", "Hitler's tattered lackey," and the "pocket Caesar with feet of clay," is the son of a blacksmith, born at Dovia di Predoppio in the province of Forli, on July 29th, 1883.

In his youth, he was a socialist but in 1914 he turned nationalist, and when he favored the intervention of Italy in the war, he was expelled from the Socialist party. When Italy entered the war in May of 1915, he joined the Army as a private. Like his friend Adolf, he reached the rank of corporal before being wounded and discharged in February, 1917.

On October, 1922, after a Congress at Naples, Musso led 40,000 Fascists in a march on Rome. Historians tell us that Benito followed the marchers later by train, fearing to risk his neck in any fighting. Musso made himself dictator of Italy in 1925.

On Good Friday, 1939, he ordered the seizure of Albania. In May of the same year a formal military alliance was concluded with Germany, and on June 10th, 1940, he brought off his famous "stab in the back" act by declaring war on France. His invasion of Greece was an unmitigated disaster.

Then, as we know, Musso lost his empire in East Africa and recently was kicked out of North Africa. Now the Allies are on Italian soil. No wonder the Italians gave him the boot.

Mr. Weustenraedt paid us a visit this evening. He is a friend of Mother from way back, as they both hail from the town of Izegem.

By chance, Mr. W. lives not two miles away from our home. He holds an important job at the Ministry of Finance and when he visits, about five or six times a year, he always has quite a few interesting stories to tell. Sometimes he shows up with information about the war so unusual in its contents, it makes me wonder. He has frequent contacts with representatives of the Nazi Finance Ministry and the Reichsbank, ravenous wolves, intent on plundering the country.

July 30th, Friday. Italy is under martial law. Mussolini is under house arrest; Scorza, the Fascist Party Secretary, and the entire Italian Cabinet are detained at a place outside Rome.

The line taken by Goebbels is that the change of Government in Italy is believed to have been due to the state of Musso's health. He was said to have been ill for some time. (Goebbels gave the same reason about Rudolf Hess, remember?)

There must be vigorous bombing going on because, night and day, masses of bombers are roaring overhead, their exhausts spitting fire sometimes visible at night. It seems that in the last few days, the USAAF and the RAF have attacked the Ruhr, specially Essen, Cologne and Hamburg. The Allies have been pounding them around the clock.

August 2, Monday. I arrived yesterday at the Youth Camp which is located on a beautiful wooded property in the village of Dworp or Tourneppe, about 12 miles south of Brussels. The building is owned by the Christian Worker Youth and was erected just before the war to provide the young workers with a nice place to meet for conferences, retreats or short, inexpensive vacations.

This youth movement is in big trouble with the Nazis for its staunch opposition to the policy of forced labor to Germany. Its founder, Jozef Cardijn, was arrested in 1942 for his forceful protests and then released. But it is only a question of time before "they" catch him again. I am told, however, that he is protected by Cardinal Van Roey and it is well known that the military authorities don't want to mess with the latter. They have enough trouble as it is and have no desire to create new problems. It has to be stressed that Belgium and for a while Northern France, are under military rule and not Nazi civilian dictatorship under a gauleiter, like, in Holland for example. The military, very harsh at times, have kept some sense of reality if not of honor.

In view of these circumstances the Youth Movement had to drastically cut its activities and can no longer use its facilities at

Dworp/Tourneppe. To avoid seeing them seized by the Occupant, they were offered to Fr. Capart who was looking around for a secluded and peaceful place for his Youth camp.

I was welcomed by the chief leader, Herman Bouton. He is a tall, lanky man with a long face and intense stare that lends him the aspect of a medieval philosopher. To me, he looks like a soul that has met a body by chance and tries to make the best of it.

We get along famously. I will be his direct assistant and, together with two other leaders, we are in charge of about fifty young boys, age thirteen to sixteen, who are in great need of good food, fresh air, exercise. As said before they are also taught the basics of deportment and personal hygiene. The other leaders are about 22-24 years old. One is Léon Lenglez, a muscular man, with a friendly, open face and slate gray eyes; the other, Jean-Pierre Roman, in sharp contrast, is short and rather stout. His features are massive and his probing eyes seem to want to see through you.

The group is divided into six packs of 8 or 9 and organized along the lines of the scouting movement. Each pack has a leader and an assistant; this means that many of these boys carry some responsibility, which allows us to discover future leaders as they prove themselves in the performance of their duties.

August 3, Tuesday. Fr. Capart is back from Brussels and after lunch he invites me to his small office. He is in a grave mood and comes directly to the point. "The Youth camp is a legitimate program," he says, sponsored by the Oeuvre Nationale de l'Enfance (ONE), an offshoot of the Ministry of Health and partially financed by it. Everything is above board. Except for two important points that are unknown to the Ministry and, of course, to the Occupation authorities. The leadership, except for Fr. Capart and myself, is entirely composed of réfractaires (forced labor evaders) or resistance fighters. They are here under assumed names, with false but authentic papers issued by the Belgian authorities, carrying authentic stamps. All of this is organized by "insiders" who, as said previously, risk prison, deportation and death for being involved in such activities.

I am not too surprised by this revelation as at home we are ready to use the same means, if needed, for brother Michel. Fr. Capart asks me not to mention this matter with the persons concerned.

The less said, the better. I agree. Furthermore to reduce the risks the three réfractaires, every evening after lights out, leave the premises and spend the night in another place. This means that I am responsible for the whole flock from around 9 p.m. to 7 a.m. I assent to that too.

Fr. Capart has another item to discuss with me, but he has to interrupt our meeting to prepare for the visit tomorrow of two inspectors from the ONE. For my part, I have to organize the troops, clean the premises and spruce up the grounds. Not to forget the rehearsing of the welcome ceremony which includes impeccable ranks and the shout in perfect unison of: "Bon-jour, Bien-ve-nue -à - Tour-nep-pe".

August 4, Wednesday. The inspectors, a man and a woman, came and went. They checked the facilities, looked up the rooms, peeked into the showers, toured the refectory and the kitchen as well as the grounds, noted the complete absence of sports equipment which the Center cannot afford, reviewed the medical files of nine very underweight boys and scribbled down their remarks.

They had lunch with us and, at the end, they made a tour of the tables, talked to a few of our protégés and finally departed, apparently satisfied with their visit.

In normal times they would have come down in an official car of the Ministry but nowadays no such luxury is available. We offered them two of our bicycles and I accompanied them on a third one with a pack leader sitting behind on the luggage rack. Down the hill we drove, and up the road about three kilometers, two miles, to the suburban streetcar that took them back to the city.

Our return with three bikes for two riders was a little awkward but we managed by riding the bikes three abreast, each one of us holding the middle one by a handle. We had to stop once to let an asthmatic steam-hissing truck pass us by...

August 5, Thursday. It was not until late last night, when everybody was asleep, that Fr. Capart and I resumed our conversation. It was a startling one, to say the least.

The subject was: The persecution of the Jews by the Nazis. This is not new; it has been going on in Belgium off and on since May 1942. Then, both Queen Mother Elisabeth and King Léopold intervened with German authorities on behalf of the Jews, with no apparent results.

About the same time, Cardinal Van Roey did not hesitate. He ordered all religious institutions to take in these unfortunates, whenever possible. He forbade any religious proselytism: this is purely an operation of charity and rescue, he said. Convents, monasteries, parish halls, hospitals, church schools and child welfare institutions, accordingly, are hiding both parents and children, most of the time separately.

"We are", added Fr. Capart, "a child welfare institution and my point tonight is to let you know that among the adolescents in our care are eleven Jewish boys. They all have new names and their new papers are the best one can get; therefore, the boys are relatively safe. Only a specific denunciation can lead the Nazis to them".

Nobody but F. Capart and Herman Bouton knows this; and myself, because I am responsible for the group all through the night. Should I not wish to take up this burden, adds my interlocutor, I am totally free to leave with the promise not to divulge any of this to anyone.

I accept and, for the first time in my life, have to face the possibility of arrest, prison, deportation, concentration camp and death. These are the penalties for hiding Jewish people in this country, courtesy of the Nazis. But what else can I do?

Run away? No! *First,* because it is the only way for me to participate in active resistance against this scum of the earth. *Second*, my activity as a "resistant" will last only one month; then I will disappear and, unless I am denounced, nobody can find me. This is because I am not paid and my name doesn't appear on any list. *Third,* although the Nazis arrest many people for anti-German activities and send them to KZ camps, the Jews are the only people who are persecuted simply because they are Jews. This pogrom (a Russian word meaning devastation, desolation) includes men, women, children, without exception. The propaganda tells us that the German Reich has to be shielded from the Jews' perverted influence and, for their own good, they are being sent to perfectly safe labor camps in the East where they will be fed and sheltered. The truth, as we know at present from serious sources, is far different.

I ask Fr. Capart whether he wishes to divulge the names of the Jewish boys. He declines, leaving it up to me to find out who they are. I know at least one of them; he has such a Semitic appearance that the kids call him "Isaac". He brushes off the allusion laughingly with the explanation that one of his grandfathers was born in Lebanon.

August 7, Saturday. Last night, I found one of the boys sleepwalking through the corridors. At first I didn't know who he was and could not therefore bring him back to his room. After a guess or two, I tucked him in his bed and the rest of the night was peaceful.

August 9, Monday. This morning I received a letter from Mr. W., via my parents, with excerpts of Mr. Churchill's speech in the House of Commons on July 27th, commenting on the great events in Italy.

"The House will have heard with satisfaction of the downfall of one of the principal criminals of this desolating war. The end of Mussolini's long and severe reign over the Italian people undoubtedly marks the close of an epoch in the life of Italy.

"The keystone of the Fascist arch has crumbled and, without attempting to prophesy, it does not seem unlikely that the entire Fascist edifice will fall to the ground in ruins, if it has not already fallen...

..."Now the external shock of war has broken the spell which, in Italy, held all those masses for so long - in fact for more than 20 years - and held them for all this period in physical, and even more in moral subjection.

"We may therefore reasonably expect that very great changes will take place in Italy. What their form will be, or how it will impinge upon the forces of German occupation, it is too early to forecast...

... "When I learned of the scenes enacted in the streets of the fine city of Palermo on the entry of the United States Army, and reviewed the mass of detailed information I have received, I cannot doubt that the main wish of the Italian people is to be quit of the German taskmasters, to be spared further and perfectly futile ordeal of destruction and to revive their former democratic and parliamentary institutions.

These they can have."

August 11, Tuesday. More news from Italy. First disclosure of how Musso was sacked came today from the official Italian News Agency. Count Dino Grandi, Fascism's diplomat No. 1 and a protégé of the Duce, proposed the sensational step at a meeting of the Fascist Grand Council, on Saturday, July 24. After a debate of ten hours, Grandi's resolution was carried by nineteen votes to seven.

There is still no official news of what has become of Musso but the rumor is persistent that he and his ministers are under house arrest.

August 13, Friday. The town of Catania in Sicily has been liberated by the British. The end is near on the island. And Churchill has promised, sort of, that the next step will be the invasion of Italy. This means "it will be a long way" before our liberation. I rather have the Allies invade northern France and Belgium.

August 15, Sunday. I get along extremely well with Herman Bouton. He is nine years older than I am, has lots of experience, is full of enthusiasm and is a great organizer. I am learning a lot from him. Daily, he comes up with new ideas that brings new life in an otherwise somewhat routine activity. He manages to find pre-war movies, puts together conferences with slides on subjects well adapted to the audience, launches great games with an interesting theme, arranges for plays, campfires before sundown and even classes for small groups. (I am in charge of the history course and French and Flemish languages .)

And so the kids are kept busy all day long, the leaders too, and there is never a dull moment.

By the way, I have spotted all Jewish boys except one by simply noting which ones never get any mail (we encourage the kids to write to their parents), by the maturity beyond their age and, at times, by the way they look at you with lusterless eyes showing the deep loneliness of a spirit, brought about by desolation in a world of blind hatred.

August 17, Tuesday. After dinner, Herman and I go out on the deep terrace. The evening is pure and calm, the coloring of the darkening sky such as no painter could reproduce. The stillness is broken only by the rustle of leaves, the chatter of a brook tumbling over pebbles of the ravine, the sleepy conversation of evening birds. There is no breath of wind; the stars are highly visible in a clear sky.

We talk about today's activities, reviewing them critically, and about the program of tomorrow. Later there is a lull in the conversation as we look into the dusky air. High above the horizon the evening star flickers like a lamp just lit. Close by is another star of constant light, much smaller.

All of a sudden, in a burst of repressed anger, Herman starts to speak about the persecution of the Jews. He states that he has just read a report, based on solid sources, describing the indescribable cruelty shown by the Nazis towards this defenseless people.

"They (the Nazis) come in the middle of the night and order the Jews to get out of their house or apartment immediately. Only one suitcase with the bare necessities is allowed for the trip. Everything else has to stay behind.

They have to "voluntarily" renounce any claim on their house, in writing, and then they are led to the freight station for "shipment". At the station each of the deportees are given a piece of cardboard with their name and number to wear around the neck. They are subjected to a thorough body search and all money, jewelry, even photographs and little mementoes, as well as any provisions brought along are taken from them.

Before daybreak the SS shove them brutally unto the train waiting to take them to an unknown destination in the East".

These scenes are taking place in France, Belgium, Holland and other occupied countries. They have been verified and are irrefutable.

And what happens to the Jews in those camps? Nobody believes the Nazi propaganda that they are well taken care off. To the contrary, persistent rumors have it that the "arbeitsfähig" (fit for work) Jews, young men and women, are directed to labor camps and the others, women with children and older people, are killed sometimes within hours of their arrival at destination.

Can this be true? Or is it just rumors? One thing is sure: among the thousands upon thousands of deported Jews, not one has come back, not one has written a letter or even a postcard. They have all disappeared in *Nacht und Nebel*.

This is the reality of Nazism. All other explanation is propaganda.

Anti-Semitism has been virulent in Germany since 1933, the year the Nazis came into power. The NSDAP official rallying word is: "Deutschland erwache! Juda verrecke! (Germany awake! Let the Jew perish!) And on January 30, 1939, Hitler told the Reichstag and the world: "A war instigated by world Jewry will lead to the destruction of the Jewish race in Europe." Can such a murderous regime show any hesitation at the extermination of the Jews?

August 20, Friday. The lack of solid news regarding the fate of the Jews or any political prisoner in Germany shows how difficult it is to get to the truth in a dictatorship. We cannot turn to the official press and radio, which is pure propaganda not to be believed or trusted. So we turn to the BBC's Belgian service, in French and in Flemish, which is widely listened to but is very fragmentary. I listen, at times, to the BBC program destined to France and also the BBC in English. All these programs are jammed (except at times the English ones) and, depending on the atmospheric conditions, they are often impossible to listen to.

Another source is the clandestine press. There are quite a few of these publications. Most of them, however, are just a two- to four-page broadside, typewritten in 6 to 8 copies and then retyped by the recipients until in the end it reaches a few hundred people. They mostly concentrate on regional news.

Except for *La Libre Belgique,* a true newspaper, printed on rather good paper, whose first issue appeared as early as July, 1940. It has continued ever since albeit on a very irregular basis. The editors, in this way, carry on the tradition of its famous predecessor of 1914-18. The Libre Belgique gives news from inside the country and from the world at large. As can be expected, this news is often outdated, nevertheless it gives us hope and confidence that the "Boche" will be booted out some day.

August 22, Sunday. There are rumors of peace negotiations between the new Italian government, headed by Badoglio, and the Allies. Are they unfounded? I don't think so. The Italian people are sick and tired of this war and there are reports of troubles in the big industrial cities of Northern Italy such as Turin and Milan. The Nazis will certainly take measures to thwart any armistice agreement.

August 24, Tuesday. Taking advantage of the proximity of the Butte of Waterloo, the castle of Beersel and even Halle with its beautiful Basilica and its famous Black Virgin of the 13th century, I would like to organize a few cultural outings. Big Chief is very reluctant to agree to such trips. There is the problem of transportation although none of the mentioned places are very far from here. Most important however Herman Bouton is of the opinion that a group of close to fifty young people on the move with their leaders, would attract unrequited attention from unfriendly and suspicious quarters.

August 26, Thursday. We came to a compromise. After lunch, I left with a group of fourteen of the older boys for a visit to the neighboring town of Halle. The suburban tramway, which connects Brussels to Halle, brought us to the medieval center of the town with its Renaissance-style Town Hall, dating from 1616, and its Basilica of St Martin, better known as the Basilica of Notre-Dame. A basilica is a Catholic church, designated as such by the Pope, which enjoys special ceremonial privileges.

It is a magnificent medieval building erected in the 14th century. The interior is so dark, one feels repelled by damp shadows and somewhat choked by the heavy odor of ancient incense which saturates the place. It is cool inside, turbulent with images of late medieval ornament, but calm withal, as though the passion that created it had all been spent and only the mystery remains, still unsolved, forever insoluble...

North of the present choir built in 1385, stands Our Lady of Halle, alone and peaceful. She is said to have miraculous powers for aiding barren women in their desire for children, so Our Lady does not lack of attention.

Like other old and greatly venerated images, the Virgin and her Child have black hands and faces. This is not the color of the wood, which is neither black nor primitively painted. Through the centuries the smoke from innumerable candles has stained and blackened not only the hands and faces of the Virgin and Child but the garments of satin and brocade. No one dares to touch so sacred an image which, year after year, gathers an overall patina of smoke and grime.

The crypt, with vaults radiating from a thick central pillar, dates from 1398 to 1402. It contained the rich "treasure" of the basilica among others a reliquary, gift of Louis XI, and a monstrance gift of Henry VIII of England (before he turned against Rome). Most of the treasure however has been removed to a safe place to protect it from the bombs and the greedy hands of the Nazis.

It was late afternoon, the sun was still warm and bright, the sky clear, a perfect day for strolling along the narrow streets of the town, walking through the park, and finally stopping for an ice-cream at one of the little cafés of the Grote Markt.

The waiter was an old man with a flat white face and heavy black-rimmed spectacles. He looked as bleak as the Behring Strait in December and greeted us with a smile that looked an unaccustomed effort for the muscles involved. He took our order: fifteen vanilla ice-creams, and went on, the smile still painted on his face. But he left behind a whiff of sulphur and brimstone.

In contrast the sun was still vivid and blinding even at this hour; the shadows were pointed, very sharp and dark blue; the sky was a resonant color as if formed of turquoise flame.

The "nephew of Gengis-Khan", as we had decided to call him, came back with wartime ice-creams that were more watery ice than cream, flavored with ersatz-vanilla that must have come from the retort of a badly trained medieval magician.

But nobody minds. The boys are delighted by this unexpected break in the monotony of the camp schedule. I think we should do this more often. It is a rather inexpensive morale booster.

My "time keeper" consults his watch and gives the signal to go; the "treasurer" gets ready to pay the bill; the "travel director" consults the timetable and counts the return tickets. Everything is under control; the "town plan reader" unfolds his maps. Most of the boys have a specific assignment, however small, and they love it! It teaches them responsible behavior and allows us to more easily spot the leaders *in spe*.

With that kind of organization, no wonder we come back on time and without a hitch.

August 27, Friday. I learn that the SS Reichsführer Heinrich Himmler has been promoted to Minister of the Interior of the German Reich - the one empire that should last a thousand years, remember?

After Hitler, Himmler is now the most powerful man in Germany. He controls the police, the Gestapo, the Sicherheitsdienst as well as the SS, and the concentration camps. Furthermore he most surely .can influence the judicial administration. He is truly in a unique position of power.

August 28, Saturday. This very morning I awoke early by the light coming through a crack in the curtained window. The gradual lightening of the room gave me a slow and sure pleasure. At first it was all gray and uncertain; gradually outlines became clear, and contours followed them. I got up and looked at the sky. A few lazy, fleecing clouds. The rest is clear, washed-out blue. A nice day in the offing!

It is my last full day here and I am briefing my successor who was my predecessor, now back from his vacation. We are preparing also for the transfer of three of the Jewish boys to another place of concealment. To avoid suspicion and perhaps detection they cannot stay permanently here. Therefore some sort of rotation has been devised whereby we convey them to another safe place. This is done by word of mouth, without any written document, letter or telephone contact. As I am going home tomorrow, I will escort them to the designated place.

August 29, Sunday. After lunch, our little group leaves for the tram stop down the hill, destination Brussels. Again to avoid suspicion the Jewish boys carry but a very light piece of luggage. They followed my suggestion to also shoulder a satchel with a few books to give the impression they are going back to school.

They are rather tense and sorry to leave their "home" where, over a period of several months, they have developed a few friendships. These they cannot pursue by correspondence: once they move to another shelter, all ties have to be broken. I invite the trio to smile and talk animatedly, as normal boys do, but encounter no success.

I am bringing them to a specific location in Brussels where they will stay for just a few hours; after a partial change of clothes, they will be conveyed to a second stop and then, after a day or so, sometimes less, to their final refuge. "Final" here means three to five months whereat they will be uprooted again.

At the tram stop we separate two by two, and climb into a different compartment but within sight of each other. They carry their own ID cards, false but perfectly legitimate, issued by the national authorities; the latter very well aware that in doing so they are helping the Underground.

In Brussels, the boys follow me, two at ten to twenty paces, the third one on the other side of the street. More precaution! It is late afternoon and roundups by the SS Einsatzgruppen or the Grüne Polizei are rare at this hour. But one never knows.

Nothing untoward happened. We arrived safely at our rendezvous. I ring the bell very briefly, twice in succession. Then, four more times, a little longer and push the heavy door open. We enter a cobbled courtyard, clean washed and not a soul to greet us.

I take out a small package wrapped in brown paper and hold it for all to see. Presently, a man appears who seems to be a shade under six feet, a man of middle years, his age attested by streaks of gray at his temples and crow's feet at the edge of his deep-set eyes; the face itself is narrow and sharp-featured.

"Uncle Robert," I say, "sends his greetings and wishes to offer you this third edition of Georges Bernanos' l'Imposture.

"Very well," he approves, returning book and package to me. "Boys, please come inside." I give them a big hug and murmur in a voice choked with emotion: "Adieu! God be with you. Don't worry; you are in good hands."

They nod with tears in their eyes and, with slow and uncertain steps, walk through a side door and disappear into the building.

At home that night, I am rather distracted and uncommunicative. Mother, noticing my silent mood asks me if I feel all right. I blame it on fatigue and go to bed early. I am thinking of the Jewish boys and all the persecuted people in Europe who are hunted down and have no place to hide.

10

September 2 – December, 1943

September 2, Thursday. It is a bright morning although the sun keeps hiding behind lazy clouds. It is warm without being hot. Our neighborhood has a freshness which has followed a little overnight rain.

The fine weather encourages me to go to the Flea Market in search of more books on Russia and the Soviet Union. I find that there is very little available on the latter but I am lucky enough to discover a Dictionnaire Russe-Français by Makaroff, St Petersburg 1899, beautifully bound and in excellent condition and *Le Bolchevisme* by Waldemar Gurian, translated from German by Jean Coster, 1933. This is the only book I can find on Soviet Russia and Communism (Bolshevism). The prize of the day, however is the *Histoire de Catherine II, Impératrice de Russie* by Jean Castéra, 3 vol. Paris, 1799.

The volumes are magnificent in their late 18th century binding, with beautiful engravings of portraits and maps. As I am a book lover, I consider these acquisitions are treasures to keep forever.

September 3, Friday. Last night we had a "Luftalarm" and the anti-aircraft guns made such a racket we thought it safer to all go down to the shelter in the basement. Swarms of planes could be heard above us. The continuous hum of the engines filled the sky for well over an hour. We lost some sleep but, fortunately Brussels was not a target. Father asserts that it is bound to happen, for our capital is a very important railroad and airfields center.

We learn this morning that the docks of Antwerp have been hit but there is no news as how severe the bombing was. Other towns, near the coast, also have suffered damage.

September 4, Saturday. The British 8th Army has invaded the mainland of Italy. Two hours before dawn British and Canadian units, protected by the most powerful naval and air bombardment,

192

have crossed the Straits of Reggio, on the "toe" of Italy.

The news is very sketchy; we will have to wait for more details. I wonder why they attacked so far down: the country is mountainous, the roads few. But who am I to question the Allies' decisions?

September 6, Sunday. I spent the day with the 66th Troop. We went by tram to the Forest of Soignes, not far from the Etangs de Rouge-Cloître (The Red Cloister Ponds). on the site of the now vanished famous monastery. Only the priory is still standing being used at present for secular purposes. I mentioned to the scouts that Hugo van der Goes (1440-1482), a very famous Flemish painter, one of the medieval "primitives" died here in 1482. His most famous painting "The Death of the Virgin" can be seen in the Museum of fine Arts at Bruges, "a masterpiece for the technical skill of its execution and the dramatic intensity of the expression".

We then proceeded farther into the forest. A group of German officers, a general among them, stopped to watch us playing games. They seemed interested and smiled. I hope they didn't mistake us for some kind of Hitlerjugend or any other Nazi youth organization.

September 7, Thursday. There is excellent news about Italy. The Nazi radio admits that the whole of Cape Spartivento, in the southeastern tip of the Italian toe, has been evacuated by German and Italian troops. The front apparently stretches from Scylla in the northwest through Villa San Giovanni and Peggio di Calabria to Melito and Cape Spartivento in the southeast. All in all about 52 miles of front but, according to my calculations, it's a long way from Reggio to Napoli (360 miles) and Roma (440 miles.)

I want to mention also the big Soviet advances all along the 600-mile long offensive front in Russia. According to the best sources available, the German armies are in full retreat from the Sea of Azov in the south, to the Smolensk area, west of Moscow. The most spectacular Russian advances are in the south, in the Donetz area.

September 9, Thursday. **Italy is out!**
Italy has laid down the arms in unconditional surrender to the Allies, utterly defeated on land and sea and in the air. This means

that about 7 million Italian soldiers have ceased to fight.

The Nazi radio broadcasted the news as follows:

"The veil is lifted from Badoglio's treacherous game. A clique of Jews and elements alien to the Italian nation have brought about the treachery against the Italian nation. Germany and Europe are strong enough to punish the originators of that crime, and German arms will carry out that punishment."

September 11, Saturday. This seems to become the most momentous month of the war. Yesterday, the Allies debarked in Salerno, about forty miles south-east of Naples and at the same time started the invasion of Corsica. I guess they will use the latter as an "unsinkable aircraft carrier" for future attacks against southern France and Germany as well as Northern Italy.

In response to the Allies' attack at Salerno, the German Army has occupied all northern Italy, including Rome and, I guess, Naples.

September 13, Monday. The Nazis are jubilant. German parachutists have rescued Musso from his mountain prison, the Gran Sasso d'Italia, which is located in the Abruzzi at an altitude of some 6000 feet.

According to the German radio, Musso is on its way to see Hitler: Adolphus the Corporal meeting Musso the Toy Soldier, what a celebration this will be!

September 15, Wednesday. Back to school. I am looking forward to this sixth and last year of secondary school, the long progress in my education and formation that will bring me to the threshold of the University.

I have developed a joy of learning which keeps my mind off the war, the perpetual hunger, the cold in winter and the loss of freedom. Not that we have to be pitied! We have been spared most of the atrocities of war. Of course, the war is not over and the future may yet bring some ugly surprises.

I met all my last year's classmates, including Wolfgang Weil, for whom, after my August experience at the Youth Center, I feel great compassion and respect. His cheerfulness is to me a source of wonder: how can a very young man show so much courage in a situation that can, at any time, be changed forever?

The school Director, Fr. A. Huysman, in an address to the whole school assembled in the lecture hall, mentions that, in view of the new air offensive by the Allies, the school is at great risk in case they decide to bomb the railroad yards of Schaerbeek/Haren. "Carpet bombing" is highly inaccurate; the fact that we are located less than three miles away from these objectives means we are in a high risk zone. We should therefore expect disruptions in our school year, including early class dismissals and even closing of the school altogether for short or lengthy periods.

This speech I feel, is more of a warning addressed to our parents than to ourselves. I know a few classmates who are looking forward to a few days of forced vacation. Despite all the privations, we don't really know what war looks like. We might soon find out.

September 20, Monday. I love historical anecdotes and I collect those that are especially amusing or meaningful. Here are some samples:

* It was a Greek envoy sent by King Attalus II Philadelphus of Pergamum (B.C. 159-138) who broke his leg in Rome and whiled away the tedium of convalescence by composing the first Latin grammar. (I wish I could get a copy.)

* Pope Urban VIII (reigned 1623-44) wrote a papal bull forbidding priests to smoke cigars!!

* After the death of Alexander the Great in June of B.C. 323, Hellenism spread with remarkable speed. The Septuagint or Translation of the Seventy, a Greek rendering of the Old Testament, was produced at the "University" of Alexandria, in Egypt, only fifty years after Alexander's death. Hellenism eventually conquered the entire Mediterranean area.

* The Duke of Wellington (Arthur Wellesley) the victor of Waterloo in 1815, died in 1852 at age eighty-three. He was buried to the sound of a nation's grief, and when the guns boomed across London, as his funeral carriage swayed through the hushed streets to St. Paul's, England said farewell to the 18th century.

September 24, Friday. It is just two weeks since the U.S. Fifth Army first landed at Salerno. Progress has been very slow. Because the country north of Salerno is very rough, the terrain greatly favors the defenders and the Germans are fighting back with machine guns, mortars and long-range artillery. Certainly those Nazis know how to fight.

September 27, Monday. Musso has spoken on the radio to the Italian people. He has announced the constitution of a "Republican State" in northern Italy to oppose the Badoglio government now collaborating with the Allies.
We don't hear much about the war in the Pacific, mostly a U.S. Navy and Marine Corps affair. By chance today, I learned that the Americans have debarked at Finchhaven, a Japanese base in New Guinea, 60 miles north of Lae, which was recently captured by Australian and American troops. The ultimate goal of the offensive is to the east, Rabaul, on the island of New Britain, a very important Japanese base.

September 29, Wednesday. On the Russian front: Smolensk has been retaken and Kiev, the capital of the Ukraine, is now within sight of the Soviet troops. The German front is crumbling but apparently the Wehrmacht retreats in good order.

October 2, Saturday. Napoli, bella Napoli, has been occupied yesterday by the Allies. Will it soon be the turn of Rome? Mr. W. told me the other day that the Allies might very well consolidate their southern positions for use as a springboard against the Balkans. This move would allow them to attack the Nazis' soft belly, avoid a murderous assault against the Atlantic Wall, cut off the Germans from Rumanian oil and, finally, join forces with the Russians for a final attack on Germany.

October 4, Monday. In French class we have, every term, a "public speaking" assignment.
This time we have to prepare a speech on an important event in Roman history that still influences our lives today. I choose: "The Roman calendar reform in the time of Julius Caesar." I have to be ready by October 26th.

October 7, Thursday. I never, never go to the movies. It's pure Nazi propaganda, either quite crude or, more often, with an implied and soft political message. At times, also, it is pure sentimentality and "Wirklichkeitsflucht" (escapism.)
But friends insisted that I go with them to see H. Steinhoff's

Rembrandt, which they tell me has artistic merit. I did join them and I must agree that it would rate an honorable mention in a setting other than that of the Third Reich.

Nevertheless I hate to pay a viewing fee which will help the UFA . (Universum Film Aktiengesellschaft.)

October 11, Monday. Throughout the night we heard the drone of airplanes and the alarm sounded twice but the FLAK was silent.

This morning while waiting for the streetcar on my way to school, I noticed long metallic strips. It is not the first time that, after the passage of bombers, one finds these strips which sometimes fall down in small bundles but more often float separately down to earth. Nobody can give me an explanation for these strange items. At first, I thought it to be some kind of message. But on close examination the strips show no trace of print or script; furthermore they are far too narrow and much too numerous to convey any message. The mystery remains but one thing is sure: it has something to do with the passage of Allied planes.

October 13, Wednesday. Russian troops have pierced in depth the semi-circular outer defense of Kiev, says the BBC. Tremendous battles, as fierce as any fought in Russia, are now going on along the west bank of the Dnieper, as the Russians attempt to widen their bridgeheads around Kiev.

Heavy fighting is going on around Vitebsk further north, and the Germans are making very determined efforts to save this bastion. Gomel is also gravely threatened by the Soviet offensive.

In Italy, the British 8th Army has occupied Termoli on the Adriatic coast. As to the U.S. 5th Army, it is engaged in heavy fighting northeast of Capua and has reached the river Volturno where the German resistance is toughening.

October 14, Thursday. Italy has declared war on Hitler. She has thus turned against her former partner a little more than one month after her armistice with the Allied Powers.

In a proclamation to the Italian people, Marshal Pietro Badoglio said that "shoulder to shoulder, we must march forward with our friends of the United States, of Great Britain, of Russia and of all the other United Nations."

Pietro must have reread Machiavellis's chapter on "How to

betray a former Ally." I would not be surprised to learn that he hails from Florence! Just kidding.

October 17, Sunday. We had planned a visit of Antwerp with the Troop but upon reflection we decided that the great port of that city is too much of an inviting bombing target. The Allies have indeed hit the town several times in the last few months.

The town of Mechelen/ Malines/ Mechlin (in Flemish, French, English respectively) is our next choice: very close to Brussels and far less dangerous to travel to.

Situated midway between Antwerp and Brussels, Mechlin is one the oldest cities of Northern Europe and has long been one of the most famous ones. For a considerable period, it was the capital of the Netherlands (the Seventeen Provinces of present Belgium and Holland) and it is still the religious capital of Belgium.

No matter from which side one approaches the city the first object to be seen is the vast square tower of the St. Rombout Cathedral. As this huge structure - the eighth wonder of the world, according to Vauban - dominates the town, so the church itself has dominated the history of the city on the River Dyle for almost five centuries.

Like many Flemish towns, Mechlin has its principal railroad station located on its very outskirts and as far as possible from the Grote Markt or Town Square. A tram is standing in front of the station but we decide to walk. At the bridge across the Dyle, we pause for a few moments to admire the fine views that can be seen here of the old Church of Notre-Dame-beyond-the-Dyle to the westward and the equally picturesque Notre-Dame of Hanswijk to the eastward.

Entering the Markt from this side we stop to admire the tremendous tower of the cathedral which here burst upon us in all its majestic grandeur.

To the architect Jan Keldermans is attributed the honor of designing the tower of St. Rombout, this architectural glory of Mechlin. Begun in 1452, work on the great tower advanced slowly. At the beginning of the 16th century, work on the massive tower was stopped for lack of funds after attaining a height of three hundred and eighteen feet.

On the outside of the tower, close to its present summit, is a clock the face of which is claimed to be the largest in the world.

We didn't climb to the top of the tower and missed the opportunity of seeing the fine carillon or set of chimes consisting of two huge bells; the oldest dates from 1498, or six years after the discovery of America. The two bells are named Salvator and Carolus, of which the larger one weighs 8,884 kilos, or almost 20,000 lbs! In olden times, it required twelve men to ring it. There are four other big bells, and forty-nine for the entire carillon (total weight 38 metric tons), most of which were cast by Pierre Hemony, of Amsterdam, the Stradivarius of bell-founders, in 1674.

As would be expected from its great religious importance, Mechlin has numerous minor churches. The largest of these is Notre-Dame-beyond-the-Dyle, dating from the 15th century, with its "Miraculous Draught of the Fishes", by Rubens, a highly colored triptych. This painting dates from the artist's best period. The Fishmongers' Guild that purchased it from the artist in 1618 for sixteen hundred guilders, certainly received good value for their money.

Another church, a small art gallery, is that of St. John the Baptist, not far from the Cathedral. Here is the fine "Adoration of the Magi" by Rubens. It was painted in 1617, when the artist was fresh from his studies in Italy, and before his success had caused him to employ a throng of students to assist in the production of his works. Furthermore, it was executed for this very church that still possesses his receipt for the final payment, written in Flemish, dated March 24, 1624, and signed by the artist, "Pietro Paolo Rubens". The price was eighteen hundred guilders.

After the defeat and death of Charles the Bold at Nancy (1477), his widow, Margaret of York, transferred her residence to Mechlin, and here she raised and educated the two children of her daughter, Marie of Burgundy: Philippe the Handsome and Margaret of Austria.

On Philip's premature death in 1506, Maximilian I, Holy Roman Emperor, again became Regent and made his daughter, Margaret of Austria, Governess-General of the Netherlands, and guardian of Philip's children. Margaret at once chose Mechlin, where she had been educated, as her seat of government. There she reigned as Regent until her death twenty-three years later. This period was the golden age in the history of the city on the Dyle, its brief day of splendor.

October 23, Saturday. The Wehrmacht is in full retreat on the Dnieper front. Dniepropetrovsk is completely encircled, Krementchug has been occupied and Krivoi-Rog is menaced. In the South, Melitopol is still in the hands of the Germans, but barely.

This latter city is the key to the Crimea where, according to the Nazi radio, the Soviets have attempted a landing on the east coast of this peninsula.

October 25, Monday. It is hard going in Italy for the U.S. Fifth Army. They are still stuck along the Volturno; the communiqué says that the Americans have occupied Alife and Piedimonte d'Alife, localities I found on the map. They are now attacking Venafro, the left pivot of the German defense line. It is a slugging match that can go on for months as the Germans are masters at defending prepared positions.

Although it is obvious to us that the Nazis are losing the war, there is no telling how long it will take and we dread the coming of another winter of war.

November 3, Wednesday.

The Plunder of a Country

The best experts in the matter, Mr W. included, tell us that the Nazis are plundering Belgium to the rate of 2/3 of its agricultural and industrial production.

After the occupation of the country in 1940, the Occupant immediately organized a system for taking over its economic resources..

For purposes of industrial production, commodity control agencies (Warenstellen) were organized with wide powers to issue regulations concerning acquisition, distribution, storing and consumption. These agencies provide the factories with materials necessary for the manufacture of their products, if and when they are working for the German war machine. The factories also find themselves under the management of factory trustees to execute orders of the occupying authorities. Moreover, every enterprise in Belgium is made subject to audit by special orders of the Chief of Military Administration.

In the field of finance, a number of decrees give the Occupant an especially privileged position. The mark was fixed at ten francs at the time of the invasion, after which it was raised to 12 1/2 francs.

These economic and financial measures are facilitated by a complete control of all the economic life of Belgium, which was put into effect by the order concerning the organization of the national economy, promulgated on February 10, 1941. This order created the framework for economic totalitarianism in Belgium and furnished the basis for integrating the Belgian economy into the Nazi economy.

In other words, Nazi Germany will continue to exploit Belgium and all other countries in her power. In the unlikely event that she wins the war, she will go on enslaving us forever; if and when she loses she will not be in any position to repay, as was proven after the Great War. Belgium will be on its own. Fortunately, we will still have our industrial infrastructure almost intact, provided of course, the Allies don't bomb it into rubble. Also, the Belgians are a hard working people and as soon as the war is over, we will roll up our sleeves and start rebuilding as we did in 1918-19.

November 7, Sunday. In the news is the retaking of Kiev, the capital of the Ukraine, by the Soviet armed forces. The Russian steamroller is relentlessly pushing forward and the Wehrmacht is unable to stop it. There are apparently too many well-armed Russians and too few German soldiers. With the Allies preparing to open a second front (but when?), Hitler can no longer win this war.

November 10, Wednesday. Brother Michel has received a summons to present himself at the "National Labor Office" for a medical examination in view of possible forced labor service in Germany. There is great anguish at home and we have lively discussions as to what should be done.

On the one hand we have the case of my godfather who went to work in Germany voluntarily and is treated more or less decently. But today there is no question of "voluntary" labor. The Nazis are mobilizing all the people they can get from all occupied countries to work for Grossdeutschland's war machine. In Belgium, the classes 1939 through 1943 have been called up and my brother is in that group.

No final decision has been made but the consensus, at present, is against showing up; however we have to weigh the consequences.

November 12, Friday. One of the collaborationist newspapers in Brussels is called *Le Soir*, and as the name indicates, comes out in the evening. Lately, because of the paper shortage, it has appeared in a simple two-page edition.

Yesterday evening, the paper was delivered earlier than usual to the regular newsstands. Some time later to everybody's surprise another batch of *Le Soir* was delivered to the same stands It was soon discovered that the first delivery had brought a fake *Soir* identical to the official one, containing virulent articles against the Nazis and their collaborators.

I managed this morning to get a copy of what is now: *Le Soir Volé* (The Stolen Evening).

It has articles on the war in Russia and in Italy, as well as national news, consisting mainly of denunciations of collaborators and promising swift retribution at the Liberation.

Left and right of the masthead are two small photographs, one showing an Allied bomber dropping its cargo, the other has a picture of Hitler his right arm raised in a defensive gesture and the caption: Ich habe das nicht gewollt! (I didn't want this!)

I am told that the military authorities are trying very hard to round up the unsold copies at the kiosks but the search must be futile. As for finding the perpetrators, they can be sure to undergo a similar frustration.

As mentioned earlier, there are at present in our country a great number of anti-nazi publications produced in a few hundred copies reaching but a few thousand people. They have a very short life: two or three issues at most. Except for the *Libre Belgique* or Free Belgium which, printed in several thousands of copies carries news from inside the country and the world at large. I usually get a copy a few days after the appearance of a new issue. I have even recently been a "carrier", transporting a bundle of five to ten copies for redistribution. It goes without saying that this is strictly forbidden and is subject to harsh penalties.

November 15, Monday. With the approval of my parents, brother Michel has decided not to present himself this week, for a medical examination at the National Labor Office. This makes him *ipso facto* a réfractaire or forced labor dodger with all the consequences: loss of ration coupons for food, textile, shoes, etc.; loss of a regular job; necessary change of identity; holing up at home or somewhere else; danger of being denounced or caught in a roundup; drastic cutoff from all contact with friends and acquaintances.

All in all, not a very happy perspective but this is the only alternative to slave labor in the accursed Reich.

Graciously, however, God limits man's vision of things within a narrow consciousness and draws the veil over the future. We are taking it one day at a time.

And Michel can ponder the Latin saying:
Sine sole dies
Sine sidere noctes
Insomnes noctes.
(Days without sun - Nights without stars - Sleepless nights.)

November 23, Tuesday. We get very little information about the war in the Pacific. But today I hear about the Allied Troops (Americans, Australians, New Zealanders) having invaded Tarawa. I could not at first find this island on the map until I looked further east and discovered it in the Gilbert Islands, in the mid-Pacific. It must have some strategic significance or harbor an important Japanese base because it is in the middle of nowhere.

November 26, Friday. For Michel, we have secured a blank identity card delivered to us with all the legal stamps from the town of Couvin. All we have to do is fill out the new name, date of birth and address. I am assigned to do this job in my best official round handwriting. The guidelines are as follows: The new name should be as close as possible to the real one. I chose CALVET. The first name: same (Michel). Date of birth: same, except that Michel is now four years younger. Address: Rue du Faubourg St.

Germain, which is the main street in Couvin. Profession: teacher; teachers are exempt from forced labor in Germany. Marital status: single. The card is a triptych, of light cardboard, greenish in color, printed in the two official languages of Belgium: Flemish and French.

The business of providing authentic "false" papers is so well organized that we had a choice of several towns. We chose Couvin because of the similarity with the town of Comines, where my brother was born. Furthermore, as we have been to school in neighboring France, we all have a "French" accent. That accent, in the case of Michel, can now be easily explained by the fact that he is a native of Couvin, a town in the province of Namur, very close to the French border.

December 2, Thursday. Mussolini has renamed his Republican State to "Italian Social Republic" with its capital at Salo, on Lake Garda. In French-speaking regions, this news is greeted with great merriment in view of the fact that, in French, the word salaud, pronounced salo, means swine or bastard. We have now at Salo, a Republic of the Bastards, or Swine!

December 3, Friday. Berlin has undergone a devastating raid by the RAF. It seems that the air offensive against the German industrial towns is relentless and increasing in intensity.

December 6, Monday. Churchill, Roosevelt and Chang Kai Chek have met in Cairo from November 22 through 27, and have agreed on a plan to beat the Japanese. (You mean they didn't have a plan before?)
According to the communiqué, the conclusions of the meeting can be summarized in four points:
1. Military operations have been agreed upon; unrelenting pressure will be brought against a brutal enemy by sea, land and air.
2. Japan will be stripped of all islands in the Pacific seized or occupied since 1914.
3. Manchuria, Formosa and the Pescadores Islands will be returned to China.
4. Korea will "in due course" regain its independence.

December 9, Thursday. Hardly is the Conference in Cairo

finished that we hear about another one in Teheran, the capital of Iran. The conference started on Sunday, November 28, and it lasted four days. Decisions reached by Churchill, Roosevelt and Stalin were announced in a communiqué, published on December 6th.

"We express our determination that our nations shall work together in war and in the peace that will follow.

"As to the war... we have reached complete agreement as to the scope and timing of operations which will be undertaken from East, West and South...

"And as to the peace, we are sure that our concord will make it an enduring peace. We recognize fully the supreme responsibility resting upon us and all the United Nations to make a peace that will command the good will of the overwhelming mass of peoples of the world, and will banish the scourge and terror of war for many generations... No power on earth can prevent our destroying the German armies by land, their U-boats by sea, and their war plants from the air.

Our attacks will be relentless and increasing.

"From these friendly conferences we look with confidence to the day when all the peoples of the world may live free lives, untouched by tyranny, and according to their varying desires and their own consciences.

"We came here with hope and determination. We leave here friends in fact, in spirit and in purpose."

This quote is only part of the communiqué I received from my habitual sources and I am not impressed. It is badly written and must have been first drawn up in Russian and then translated by a drunken interpreter just out of a one-year Russian course.

I am also suspicious of sentences like "according to their varying desires and their own consciences"; this leaves the door wide open to all kinds of fantasies and tyrannies. Why not just say "according to democratic rules summarized as follows... and then enumerate the four or five points which constitute a democratic process: freedom of speech, freedom of elections, etc.

However, I take very seriouly the military aspect of the communiqué. But on the political front it is nothing but wishy-washy talk.

December 20, Thursday. Not much time for the diary because of the exams. On December 16, the Americans invaded New Britain, the island east of New Guinea; their goal is certainly the important Japanese base of Rabaul.

Franco has dissolved the Falanga, the fascist party in Spain. Does the Caudillo feel that the international political wind is shifting and blowing in quite a different direction?

December 24, Friday. Free at last from exams and school. I have resisted all attempts to take over my position at the head of the class. Classes resume Friday January 14, at 8h30.

The news of the day is the promotion of General Dwight Eisenhower to the post of Supreme Commander of all Allied Forces in Europe. This means he will be in charge of the Second Front: the invasion of Festung Europa some time next year. The earlier, the better. General Eisenhower was the commander of the American troops during the invasion of North Africa, and I guess also in Sicily. I know next to nothing about him.

December 27, Monday. Christmas Eve and Christmas Day were celebrated at home, a very subdued affair.

On the assumption that the Nazis will not conduct any round-ups, Michel and I, before curfew, went on a two-hour walk which did my brother a lot of good after weeks of being cooped up at home.

Soon, we were strolling through silent back streets that, with the coming of darkness and the blue lighting, appeared to have retreated beyond present times to the Middle Ages.

Without warning, the frosty mist drifted in low curling wreaths across the open space, now drawing close an impenetrable curtain of white vapor, and again lifting to reveal glimpses of moving shapes, portions of buildings, hints of boundaries more suggestive than complete disclosure.

Michel was elated and as excited as a young child who is let go after a long day in class. He was blowing light vapor through his mouth, jumping over imagined obstacles and splashing in invisible puddles. What a treat it was for him!

We talked about the future, what we planned to do after the war. Food came first in our discussion. We tried to imagine what white bread tasted like and then we concocted a real feast. Along one side of the room, a table covered with a white cloth on which the edibles are displayed: cold chicken in aspic, a large game pie, sliced cold tongue and a fine, cooked sirloin of beef. Besides these were a multiplicity of smaller dishes containing such delicacies as pickled eggs, pickled asparagus, artichokes, anchovies and prawns, apple tart and praline-flavored ice cream. Invited guests would help themselves to supper, pouring their own drinks: champagne and fine French wines.

What a mouth-watering dream! The bubble burst when the penetrating cold brought us back to reality and we switched to our plans for the future: Michel hoping to start a printing business and I preparing for the University and perhaps an academic career.

Right at that moment the sirens wailed and soon after, the familiar sound of approaching airplanes could be heard. Another raid on Germany and this on Christmas Eve! We reflected that even in the Great War, which was bad enough, both sides suspended hostilities during that night. But not in this conflict. People will die tonight while trying to commemorate the advent, two thousand years ago, of the Prince of Peace.

The FLAK did not open up but, as a precaution, we returned home where a more modest feast was expecting us. This is our fourth war Christmas and the mood is not great. We don't complain, however. We know that many people all over the world live in worse conditions. We are not free, we suffer from the cold and are undernourished, but we are not starving and, for now, we have been spared the Allies' carpet bombing which the Germans have been quick to call "terror bombing" and which I call "indiscriminate bombing".

December 30, Friday. The BBC has announced that units of the British Home Fleet has caught the 26,000-ton Nazi battleship Scharnhorst and sank her in a battle off North Cape, Norway. This is the biggest naval defeat suffered by Germany since losing the Bismarck, in 1941. The ship was trapped when it tried to intercept a Russian-bound convoy. The battleship was armed with a main battery of nine 11-inch guns and carried a crew of 1,461 officers and men.

My encyclopedia tells me that Gerhard Johann David von Scharnhorst, after which the battleship is named, was a general (1755-1813) who organized the Prussian army to fight Napoléon in 1812-13.

11

January 2 - April 27, 1944

January 2, Sunday. The very cold weather is with us. As there is no possibility to get warm premises for our Scout meetings, I have decided to suspend them until the weather improves a bit. Furthermore, a majority of the boy scouts do not have the warm clothing for a one-day hike, anywhere. We had a short get-together on December 26th but everybody was shivering and I dismissed the Troop until further notice.

January 3, Monday. Thanks to Father who has provided the coal, during this Christmas vacation I can use the "office" downstairs which can be heated by a small stove.

It allows me to spend many hours in somewhat comfortable surroundings catching up on my reading, especially that of the Russian writers I discovered last year. I have read Tolstoy, Turgenev (name spelled in many different ways) and parts of Gogol. It is however Tolstoy with his "War and Peace" who gets the prize.

My interest in the country of Russia and its peoples has not abated. Like everyone else, I am amazed at the fierce resistance the Red Army has meted out to the Nazi onslaught despite grievous early defeats. Where did the Russian people find the strength to stand up to the Nazis at the cost of countless lives? Is it their love of the Communist régime or is their attachment to Mother Russia? To answer these questions I have started to study Russia's history as well as the ideology of Bolshevism. I have the books for it and I plunge into them at every opportunity.

January 6, Thursday. The Russian battlefront is moving steadily towards the west and is now closer to Berlin than it is to Stalingrad. The time is in sight when the Russian front will become the Polish and Rumanian fronts, and then the German front.

All reports and comments we receive from Berlin dealing with the Ostfront are couched in the grimmest terms. There is not a word of comfort and hope anywhere. And broadcasts for home consumption is a recital of the "impossible conditions" facing the German troops.

January 8, Saturday. The great air offensive by the Allies against Berlin is now in its seventh week. So far the German capital has been hit ten times and the results are devastating. Two days ago Hitler's Chancellery, center of Government and symbol of the Nazi Party's rise to power, was bombed and lies now in ruins.

It is obvious that the RAF, in an effort to crush the German civilian morale, is systematically bombing and destroying one Berlin district after another. Non-stop evacuation, mostly of women and children, is reported to have reduced the population from four million to one and a half million. So it seems the RAF is mostly hitting empty buildings.

January 10, Monday. Count Ciano, son-in-law of Mussolini and former Minister of Foreign Affairs in Fascist Italy, and Marshal De Bono, former head of the Fascist Militia, have been condemned to death by the tribunal of the Republic of Salo, in Verona.

January 14, Friday. Return to school. As a consequence of the Allies' bombing offensive not only in Germany but also in northern France and western Belgium, drastic measures are being taken at school. For five days in a row, we will be drilled in air raid precautions. The shelters have been reinforced but to me they look pitifully inadequate. A direct hit by a big bomb and few of the more than four hundred students and teachers will survive.

It is more and more difficult for me to get to school on time despite the fact that I now leave home earlier. The problem is that the streetcars break down at an alarming rate; they also stop running when the sirens, in their mournful tones, announce an air raid. To top it all, when by chance they run normally, they are so full it is difficult to squeeze in. And I often reach school so bedraggled and tired that I have a hard time concentrating.

January 14, Friday. Weather report last night. Fine and cold; some low cloud banks; temperature minus 8 degrees C.

January 17, Monday. Nowadays in Brussels it is not unusual to experience a power failure. Domestic gas is rationed to two hours a day. Last Saturday nobody was especially surprised to have to go through another electricity cut.

It appears however that this power outage was the result of an important sabotage effort to paralyze the main industrial sectors of Belgium. This was achieved by the blowing up of a significant number of electric transmissin towers (60 to 70, it is reported) thereby halting production in a number of industrial plants in this country, and jamming rail communications between Germany and the Nazi troops on the Belgian coast and Northern France.

January 22, Saturday. Mr. W. has done it again. To my question as to whether or not there is an anti-Nazi movement in Germany, he responds with the following note which I received this morning.

"A warning to Nazi Party leaders that the German Army is planning a *putsch* (German for revolt or uprising) to overthrow Hitler and make peace has been circulated by Erich Koch, a prominent Gauleiter and one of the party's bigwigs."

This is stated in the Gazette de Lausanne, which quotes the circular letter sent out by Koch: "The Führer is in danger. Parties of reaction are trying to displace him and establish a military dictatorship under which Germany would immediately start peace negotiations against the will of the people".

In an attached note, Mr. W. comments: "There have been several peace overtures by Germany to Great Britain in the past but they all have been turned down. None of these proposals will be taken seriously until the Germans get ready for unconditional surrender. This has been confirmed officially by London and Washington, in the last few weeks."

January 25, Tuesday. The Allied advance is not proceeding ahead very fast. This perhaps is the reason they have decided to leapfrog the Germans and land American and British troops in Anzio and Nettuno. From that bridgehead the Allies are only about forty miles from Rome and, unless the Wehrmacht can very rapidly establish a defensive line, and they have shown to be very adept at this game, we can expect the Italian capital and the Vatican to be liberated in a few days.

January 28, Friday. Father has brought back a magnificent loaf of bread, baked in a friend's farm near Groot Bijgaarden. It is made in a combination of light and dark brown wheat flour that gives the slices a beautiful marbled aspect. We receive each a thick slice for dinner together with a delicious pea soup. Verily, this evening gives us an adumbration of Heaven!

February 2, Wednesday. The success of the Soviet armies has accredited the idea among some of my friends that Marxism is the future of mankind. However my opinion is that, in the light of history, it is regressive. Collectivism, with its violent measures of repression, is nothing new. It has appeared during the last 6,000 years whenever man has become tired or afraid of freedom.

Nevertheless, in this country and other places as well, thanks to a clever propaganda, there are some people so blind to reality that they prefer to toy with the recipes of visionary doctrine, no matter how unpalatable they have proved to those unhappy peoples who had to swallow them.

I hope that when the day of Liberation arrives, the Belgian people will not listen but will repudiate with scorn the tawdry bait of impractical and ruinous theory. Our society and our economy had, before the war, no need for the witch medicine of Marxism and will reject it even more forcefully after this conflict. Helping the Russian people in its fight against the cursed Nazi threat is one thing, supporting the detested Communist tyranny is another.

February 5, Saturday. Howls of protests, from the Cardinal, the bishops, the clergy and the entire Belgian people, greeted the news that the military authorities have decided to confiscate all church bells in Belgium to be sent to war plants in Germany for use in the armament industry.

Cardinal Van Roey has condemned this move in a pastoral letter read at all Sunday masses in all parishes of the country. The authorities seem to have been taken aback by the unanimous resistance against this move by the entire population.

After negotiations, it seems now that, although the order still stands, the bells more than a hundred years old will be spared. General von Falkenhausen, the Military Commander in Belgium, understands very well that there is a limit to the exploitation of this country. He is well aware of its strategic and economic importance. Disorders will for sure be suppressed (they have all the guns) but any disruption of the present system would be very harmful to the Nazi war effort.

February 10, Thursday. Today, after numerous delays, I had my turn at 'public speaking' in front of the class on an important event in Roman history. A summary of this presentation follows.

The Reform of the Roman Calendar
under Julius Caesar

During the visit of Cleopatra to Rome, in the years 47-46 B.C., an event of the greatest importance took place in which she was associated, an event that has influenced the lives of mankind ever since. This was the reform of the calendar.

The year had fallen into confusion and Julius Caesar (100 - 44 B.C.) decided to start it afresh with the Julian Calendar, which remains the basis of our present system. Some of Egypt's court astronomers were invited to Rome to devise a new calendar based on the Egyptian one of Eudoxus. Among these astronomers was Sosigenes, the most celebrated astronomer in the land of the Pharaohs; and it was with him that Caesar collaborated.

The year before the new calendar came into operation must have been endless: it contained an additional ninety days! Then, the first Julian calendar began, with its days distributed between months of either thirty or thirty-one days, except February which originally had twenty-nine days and thirty every fourth year. The month Quintilis was named July in honor of Julius Caesar and so, it seemed, the new calendar was fixed.

In the succeeding reign however, in order to gratify the vanity of Augustus (Octavianus 63 B.C.-14 A.D.) the thirty-day month Sextilis, was named August. As it was felt to be beneath his dignity that August should be shorter than Caesar's July, a day was taken from February and added to it. This is why, to this day, February has twenty-eight days and twenty-nine in each leap year.

February 14, Monday. Berlin reports of the northern battles at the Russian front, relayed by radio Brussels, are uniformly gloomy. They estimate that the Russians or rather, the Soviets (the Nazis never mention the word "Russian") are using 40 infantry divisions and 20 tank formations, to drive up from Novgorod to Kronstadt Bay (Leningrad).

The goal of this offensive is to smash the entire Northern front and liberate Leningrad.

February 16, Wednesday. The siege of Leningrad is definitely lifted. It lasted for 872 days at the cost of untold lives - military and civilian.

February 17, Thursday. From the Nazi controlled radio Paris, a few days ago, comes a fantastic account of aerial "torpedoes" falling on panic-stricken Londoners. This is the latest German propaganda attempt to make the British think that now has begun a full-scale retaliation of the Berlin bombings.

But is it propaganda? And why the mention "torpedoes" and not, if it was a bombing raid, talk of "bombs"? And why would Joseph Goebbels be especially interested in mentioning this raid? Strange... But many strange things have happen in this war and most of them are left unexplained.

February 21, Monday. I have already mentioned, that due to the lack of fuel, we stay in the kitchen which is a most pleasant room and the easiest to heat properly. The living room is almost never used in winter. At the moment, I suffer from frostbite on hands and feet, because of cold and moisture; I try to keep them dry and warm but it will be a losing battle until spring brings milder weather.

February 23, Wednesday. The landings at Nettuno and Anzio, south of Rome, have not provided the opportunity for a breakthrough. As a result, the Allies are stalemated on what the Germans call the Gustav Line, along the Garigliano and the Sangro rivers, with Monte Cassino in the middle.

Cassino? I consult the Encyclopedia. Yes, it is the site of the famous Benedictine Abbey founded by St. Benedict. He came to Cassinum from Sublaqueum, now Subiaco, around the year 500 A.D. and built the abbey upon the ruins of a Roman temple dedicated to Apollo, the god of light. Benedict died, according to tradition on March 21, 543. His fame brought throngs of pilgrims to Cassinum and the abbey grew and grew to accommodate them all. It is now of enormous size and contains wonderful works of art. The Germans and the Allies of a common accord should spare this abbey: so much has already been lost, so many treasures destroyed forever in this horrible and never-ending war.

February 26, Saturday. If anything, this war has greatly improved my knowledge of geography, especially in the Far East. I am told that in the Pacific the Americans have occupied Eniwetok. Never heard of it, of course. Fortunately, I am given the indication that this island is located in the Marshall archipelago consisting of 24 atolls for a total of 74 square miles. Very small indeed. Somehow, it must have some strategic importance. It is very far east in the Pacific; could it have been used by the Japanese for a planned attack on the Hawaian islands?

February 28, Monday. The Americans have placed an embargo on the sale of petroleum to Spain. I didn't know the USA was providing the Spaniards with any type of fuel, least of all petroleum. Why this decision now? Are the Americans afraid that this precious fuel might be resold to the Nazis? No! The U.S. certainly knows exactly Spain's requirements and doesn't supply one liter above those needs.
Are they afraid that Franco will join the Axis? The Caudillo has no reason to join an Axis that is no longer in existence and whose victories have turned into defeat after defeat. Franco had a chance in late 1940 and, wisely, didn't chose sides. Perhaps the intention is to inflict punishment on the Spanish people for supporting Franco and his dictatorship? I don't understand.

March 1, Wednesday. I have just been shown photographs of the monastery of Monte Cassino utterly destroyed by Allied bombs. *Necessitas non habet legem* says the Latin proverb, or "necessity has no law," and the commanding generals took upon themselves the responsibility of another cultural disaster. Can we expect the same for Rome, Venice, Florence and other old artistic towns of Italy? We can truly say: the savagery of war knows no bounds!

March 1, Wednesday. A letter from sister Rosa from Armentières brings startling news. Her husband, Jules Wille, has been released from his Stalag POW camp for reasons of failing health, which is life threatening and cannot be treated in camp. We don't know how seriously ill he is, but surely they would not release him for just a bad cold.

March 9, Thursday. As I walk to school along the rue Royale towards the St. Mary's Church with its distinctive green cupola, I notice a building the front of which is drenched in a sea of red bunting dotted with white circles offsetting black swastikas. At the height of the second floor a big banner proclaims black on white: SO SIND DIE SOWJETS! Right and left of the entrance are two posters, in French and Flemish, explaining that behind these doors is an exhibition intended to give the visitor "The truth about the Soviets". I am interested in what the Nazis want us to know about the Soviet Union. A lot of propaganda, it goes without saying but perhaps also basic information, which I need. After four years of Nazi indoctrination, I have learned to separate the wheat from the chaff. As I have the afternoon off from school, I decide to have a look.

After class, I direct my steps toward one of the soup kitchens organized by the municipality offering, for a few francs, an "off the ration" meal. I am presented with a strange-looking goo which the lady-server, in a burst of enthusiasm, calls "beef stew". I don't want to be downright impolite or overly sarcastic, so I take the plate without uttering a single word. I know there is no meat in it, perhaps a few cubes of Maggi bouillon for flavoring, a few indifferent potatoes, a good amount of the hated rutabagas and some cabbage. I sit down, sprinkle the "stew" liberally with salt and pepper, a sure way to improve the taste; with the help of a glass of saccharin-assisted lemonade I swallow the concoction, not for pleasure but to calm down an insatiable stomach.

A Nazi Exhibition

The visit is free for students. The only person in attendance is a civilian, tall and lanky. His features are pinched, with cold, probing eyes. He appears withdrawn and self-contained. He is trying to smile but he smiles with the lips, not with the eyes. Without a word he hands me a free ticket and a tired gesture directs me to the visitors' book. As I have no intention of

215

revealing my identity, I coolly write down, in the space left between two names: Adolphus Van Braunau. (Our dear Adolf with the funny mustache is born in Braunau, Austria, on April 20, 1889.) Under "profession" I scribble mythologist and proceed with the tour.

According to the brochure, the exhibition is organized in five sections: The Communist Party, the Soviet Police State, the Katyn Massacre, the GULAG, the Judeo-capitalist plot and the gallant fight of Germany against Boshevism and its plutocratic allies.

1. The Communist Party of the Soviet Union.

Long awaited, heralded in advance for many decades, desired by many segments of the population, the first successful Russian revolution took the nation by surprise. On March 2, 1917, Emperor Nicolas II abdicated after ten days of confused rioting in Petrograd, as Sankt Petersburg had been renamed in 1914.

For eight months after the abdication some semblance of power was uneasily wielded by a Provisional Government of newly-appointed Ministers, chiefly liberals formerly prominent in the Duma (Parliament).

On 25 October (7 November, new style) 1917, the Bolsheviks seized power in Petrograd by an almost bloodless coup, while Moscow saw a week's hard fighting before Lenin's adherents made themselves masters of the city. In most other parts of the former Empire their revolution was something of which people read in the press.

The leading organ of the new government was the Council of People's Commissars who performed the function of Ministers. They were fiteen in number at the outset, all Bolsheviks, and worked under Lenin's chairmanship. However Lenin did not command anything approaching majority support in the country at large, for the number of Bolshevik Party members was tiny, though it is also true that enthusiasm for Bolshevism was widespread among people who were not necessarily party members. Therefore, for quite a few months, Lenin had to share power with leading socialists. Soon Lenin got rid of these "allies" and the first signs of a harsher approach were not long in appearing.

In December 1917, the suppression of political offenses against the new order was put on a more regular basis when the Council of People's Commissars established the Cheka (the All Russian Extraordinary Commission for Combating Counter-Revolution and Sabotage), which has remained the official political police organ, under different names: GPU - OGPU - NKVD - to this day.

2. The Soviet Police State.

The Soviet political police expanded throughout Russia and became responsible for far more political arrests; the number of victims defies exact computation. The Cheka (I will call it NKVD, its present name) did not execute its victims in public but these executions lost nothing in terror-inspiring quality through greater secrecy. Hangings, drowning and various other former of deaths were recorded in horrific detail, but execution by shooting through the back of the head, a procedure calculated to make the victim's face unrecognizable, became the standard practice.

3. The Katyn Massacre.

Besides these cellar shootings, numerous mass executions also took place in convenient waste areas outside the towns, where the condemned were dispatched by revolver, machine-gun and bayonet, after being forced to dig communal graves. This is how the Polish prisoners of war held in three camps in the west and center of European Russia were executed. The exhibition devotes a full room to this massacre.

According to the Nazis, in April 1940 the inmates of the Kozelsk camp, over four thousand in number, were taken by the NKVD to the forest of Katyn, ten miles west of Smolensk shot, one by one, in the back of the head and buried in a mass grave.

Three years later, the Germans, then in military occupation of the area, found the grave and published details of the shootings and numerous photographs of the victims. The Soviet authorities retorted by accusing the Germans of perpetrating the massacre themselves. I have discussed this matter several times with some friends and we all agree that, in view of the Nazi reputation, it should not come as a surprise to us if they were the perpetrators. However an impartial investigation by representatives of neutral countries have established at least one fact: the corpses show, without the shadow of a doubt, that they were killed in the spring or summer of 1940. The Nazis reached the Smolensk area and occupied the city on July 16, 1941.

4. The GULAG.

Once sentenced, the "enemies of the people" face new ordeals by rail transit to concentration camps which are the most characteristic feature of the Stalinist State, as it is of the Nazi dictatorship. They are operated by an organization called GULAG (Main Administration of Camps). Furthermore the GULAG adopted the policy of exploiting concentration camp labor as a major element in the task of building up the economy.

Officially known as corrective labor camps, an immense pool of slave labor is theoretically dedicated to the rehabilitation of political prisoners and other criminals "through honest toil" and are celebrated as such in Soviet publications. These camps are located in the Arkhangelsk area as well as in Eastern Siberia. According to the exhibition brochure, the number of people held in these camps runs into the millions.

5. The CRUSADE against Bolshevism and Jewish plutocracy.

The Nazis declare they are the avant-garde in the fight against Bolshevism, in the East, and plutocracy and international Jewry, in the West. These two have joined forces to colonize the entire world, enslave the nations and destroy European civilization.

At first, the Crusade against Bolshevism attracted considerable support in Western Europe. Large contingents served on the Eastern front in 1941 and 1942, from Rumania, Hungary and Italy. France has sent its Blue Division and Spain its Condor Division. Latvia, Estonia, Lithuania did furnish a few thousand volunteers. Recruits have come from Belgium, the Netherlands and Scandinavia. They include Nazi sympathizers, anti-communists and adventurers. At first they joined the Wehrmacht but at present they all have been grouped, in their own units, in the Waffen-SS. With the grave defeats on the Russian front the enthusiasm has cooled quite a bit and the volunteers have become a scarce commodity.

Please note: this last comment is not to be found in the brochure.

The tour of the exhibition ends with the projection of a film on "International Jewry".

It starts with the display of a map of Europe showing the Jewish menace in the form of an octopus with the head in Russia and Poland, its tentacles expanding slowly in a westward direction until they engulf all of Western Europe: Italy, Spain, Great Britain, the Low Countries, France and Germany, with one very long tentacle encircling North America.

Then comes a long and frightening sequence in which the Jews are likened to rats, filthy rats, scurrying out of sewers and dark cellars in growing numbers until they invade every part of the countryside.

Another sequence follows showing sly Jews, repugnant Jews, abhorrent Jews, detestable Jews, scheming Jews; the typical Jew in profile, the Jew with the crooked nose, the rich, fat Jew, the Jewish plutocrat in morning suit, high hat and cuff links marked with the dollar sign, smoking a big cigar in the form of a zeppelin airship.

The two sequences then slowly merge, Jews and rats, rats and Jews, Jews and raw capitalism, Jews and exploitation, until the message, unexpressed, becomes clear: this vermin has to be eradicated.

March 12, Sunday. Golden afternoons are not many in Belgium but this is one of them, still and clear, the sun warm in a light-blue sky bereft of clouds. The view across the sun-streaked woods of the Forêt de Soignes is quite breathtakingly lovely, a vista to warm the hearts of all but the very sick, the very near-sighted and the incurably pessimistic.

Thanks to the balmy weather, the 66th Troop did spend most of the day in the woods. A sense of peace is mingled with the mute noise of airplanes, far away, the day's warm air and the brilliance of a great afternoon. Around us strolled the people of the city, relaxing from their own worries for a few fleeting hours as is their due and proper right, far removed from war and deprivation.

March 14, Tuesday. I did not fail to give a detailed account to my parents, brothers and sisters, of my tour of the exhibition "So sind die Sowjets". Here is my report.

As I was leaving the exhibition's premises, the caretaker approached me, his face made even longer with its powerful nose, prominent cheekbones and his deep-seated eyes with all the warmth of a hooded serpent. "Sir", he said, "I noticed that you are a myth... euh!, mytholo... a mythologist. I am much interested in knowing more about this new science. Could you explain it ?"

"Well, monsieur it is, as you have guessed, a brand new science. It comes of course from Germany and its main thinking heads are

219

the well-known Adalfar Kritler, Dr Heinrich von Grimmler, not to forget Dr Joseph von der Göbel-Taugnitz (Misfit!). But, without a doubt, the greatest of them is Adalfar whose seminal work "Sieg, Heil und Niederlage" will remain influential for a thousand years.

"Quite interesting, Sir, how come I never heard of this interesting development?"

"Well, you know how it is. Our country is rather behind the times and not willing to keep up with the latest scientific approach regarding the great human problems of grand theft, murder and lunacy. But this is changing. Furthermore, I wish to help you. Will you be here tomorrow?"

"Yes, Sir."

"Here is what I intend to do. I will bring you some literature, about these great stinkers...euh! I mean thinkers, - sorry for the lapsus linguae - it will enlighten you about the momentous events of our day."

"Thank you very much, Sir. Goodbye, Sir..."

Unfortunately, nobody at home bought my story. Too much *pathos* and too much *mythos*.

March 17, Friday. General Dittmar, of the Wehrmacht, is the official military commentator on the Nazi radio. His comments are sometimes unorthodox in the sense that they do not reflect the permanent optimism of Goebbels' propaganda machine. Two or three days ago, general Dittmar did admit that, on the Eastern front, things were not going well. In Russia the thaw period has set in, a time when all roads are turning into a sea of mud. This, says Dittmar, favors the other side and "we should expect more severe setbacks" until the arrival of dry weather.

March 20, Monday. Despite the "mud," the Soviet offensive continues. These guys seem to have an inexhaustible supply of men and equipment. The latest news tells that the Russians have crossed the river Bug, meaning they are not far from Odessa and pushing towards the Rumanian border!

March 22, Wednesday. The Wehrmacht has occupied Hungary to avoid this country's defection to the Allies, as in Italy. At the same time it seems that the Russians have now penetrated into Rumanian territory.

March 24, Friday. Easter is two weeks away and as of Monday we will start the second term exams on this, my last, year of school. Before I plunge into the books I wish to give a description of the German military uniform as compiled over the last few months.

The German Combat Uniform

The combat uniform of the Wehrmacht is of feldgrau (field gray) or forest green color. The jacket has a stand and fall collar with pebble-finish buttons on the front and epaulettes. Cuffs are French turn-back style.

Officers' rank insignia are worn on the shoulder boards while non-com officers wear their rank insignia on the sleeves. Shoulder boards and collar tabs have edge piping in a variety of colors to denote the branches of services (green for infantry, red for artillery, yellow for the air force...)

Before 1942, uniforms were made of excellent quality wool. Since last year however the quality has deteriorated markedly. There came also a no-frills tunic: no French cuffs, no dark green collar, no scalloped and pleated pockets. On the right breast is sewn the German eagle perched on a wreath encircling a swastika.

The enlisted men wear trousers of the same color as the jacket with the legs narrowing slightly at the ends to facilitate the insertion in the jackboots. The soft caps have also undergone changes during the last few years. The 1938 model was made of field gray wool with no buttons in the front and no visor. The front was decorated with the black, white and red cockade surmounted by the eagle with piping of the branch color. In 1942 a new model was introduced with two buttons in the front, allowing earflaps to be buttoned under the chin.

Last year, 1943, the visored field cap, formerly worn only by the alpine troops, became standard for all branches of the Wehrmacht. The only difference is the slightly longer peak. German boots are the traditional field marching boot (jackboot) with hobnails, hoof irons, and sometimes toe-plates. Being hit with one those boots is a painful experience. The finish is either pebbled or smooth. Officers use the riding-style knee boot with similar sole protection.

Again in 1943, material shortages led to the replacement of the jackboot by the short lace-up boot. This boot is usually worn with short leggings, fastened with a buckle.

Lately, the German soldier has been wearing a surprising variety of camouflage clothing: field cap, tunic and parka. To this add the famous, awe-inspiring helmet, the symbol so to speak of German and Nazi might. All branches use the same helmet except paratroopers and tankers; the 1938 model replaced the Great War coalscuttle type with its ugly side vents. The helmet is streamlined and, the experts tell me, offers excellent protection.

In the Wehrmacht the left side is marked with the Imperial eagle and the right is adorned with a simple badge in the colors black, white and red, diagonally disposed. The Luftwaffe's badge has an eagle in flight holding the wreathed swastika in its claws. The Nazi units, SS and so forth display the party badge: red with a white circle and black swastika in the middle.

April 1st, Saturday. Late in the afternoon, I came home from the library shouting: "Turn on the radio, please, fast, tune in to Radio Berlin."

"What's the matter?" asks Mother.

"At the library, they were discussing the news from Berlin Radio that Hitler had a heart attack and is in very critical condition. Hurry, let's tune in."

The speaker, in a lugubrious voice, recites an official communiqué mentioning yesterday's air raid on Berlin, which he describes as "Terror Angriff" or terror raid. He goes on with further news about the Wehrmacht's successful defense in Italy and the heroic resistance of German troops in its Crusade against Bolshevism.

The news goes on and then it's over. Not a word about Hitler. Are they trying to keep this momentous event under wrap? We switch to other stations. Nothing... In an innocent voice I ask mother: "What day is it?". She looks at the calendar: "Well, it's March 31st." "Are you sure? It says Friday March 31st, and today is Saturday." Mother removes the leaf: April 1st. "Fool's Day" I exclaim.

Mother is not happy. The news had brought such hope, now quashed. And nowadays we live on hopes, tiny, tenuous ones keeping us going, especially mother who has for four long years borne the responsibility of feeding the family, keeping it together in a time when every day starts with new problems, new troubles, intractable and sometimes insoluble...

The innocent joke backfired. I should have thought of something less sensitive. "Sorry Mother". I apologize and give her a short note that says: Laughter, the great enemy of despair.

Mother is back at work and, with somewhat of a guilty conscience, I take a good look at her. She is an attractive lady, rather tall and thin, with pink cheeks, blue eyes often with a little twinkle in them and a gentle rather fussy manner. She never uses make-up and does not look her age. Anyone looking at her is struck by the subdued radiance of her beauty. The exquisite line of cheek and jawbone, the hair which falls loosely and naturally to frame her face, the fine eyebrows, the warmth and sweetness of her smile, all exude a subtle magic...

April 3rd, Monday. Our French teacher, always planning ahead, asks us to choose a subject for our main (and last) essay in the forthcoming term. He wants us to visit a famous site, a great museum or an old church, or else expound on the life of a famous personage. We should write it up in the form of a serious magazine article. We have to pick our subject by April 20 and it has to be remitted before Friday, May 19.

April 6, Monday. We were delighted about the happy return of Jules Wille from a POW camp in Germany, but my parents want to get some first-hand information about his health and all the details of his more than four years of captivity at Stalag IIA, B.357. They have, therefore, decided to send me as the representative of the family for a visit at Armentières, to bring Jules and family our love and best wishes, and to get all the news about his experience in Grossdeutschland. I plan to leave on April 14 and be back April 17.

I go to Mass early with brother Michel who wears a hat (not in church!) in a futile attempt at disguise. We don't meet anyone familiar except Monsieur Pelletier, a good friend who is in the know. He is a somewhat fallow personage under the influence of his redoutable wife who orders for him his suits, his books, his shirts and his ideas. We talk for a while and this short outing is pepping up Michel in the most wonderful way. So much so that, in late afternoon, we go out again and walk to the Rivieren Castle, in Ganshoren, not far from home.

We enter the blossoming park where the trees and bushes lose more and more their contours and turn to smoky shadows in the deepening dusk. The sky above is filled with screaming swifts that dive and soar, filling the air with a shrill clamor that dominates the evening sounds and, may be, the applause of a distant audience.

April 10, Monday. This is a busy week for me. Tomorrow I intend to visit sister Simone who is now a novice at a nun's congregation in Antwerp. And Saturday, I leave for Armentières, France.

April 11, Tuesday. Sister Simone resides at Rode Straat or Red Street, close to downtown Antwerp, near the Paardenmarkt or Horse Market. The complex consists of the convent, plus a large building built in the 19th century at the back of the Protestant temple, as well as a series of small houses fronting the Paardenmarkt. These houses date from the 16th and 17th centuries.

I ring the bell that resounds loudly in an immense corridor and am led to the visitor's parlor. My sister appears, radiant in her ample white and black robes. An excellent lunch is served which makes me think that I should visit my sister more often! (Just kidding.)

After lunch we talk at length until it is time for Simone to go back to her duties (she is a nurse); I will see her again at supper.

I decide on a walk that brings me to the St. Jacob's church built in late flamboyant Gothic, begun in 1491 and not finished until 1656. This church is of interest to me because it contains the chapel of Rubens (1577-1640), with his grave and that of several members of his family. One of his most famous paintings representing "Our Lady and the Saints" (1634) is kept here.

I do not enter the church, however, for I know that the paintings have been removed to a safe place because of the danger of destruction by bombing or thieving by the Nazi bigwigs. So leaving the church I proceed to my left along the Lange Nieuwe Straat, toward the magnificent Cathedral of Notre Dame, and the full gables of the quaint old houses surrounding her, which blush in the declining sun.

The Cathedral, well worth a lengthy visit, is the largest and one of the most important Gothic churches in this country. It was started in 1352 and completed in 1411. The Tower, the masterpiece of Antonius Keldermans and Dominic De Waghemaekere, was only finished in 1530. The spire is 123 meters or 406 feet high. For those with strong legs and good lungs there is a beautiful view from the top gallery that can be reached by 622 arduous steps. The chimes of the cathedral are famous and, before the war were played by the most celebrated "bell ringers" of the school of Mechlin. There are 47 of them (bells, not bell ringers), the largest is from 1507 and weighs 16 tons! It is named Keizer Karel in honor of Charles V (1500-1556), who made his Joyous Entry into Antwerp in 1515.

The cathedral has had an eventful history. In 1554, Philip II held a Chapter here of the Order of the Golden Fleece. In 1566, the iconoclasts smashed all the statues and works of art. In 1794, the church was stripped of all stained glass windows, the paintings and the stalls in the choir. Public worship was not allowed again until 1802, and the paintings of Rubens, stolen by the French, were not brought back until 1816. These same paintings have been removed to a safe place awaiting the end of this dreadful conflict.

April 12, Wednesday. I came back to the convent from my tour in time for early supper with Simone and another long chat until Evensong in the chapel. By nine o'clock I was in my delightful late medieval little room, which I proceeded to inspect. First of all, there is evidence, judging by the door's height, 5 feet 4 inches at the most, that people around 1500 were not very tall. I had to bend to enter the room that contained a bed, a washstand and a magnificent cupboard, beautifully carved.

I also noticed that the house has settled rather heavily to one side so that the room felt like the cabin of a boat at anchor, pushed to one side by wind and current. When I climbed into bed, I was reminded of the short size of my ancestors. Although I am not tall (about 5ft10) my feet were sticking out and to keep them inside the confines of the bed I had to bend my knees, fetus-like. Furthermore, the tilt of the room made me slide slowly toward the edge. I had to place a heavy Renaissance chair against the bed as an improvised railing to keep me from sliding to the ground. Nothing untoward happened to me however and I slept soundly all through the night.

After Mass a super breakfast awaited me consisting of petits-pains made of white flour, something I have not seen in years, plus ersatz coffee, home-made jam and a small fruit tart with one candle, in honor of my birthday. First class treatment, indeed!

By nine o'clock I was at the Plantin-Moretus Museum only to find out that it opens only at ten. I spent that waiting hour by having a look at the House of Peter-Paul Rubens, situated appropriately enough in the Rubens Street. The artist acquired it in 1610, enlarged and inhabited it from 1615 until his death, May 31st, 1640. The House has been completely restored to its original aspect but I had to be content to tour it from the outside.

To those who are interested in the noble art of printing, this town possesses one of the rarest treasure houses in the world. It is the Museum Plantin-Moretus, for three centuries the head office and workshop of the great printing-house whose name it bears. Christopher Plantin, the founder, was by birth a Frenchman who came to Antwerp in 1549 and resumed the trade of printer he had learned in France.

I spent almost three hours at the Museum and got so interested that I decided to take it as the subject of my essay for French class. I gathered all the information available and promised to myself I would be back.

I missed lunch at the convent but it had been kept for me. I ate in a hurry, said a hasty goodbye to my sister. Laden with a few parcels of food, I rushed to the station and arrived home well in time for a birthday party.

April 14, Friday. I am on my way to France, catching the train to Kortrijk (Courtrai) via Denderleeuw and Oudenaarde. As we pass the Wevelgem airfields, I note that they seem quiet. No longer can you see swarms of bombers on their way to England. No longer are Messerschmidts 109 or Focke-Wulfs 190 to be seen roaming the skies in their camouflaged colors of light gray and dark gray patches gradually blending into the light blue undersurfaces. These skies are now the almost exclusive territory of our Anglo-Saxon friends. We all, in this train, keep a watchful eye on the pale moving sky dotted with wool-fleeced clouds. The gentleman next to me, very nervous, pours and tosses back in one draught enough spirits to put an abstainer to sleep for a month.

Fortunately nothing happens and we arrive in Courtrai in one piece. My connection to Armentières consisting of three antiquated railroad cars and a locomotive, plus tender (guaranteed to date back to Stephenson), is waiting, puffing and steaming from all orifices. We leave on time however and we chug along; the dutiful little dinosaur stopping at every station it can find on its way: Menen, Wervik, Komen or Comines (where I was born!), Warneton, Pont-Rouge, Le Touquet and finally Armentières, where Rosa, Jules and little Charles are impatiently waiting. It was quite a reunion with great smiles, tears, slaps on the back and talk, talk which lasted well into the night.

April 15, Saturday. Jules Wille was diagnosed at the infirmary of Stalag IIA with a very bad case of sinusitis.. As there was no hospital bed available for him in Germany, the Commandant of the camp decided to send him back to his family in France. This was last February. By March 14, Jules was on his way back and arrived home, greeted as a hero, on March 18.

He was immediately admitted in the Armentières hospital where, after a few days of testing, it was discovered that although his case is serious there is great hope for full recovery. Jules was placed on a wholesome diet and, though not healed, he was allowed to go home two weeks later. Although still rather weak and very thin, his liberation from the POW camp and reunion with his wife and child has worked out wonders. I find him elated but nervous. After four years of captivity he is trying to readapt to civilian life: from the freedom of moving about everywhere he pleases, to eating off beautiful plates and even to sleeping in a soft bed, (too soft, he tells me). He is back home at the rue Bayard where he was born 29 years ago.

I ask my brother-in-law about his odyssey as a POW but he only wants to forget about it. He mentions however that despite all its negative aspects, the experience was not a total disaster. He developed great friendships to last a lifetime. His jailers were decent human beings who did not want to aggravate an already bad situation. As a matter of fact a guard once told him: "Wille (he pronounced it Vil-lay), you are lucky, you will come out of this war alive; as for me I shall be sent one day to the Russian front, never to return. I wish I were a prisoner of war."

I encourage Jules to write down the story of his life as a POW but he confesses he cannot do it. I explain that he should gather all the information he possesses: letters, postcards exchanged with his wife and others; official papers; his threadbare uniform; notes he should jot down as they come suddenly to his mind, helped by friends' questions or by a special event. I suggest he starts right away but the response is negative: "Not now, I am too tired mentally."

In the afternoon, all four of us take a walk to the park. (Grandma stays behind to prepare supper and Grandpa will "supervise".) It's not really a park but a British military cemetery, beautifully laid out as a park where the people of the neighborhood can take a walk, weather permitting.

It is not a big cemetery, about three hundred tombs aligned for an eternal parade. Each soldier has a separate resting place, with name, age, rank, regiment, time of death. If unknown, the headstone bears the words composed by Kipling: "A soldier of the Great War known unto God."

The cemetery is walled and planted as an English classic garden. In the middle is a very simple monument with the Cross of Sacrifice and a symbolic altar, the Stone of Remembrance, bearing the inscription, also of Kipling:

THEIR NAME LIVETH FOR EVERMORE

There are more than six hundred of these cemeteries disseminated throughout Flanders and Northern France. In the town of Ypres, for example, at the Porte de Menin is a big arch with the names of 58,600 English soldiers who fell in the Ypres Salient, and who lie in unknown graves.

The weather is rather cold and we wear heavy coats. We sit around for a while, taking in the weak sun, but soon we walk slowly along the tombs, reading the names of officers, non-coms and soldiers, many of them, I notice, are from the 1st Somerset Light Infantry. The average age is 20 years, the age of Jules' father "mort pour la France" on October 6, 1915, at the Butte du Mesnil, during the battle of Verdun.

We take a few pictures, and as we leave I am reminded of the poem by Major John McRae, who later died not far from here, on the Ypres front, entitled: "In Flanders Fields."

In Flanders Fields
We are the Dead. Short days ago
We lived, felt dawn, saw sunset glow,
Loved and were loved, and now we lie
In Flanders Fields

Take up our quarrel with the foe
To you from failing hands we throw
The Torch; be yours to hold it high
If ye break faith with us who die
We shall not sleep, though Poppies grow
In Flanders Fields

April 16, Sunday. Robert Leroy comes to have lunch and spends the rest of the afternoon with us. We reminisce and talk about his father, who died very suddenly in 1941, aged 41. His mother had to leave the apartment that came with the post of Director which his father held at the textile plant of Motte Frères. They now live in Armentières. They have a hard time living on a small pension; the high black market prices don't help. I cannot but reflect that until his father's death, Robert had a pretty easy life but now our family of eight children is better off than they are, *ceteris paribus*, (other things being equal).

We talk about the future and he mentions his application at the Arts et Métiers School (Industrial Arts and Crafts) in Lille, one of the best in the region, where he intends to study chemistry.

At this point, the mournful sound of the air alarm siren rends the air, but no one seems unduly concerned. It happens so often, nobody pays much attention anymore. This is because we are sitting here at almost equal distance - about 15 miles - of three airfields: the one at Wevelgem, to the northeast, one at Merville to the west and another near Lille, to the southeast. These are a favorite target for the Allied fighters, coming low and strafing every plane on the ground, fuel depots, military vehicles and buildings.

Their machine guns and cannons wreak havoc with anything that resembles a military target. Unfortunately they also kill and maim civilians. This is more and more resented by the population. I am told of a Hurricane, of the fighter-bomber type, which in one burst pulverized the roof of a farm covered with very heavy tiles, killing two cows... The farmer and his family were spared, but many other people were not so lucky.

Robert leaves us after a light supper. We plan to meet again, God willing, in September, before we both start a new stage in life.

April 18, Tuesday. I came back safely yesterday. We were neither strafed nor bombed. Some people were anxiously scrutinizing the skies as if this can help. These planes are so fast they are upon you, blazing away, before you can spot them.

I find that people have now adopted the Nazi slogan: *SIE KOMMEN.* Yes, they are coming. The opening of a second front is near; but when and where? When? I estimate some time in May when the weather is favorable and the North Sea less agitated. Where? Logic dictates as close as possible to the German border to end the war as swiftly as possible. This means an attack along the coastlines of Holland, Belgium and France. Holland is out because the hinterland can be so easily flooded. Belgium has beautiful beaches perfect for a landing operation but I hear that the coast is heavily defended and the North Sea is too often unforgiving. Furthermore the Belgian coast is only 45 miles long; this is probably not sufficient for a large-scale operation. It can be prolonged, of course, to Dunkirk, Calais, Boulogne, Le Touquet and Abbeville in France. But these are the areas where Rommel will be expecting them. The distance between Dover and Calais is only 22 miles; between Folkestone and Boulogne, 26 miles!

Further west the distances increase but they are not insurmountable. From Brighton to Dieppe is 67 miles; Southampton-Le Havre, 114 miles; Southampton-Cherbourg: 83 miles. Where will it be? My guess is between Abbeville and Le Havre with a sideshow at Dunkirk, Boulogne and Calais. But please don't tell anyone! Von Rundstedt and Rommel and the Generalstab in Berlin should not know about this great piece of military planning!

April 19, Wednesday. Back to school and my last term at Sainte-Marie. We are advised that in case of "military operations" in Belgium, classes will be canceled until further notice. Furthermore the seniors are encouraged to matriculate at a university as soon as possible to avoid being drafted as "unemployed" in the Forced

Labor Battalions, in Germany. I decide to pay a visit at Louvain University without delay.

April 22, Saturday. I am behind the times; last week, the Nazis took over the Ploesti oilfields region in Rumania. These fields are vital to the German war effort and it appears that they are now less than 200 miles from the advancing Russians. I expect the Germans to hold on to the Ploesti area with all their might. I wonder what they will do if they are lost. It is known that they manufacture synthetic petroleum but surely production is not sufficient to cover their tremendous needs.

Meanwhile, the Wehrmacht has abandoned Odessa, on the Black Sea: the last big Russian city they still occupied.

April 27, Thursday. I am now a member of the Défense Passive (Civil Defense) in which I will serve as a part-time air raid warden. The DP is divided in two groups: the wardens, full-time or part-time, and the Rescue Service manned by professionals such as firemen and members of the building trades.

As warden, when on duty I am responsible for rescue when possible and first aid until the Rescue Service arrives. At that point my intervention switches to post-raid services such as directing the homeless to a Rest Center. I have been handed an armband and an official pass that allows me to move around even when curfew is in effect.

The DP is being beefed up because the Belgian authorities are convinced that. sooner or later, the country will experience increasing bombing of military and economic targets especially ports, waterways and railroad centers. They know about the loss of life and havoc created in Germany by Allied bombing. This can happen in Belgium as soon as the second front is opened. And it is almost a certainty that our country will be the theater of military operations with all its consequences. It has always been that way in the past, and there is no reason to think that we will be spared this time.

12

May 1 – July, 1944

May 1, Monday. We have a day off in school at the occasion of a Teachers' Conference; this is an opportunity for me to pay a visit to the University of Louvain.

I take the inter-urban tramway which is preferred to the train, the latter more likely to be a target of bombing or strafing.

The streetcar is jammed beyond capacity. Here I am pressed against the rear window, hardly able to move a finger, feet stuck under a great number of parcels, packages, bundles, suitcases and even a small green trunk. All these are property of the black marketeers who have invaded this relic of public transportation. A few of them are outside, perched precariously on the buffers between the two tramcars, holding on for dear life.

These people are actively pursued by the black market police, an intervention much resented by the public for three reasons: *First,* the black marketeers are treated as heroes because they help feed the population; *second,* the inspectors, who operate mostly at train stations and inter-urban terminals, are suspected of collaborating with the Occupant; *third,* they (the inspectors) are accused of appropriating for themselves the confiscated goods which are supposed to go to hospitals, hospices, orphanages, etc.

Brussels and Louvain are only 30 kms (about 20 miles) distant but there are lots of stops. It takes close to two hours before we reach the terminal at the railway station. This town of about 40,000 inhabitants was founded in the ninth century. It was severely damaged by the invading Germans in 1914. The University Library, with its collection of priceless Arab manuscripts and incunabula (early printed books), was burned to the ground. Rebuilt with the help of America, it was again destroyed during the German advance on Brussels, in May of 1940. It is now just an empty shell.

The University was founded in 1425 and became one of the great centers of learning in Western Europe. It was home for great celebrities such as Pope Adrian VI - Adriaen Boyers of Utrecht - (1459-1523), Erasmus, Justus Lipsius the famous professor, Vesalius, Mercator and Ortelius, geographers. It was also the most solid bulwark against the rise of Protestantism in Northern Europe and, later, the most active base for the Counter-Reformation.

And here I am at the administration offices, 519 years later, asking to join the thousands of students and professors who preceded me. I had all the necessary papers and was right away issued a temporary student ID card, to be replaced by a definitive one as soon as the papers are verified with the school authorities.

After these formalities, I direct my steps towards the Rue des Récollets, close by, for a visit to the Jesuit College. It consists of a series of houses acquired over the centuries, connected with each other by a bewildering series of passages, stairs and small gardens which give a kind of medieval cachet to the entire structure.

The goal of my visit is the Jesuits' Library where the fathers hide a magnificent collection of manuscripts and books. Here are examples of early French, Flemish, Dutch and Italian printing. There are Aldines, Plantins, Elseviers. There is also an interesting collection of incunabula (books printed before 1500), coming mainly from Louvain itself where the printing press was introduced in 1473 by Johann Westfalen. Here also is the Biblia Regia, in six languages, edited for Plantin by Arias Montanus, aided by a host of learned churchmen of Europe.

The printing of this Bible began in 1568 and was finished in 1572. The languages are: Latin, Greek, Hebrew, Syriac and Chaldean plus French. In addition it has detailed appendices including Hebrew, Chaldaic, Syrian and Greek grammars and vocabularies. The book is filled with full-page illustrations made from copper plates. The eight big in-folios are Plantin's masterpiece and the most important work ever produced in the XVII Provinces (present Belgium and the Netherlands) by one printer.

What a magnificent silent world of books. They start to speak to you as soon as they are opened. The most precious of them, following the medieval tradition, are still solidly attached to the reading table by a long chain to prevent any undue "appropriation" by an enthusiastic and fanatic collector.

Before catching a six o'clock tram I have time enough to go and admire the splendid façade of the Town Hall, one of the most beautiful non-religious edifices in Belgium. Begun in 1148, it was finished in 1459, the work of Mathieu Van Layens. It was damaged in 1914 but is now restored. It is a huge reliquary in elegantly carved stone with a profusion of turrets, pinnacles, dormer windows as well as about 300 niches set in the wall with statues replaced in the 19th century.

My next stop was the St. Peter's church, also badly damaged in 1914. In peacetime one could admire "The Last Supper" of Thierry Bouts (around 1468) but it is now in a safe place, waiting for less perilous times. To the left of the transept sits enthroned the *Sedes Sapientiae* or Seat of Wisdom, a statue of Our Lady dating from 1441, the Saint Patron of the University, whose effigy is reproduced on its Great Seal.

Oh! I notice I am a little late and speed to the terminal, but what a crowd! I cannot even get near the tram. I have to wait for the next one that ended up being full but not too crowded.

May 6, Saturday. I spend a good deal of the afternoon at the local Red Cross for a refresher course in first-aid. We are about a dozen people plus the two nurses in charge. This is our first lesson and it deals with bandages: of the knee, heel, foot, head (crossed - monocle and binocle) and chest. No big deal! We practice this with the scouts on a regular basis. I was through with my bandages in no time and this gave me leisure to look around. One of the nurses is very attractive indeed. Her silver-blond hair shimmers like a halo against the pale sunshine slanting sideways through the window. She wears a Red Cross uniform, very becoming. The whole effect is colorful and gorgeous. I am sure that all the male participants will be back, next week.

May 9, Tuesday. I witnessed a sad event this morning. As I was proceeding to the tram stop to go to school, I noticed a rather big group of people disposed in a circle, in front of the La Madeleine church. Such an assembly is unusual as all public meetings of more than five persons are strictly forbidden. Curious, I approached and discovered another group within the big one. It consisted of a squad of German soldiers and a few local policemen of somber mien, there to protect about a dozen workers whose job it was to extract the two bells from the church tower.

The gathering was murmuring protests but remained orderly; the soldiers, although armed, were not menacing. With the help of a crane and a huge inclined platform, the workers were slowly bringing down the bells, one at a time.

It was a painful moment which made me reflect that this latest case of Nazi robbery cannot help the Germans very much. I rather think that they want to punish the Belgian people for steadfastly refusing to collaborate in the creation of the "New Order" in Europe.

We hate the Occupant more and more. There is very little we can do except for civil disobedience which we practice at every opportunity. We also let off steam by using, in referring to them, a series of insulting epithets such as: Boche, Fridolin, Frisé, Fritz and, in Flemish, the most common is Mof, or Moffen (in plural.) Another one is Doryphore ("Spear Bearer") or Colorado beetle, in reference to the parasite that attacks the leaves of potato plants - the Germans stealing most of our potato harvest.

May 10, Wednesday. This is the fourth anniversary of the German invasion. At this occasion I find people both nervous and hopeful. We are all expecting the Allied invasion any day now. Our Nazi-controlled newspapers are full of "don't-you-worry-we-are-ready" stuff. Photographs show midget Marshal Rommel (very popular and very overstated, if you ask me). You see him strutting up and down the Atlantic Wall with all his medals and his baton, looking as if he were suffering from dyspepsia (may be he does).

Some people around me insist that it took the Germans a full three years and more, in peacetime, to build the Siegfried Line which is approximately 300 kms long or two hundred miles. The Atlantic Wall or Festung Europa stretching from Vlissingen in Holland to Biarritz in southern France extend over more than eight hundred miles. And they started building in earnest at the end of 1942. Even if we take the areas most likely to be attacked, between Knokke and Cherbourg, about 800 kms or 500 miles, there is no way the Nazis can have the materials, the equipment, the personnel to build this Wall; and where will they find enough seasoned troops to man it. This is what I am told.

May 12, Friday. My essay on Plantin-Moretus is getting along wonderfully. I will be ready by May 19th. At school, we are again advised that in case of military operations on the soil of Belgium, all classes will be suspended until further notice. In the event of this term being cut short, we are assured it will count as a fully completed one toward obtaining the high school diploma.

May 17, Wednesday. My friend Wolfgang Weil has not appeared in school since May 3rd and nobody knows what happened to him. At first I thought he might be sick but now I wonder. Our main teacher has no explanation for this prolonged absence, I decide to ask the Director of the school: "Where is Wolfgang Weil?" The answer is immediate and short. "Don't worry, Wolfgang is all right and in good hands." This allays my fears and I don't need any further explanation. I know he is in hiding and relatively safe.

May 20, Saturday. In Italy, the Allies had a hard time, after their landings at Anzio and Nettuno, pushing up north against a very determined Wehrmacht. This shows how tough a fighting machine the Germans still are despite their heavy losses on the Eastern front.

It now seems that the deadlock along the Gustav Line, which has lasted for months, has been broken. A special communiqué announced yesterday that Cassino and the monastery on top of the mountain behind the town have been captured by the British Eighth Army. The next goal is, of course, Rome. Hopefully, the Germans will not try to defend the Eternal City, street by street, and destroy it like a second Stalingrad. However, I think the Wehrmacht doesn't have the troops and equipment needed for such a siege.

May 23, Monday. In due time, I delivered my essay on the Plantin-Moretus Museum, and here are some extracts.

The Plantin-Moretus Dynasty of Printers

To those interested in the noble art of printing, Antwerp possesses one of the rarest treasure-houses in the world: the Museum Plantin-Moretus, for three centuries the head office and workshop of the great printing firm whose name it bears.

Christopher Plantin the founder, was by birth a Frenchman, born in the vicinity of Tours in the year 1514. Fleeing from the plague with his father to Lyons he ended up in Caen in Normandy, where he learned the art of printing. In 1549, with his wife Jeanne Rivière, he came to Antwerp and the following year was enrolled as a citizen, and a member of the famous guild of St Luke and as a printer.

There were at the time no less than sixty-six printing establishments in the Low Countries, of which thirteen were at Antwerp, some of the latter rivaling the best printers of Paris, Basel and Venice in the beauty of their productions. During the next seven years, Plantin's presses turned out a limited number of works. In 1563 he organized a company consisting of himself and four partners. While this arrangement lasted, from 1563 to 1567, more than two hundred books were printed and forty workmen kept continuously employed. His work was already considered notable for the beauty of its type and excellence of the paper used.

Soon after the partnership was dissolved, Plantin undertook what was destined to be the greatest work of his career, and one of the most famous in the history of printing, the famous Biblia Regia. This was the edition of the Bible in four ancient languages, Latin, Hebrew, Greek and Chaldean. The Hebrew type was purchased from a Venetian printer, while the last two were cast expressly for this book. His friend Cayas interested Philip II in the project, and the monarch sent the great scholar Arias Montanus from Alcala to supervise the work. At the suggestion of Cardinal Granville, Syriac was added to the other texts so that, including French, there were six languages in all. The first volume of this "Polyglot Bible", as it came to be called, appeared in 1569, and the eighth and last, in 1573.

Besides the Biblia Regia, Plantin, now at the height of his fame, managed to turn out a vast quantity of printed matter. While the largest printers at Paris employed no more than six presses, Plantin kept twenty-two constantly at work, had agents at Paris and Leyden, and sent a member of his family every year to attend the fairs at Leipzig and Frankfurt. In 1575, his office is said to have had seventy-three different kinds of type, weighing over seventeen tons.

The Plantin Press was located at various places about the city until 1576, when it was established on the Hoogstraat near the Sint Jans Poort. Three years later Plantin purchased the premises occupied by the present museum, extending from the Hoogstraat through the Friday Market, with a large gateway opening into the latter. Plantin had been only eight months in this new location when the Spanish Fury (a mutiny of unpaid mercenaries) broke out. For a time Plantin had to leave Antwerp, going to Leyden, where he met Justus Lipsius, and was made printer to the University. After the siege he hurried home, but a short time later his health began to fail.

It was in his house on the Friday Market that the dying printer gathered his family about him. His only son had died in infancy but his five daughters had all lived to be married, three of them to men associated with him in the printing shop. The eldest, Margaret, married Frans Raphelingen, the chief proofreader and an able linguist; while the second, Martina, married Jan Moretus (Johannes Moerendorp) the father of a long line, of which the eldest sons bore the same first name so that they came to be distinguished by Roman numbers, the first being Jan Moretus I, and so forth, like a line of kings. On July 1st, 1589, Christopher Plantin, this "giant among printers" breathed his last, and was buried in the ambulatory of the cathedral, his friend Justus Lipsius writing the inscription for his tombstone.

His successors fully maintained the noble tradition he had started. Jan Moretus I ruled over the destinies of the house until his death in 1610, leaving it to his two sons, Jan II and Balthazar I. The latter was the greatest of the dynasty printers, after Plantin and Jan Moretus I. He was a warm friend of Rubens (d.1640) who illustrated many of the publications of the house during this period. In the fourth generation, represented by Balthazar III, who ruled for half a century, from 1646 to 1696, the family was ennobled but after this period the house confined its output and commerce to missals and breviaries, under the monopoly granted by Philip II for the countries under the rule of Spain.

In 1800, under the French occupation, the printing office ceased operations. It resumed activities on a small scale once or twice during the nineteenth century, but finally closed in 1867, after an existence of three hundred and twelve years. In 1876 Edouard Moretus sold the entire establishment, with all its priceless collections and furnishings to the city of Antwerp for the sum of

1,200,000 francs, a big sum at that time, to be maintained as a museum.

May 26, Friday. In a letter, Fr. Capart enquires whether I would be willing to help him for two or three weeks in July or August, at his Youth Center in Tourneppe. My answer is "yes, unless we are overtaken by unforeseen events." This is the caveat everyone places on any project, even short-range ones.

May 27, Saturday. Radio Berlin, earlier in the week, quoted Field Marshal von Rundstedt, the German anti-invasion chief in France, as saying: "Invasion will begin any moment now."

May 28, Sunday. This is Pentecost or Whitsunday. The situation is extremely quiet, the lull before the storm, except for the deep throated humming of squadrons of planes on their way to Germany. Coastal Belgium and Northern France are bombed and strafed on an almost continuous basis but Brussels has been spared so far. It is only a question of time however, and people are rather impatient to know when the second front will finally become a reality.

The weather is relatively favorable for an invasion: General improvement and promising outlook: sunny. Temperature: high, 19 degrees C, low clouds. Visibility: fair. Westerly winds.

May 29, Monday. Great news from Italy, at last! A Berlin communiqué announces that Field Marshal Kesselring has been forced to retreat after the breach of the Gustav Line. This line, according to the information I could piece together, is a series of concrete defensive works built by the Todt Organization This is why Kesselring has been so successful in keeping the Allies from quick victory. Looking at the map I can see that it took the Fifth U.S. and the Eighth British Armies five weeks to advance 310 miles from Reggio di Calabria to Capua, north of Naples and seven months to finally pierce through the tough Gustav Line also called, I discover, the Hitler Line, about 50 miles away. The Germans have now issued the statement that they are fighting the Americans in Velletri, only 25 miles from Rome. The road to the Italian capital seems open.

June 3, Saturday. The northwestern suburbs of Brussels have been subjected to a brief but heavy bombing by the American air force. I was at home and could hear the muted explosions to the north of us. Although our section is not affected by the raid, I dress in my old clothes, not forgetting my armband, and in no time, I am on my bicycle to join the local DP post for rescue and stretcher party. I usually don't take my bike for fear it might be confiscated by roaming Nazis, but this is an emergency. At the post, a dozen or so of mostly middle-aged men plus the two Red Cross nurses, are getting ready for action.

We are directed to the stricken area and at first we encounter nothing but deserted streets and soon we pass ambulances rushing to hospitals and fire trucks dashing to the fires. Further on, we are stopped by a policeman who redirects us toward the scene of the worst "incident". We alight from our antiquated vehicle and, laden with our folded stretchers, simple digging tools and first aid implements, we approach a block of buildings that has been severely hit. As we get near, a fine milky cloud of dust start to fill our noses and throats, muffling any sound. We don our dust masks and penetrate the zone.

The spectacle of this part of the town is stupefying. It is nothing more and nothing less than a huge pile of rubble. The streets are blocked by chunks of masonry and concrete from buildings blasted to pieces. We are the stretcher party and are supposed to stand by until the casualties are brought out, or the ruins are safe to enter; we refuse to remain idle and start helping our more expert colleagues. These "heavy rescue" men are mainly building trade specialists: bricklayers, masons, plumbers, carpenters and roofers who know how buildings are put together and apply their techniques in reverse.
Being a little late, we discover that most of the serious casualties have been led away. Our nurses are assigned to a mobile first aid unit and we join a team of heavy rescue workers with the peremptory order not to take unnecessary risks and strictly follow instructions.

I am now facing what once was a huge brick building that has dissolved, with the peculiarity of that type of housing, into a compact smoking pile; underneath it an unknown number of people are trapped, dead or alive. A little further up the street is a three-story house, of which all the floors have collapsed in layers into the basement, crushing to death and burning an old couple near their kitchen range.

After ninety minutes of backbreaking digging and a few short pauses, our rescue team chief calls for a break for food and drink after which he directs us to the boulevard where a bomb has collapsed a group of stately mansions.

We are told that a few people are trapped beneath the huge debris. Our leader calls for silence as to better hear the muffled cries which should lead us to the victims. After a few minutes we do indeed hear the faint moaning under a heap of rubble at the house, second from the left. After removal of loose stone and brick we could hear more clearly the voice of a woman calling for help. We dig further and find that she is trapped with her little girl under the collapsed concrete roof of the cellar. Despite our efforts, for lack of adequate equipment, we do not succeed in extracting mother and child out of their perilous situation.

We ask for heavy equipment but it seems that none is available for the time being. We clear more debris, start digging a hole and the woman's voice is a little clearer. Through a small opening we slide to her two rubber tubes to help them breath a little easier. The mother is pinned down and cannot feel her legs; the little girl is alive but her breath is shallow and irregular. We take turns talking to the mother trying to keep up her spirits; she is much concerned about her daughter and fears that life is ebbing away from the child.

We continue our digging and clearing but it is very difficult and dangerous. An attempt from the opposite side is soon abandoned when it is found progress is even slower and even more dangerous.

An hour goes by and still no sight of the heavy equipment and the digging experts. We keep talking to the mother, very brave, but her voice is faltering and we fear for her and her daughter.

At long last! there comes the heavy rescue team. These professionals negotiate the wreckage with care and yet with amazing speed. In less than thirty minutes they extract the mother with broken limbs and in very bad shape. It takes longer to get the child out. Life has departed from her; her eyes and lips are puffed, she has suffocated to death. A little curly angel, innocent of war's crimes and tragedies, has paid for us and gone to heaven.

I carry her, limp in my arms, a featherweight, down the broken ruins to the waiting doctor hastily summoned. He confirms what I already know: she is dead. I burst into tears, inconsolable, as she is taken to the makeshift morgue. It is not my first encounter with death but it is my first battle with death and my first defeat at the hands of the Angel of Death. The doctor, disheveled, his face covered with grime, places a hand on my shoulder: "Pull yourself together, boy! or you will fall apart. This is not an easy job. I recommend you take a break, or better call it a day. Go to the mobile canteen for a snack and wait for the relief team due very soon."

We are relieved fifteen minutes later and it is a very subdued and exhausted team that returns to the local post. Dusty and hungry, thirsty and beaten, we are served a nice meal and a strange concoction called "coffee". A warm shower seems to revitalize most of us. I retrieve my bike and in a somber mood, my muscles hurting from the exertions of the last few hours, I reach home where I recount the events I just lived through.

June 5, Monday. Brother Lucien shakes me awake: "The Allies have liberated Rome," he shouts and disappears downstairs, in velvet paws, like a cat.

It is true. The U.S. Fifth Army did reach the heart of Rome yesterday evening, after some resistance in the outer suburbs by the German rearguard. The German main army is apparently retreating fast north of town and it looks like the enemy is making a big withdrawal to far behind the Eternal City. No other details are available.

Meanwhile, the Allied air forces did spend the weekend hitting military installations, almost non-stop, all over western Belgium and northern France. We can expect our share of bombings in the next few days.

June 6, Tuesday. Our neighbor next door rang the bell this morning, something she rarely does and, all excited and out of breath, tells us to tune to Nazi-controlled Radio Brussels. She is an immense dumpling of a woman, immovably fixed in an armchair conveniently placed so that she can, from her window, the radio permanently switched on, listen and observe all that is going in the world outside.

It appears that the German news agency has flashed the word to the world that *AN ALLIED INVASION* of western France has begun with parachute troops spilling out of the dawn skies over the Normandy peninsula and seaborne forces landing in the Le Havre area.

Another German news report says that the long expected invasion has begun in the first hours of this morning and it adds that no Allied landings were made "yet" at Calais and Dunkerque. This obviously is an indication that the Nazis are expecting Allied assaults along the line Dunkerque-Le Havre, a distance of 150 miles.

On my way to school I find people unusually loquacious but in low tones. They all heard the news and have only one question: Is it the real thing? At school there is no other talk. And then the wildest rumors start to circulate: The English fleet is cruising along the Belgian coast; the Americans have landed at Dunkerque, France, and in De Panne, a few miles to the east, in Belgium. None of it can be confirmed.

Between two classes, one of our teachers comes up with the information that the BBC, quoting German sources, has announced the invasion. There is no official confirmation from the Allies.

Then later, we hear of *Communiqué No. 1* from General Dwight Eisenhower's headquarters announcing what we already know: Allied troops have begun landing on the northern coast of France.

A second announcement followed from SHAEF, the Supreme Headquarters of the Allied Expedition in France, telling us that General Bernard L. Montgomery is in command of the Army group carrying out the assault. This army group includes British, Canadian and U.S. forces. Montgomery will face Hitler who is taking personal command of all the anti-invasion operations. The other German commanders are: Field Marshal von Rundstedt, commander-in-chief; Field Marshal Erwin Rommel, Inspector General; Generaloberst (Colonel-General) Hugo Sperrle, in charge of the Luftwaffe, Generaloberst Johannes von Blaskowitz, acting deputy to Rommel and commanding general of Army Group "G", whatever that is.

The whole day in school has been a cacophony of joyous but restrained babble. No classes were taught; the teachers, even the most dedicated ones, didn't even try. They ended up showing maps and providing their own personal commentaries. No matter how tentative and possibly very wrong, they were received with the greatest attention.

We are also told that Hubert Pierlot, Prime Minister of the Belgian Government in exile, has made a speech, I don't know when, telling us: "The hour so long awaited by you is near. Preliminary operations for the liberation of Europe have begun. The first assault is the certain signal of your deliverance. The moment of supreme combat has not yet come." Well, it doesn't say much, does it? I say so but I am rebuked as being too critical. I retort that if the Prime Minister, whom I consider a shallow personage, has nothing to say, he should shut up.

Back home, I listen to both the BBC (terrible jamming), Radio Brussels and the German radio services. I find that the Allies, understandingly, don't say much but the Germans give more detailed information. These are military communiqués not repressed by Goebbels' Propaganda Abteilung. I take my map of France and note the following:
* Landings continuing all day in the Seine Bay, the stretch of the Normandy coast between the ports of Cherbourg and Le Havre.
* Strong American airborne forces jumped between Barfleur and St. Vaast-la-Hougue, about 15 miles from Cherbourg.
* Landing barges at Ouistreham, which I find at the mouth of the river Orne.
* Sharp fighting at Caen, about ten miles inland.
* Tanks have been landed at Arromanches, midway on the Seine Bay coast.
* Parachutists landing around the estuary of the river Vire.

The news about the invasion has completely eclipsed the war in Italy and the liberation of Rome. There has been very little fighting and the city has been spared. The Wehrmacht is retreating north precipitously. It seems that the next front will be the Leghorn (Livorno)-Florence-Rimini line, along the Arno river valley, 160 miles north of Rome. Would it not be ironic to see the Italians liberated before we are?

June 7, Wednesday. Brothers Michel and Lucien, as well as sisters Leona and Marie-Thérèse, complain that I monopolize the radio set at home! They are right. As a matter of fact I was up early to get the latest news in French, Flemish, German and English. The best source so far is the German radio. It has the ring of truth; it seems to be summaries of reports from field commanders to their superior officers. Here is what I could gather:

* Powerful paratroop formations dropped behind Boulogne and north of Rouen. Other paratroops have a firm grip on a 19-mile stretch of the Cherbourg-Caen road.

* The Allied bridgehead is said to be fifteen miles long and several miles deep on both sides of the river Orne and northwest of Bayeux, between Caen and Isigny.

* Troops landed from hundreds of ships attacking Arromanches and Ouistreham. Cliffs scaled by ladder, and tanks landed.

* Paratroops made twelve landings from Cherbourg to Boulogne. First and Sixth British and 28th and 101st American airborne divisions engaged.

* Allied troops try to break into Carentan, west of Isigny.

* German military commentator, Sartorius, says the offensive has extended to the entire Normandy peninsula.

Churchill's speech in Parliament and midnight Allied communiqué say absolutely nothing. I understand that they have to be careful not to divulge any moves that would alert the Germans to what the real objectives are.

In school, the excitement is at its peak. It's buzz, buzz, buzz! I have brought my map plus my notes and we discard French, History or Math to discuss what might be the most important event of our lives. The teachers don't mind. Impossible to concentrate; our thoughts are with the Allied troops in Normandy.

June 9, Friday. Situation very fluid on the new front. The Allies' communiqués are inscrutable and the Germans announce vigorous counterattacks but again, no detail. Fair enough but it doesn't still our hunger for concrete news.

June 10, Saturday. An example of a communiqué from the Allies Supreme Headquarters.

"Repeated enemy attacks against the 6th Airborne Division have been repulsed. The American bridgeheads are being gradually enlarged.

"The enemy is fighting fiercely, his reserves have now been in action along the whole front.

"With the safe and timely arrival of merchant convoys and improvement in the weather, unloading of supplies is proceeding at a satisfactory rate.

"During the early hours of today, E-boats were attacked along the French and Belgian coasts by coastal aircraft. The enemy air effort is as yet on a limited scale, but some opposition from FLAK has been encountered.

"Ceaseless patrols were maintained over the immediate battle positions by our fighters and fighter-bombers. Rocket-firing planes attacked a tank concentration near Caen."

Notes. a) This communiqué was copied in shorthand, courtesy of a schoolmate's sister.

b) What is an E-boat? It is really a S-boat for Schnellboote, in German. It is a very fast torpedo boat, with a maximum speed of 42 knots. (Source: Signal magazine.)

June 12, Monday. Classes are now back to normal. However the breaks are spent discussing the communiqués and the scanty news: lots of smoke and very little fire.

June 14, Wednesday. In a London broadcast last week, a spokesman for General Eisenhower said: "A new phase of the air offensive has started. It will affect the entire coastal region situated not less than 35 km (22 miles) inland from France and other coastal countries. People will be advised by special announcements dropped from Allied planes."

The spokesman concluded with the advice that those able to leave the 22 mile-deep coastal belt should do so at once, adding that those who cannot leave now must do so when the Allies give warning.

Looking at my map of Belgium, the coastal belt would start approximately at Poperinge on the French border to Terneuzen in Holland via Langemark, Hooglede, Aalter and Eeklo. That would include the important city of Bruges as well as the coastal towns of Ostend and Knokke plus the port of Zeebrugge.

This broacast leaves me puzzled. Why this warning? We all know we are at risk and not only in a 22-mile coastal zone. Is this smoke and mirrors to confuse the Germans?

June 16, Friday. The British are progressing slowly on an east-west line Caen-Villers-Bocage–Caumont-Carentan. Further west, the Americans have taken St. Sauveur-le-Vicomte and are threatening to cut off Cherbourg. American forces have also advanced to Montebourg and are only a few miles from Valognes the last town before Cherbourg.

Good! It looks like the Allies have been successful in establishing and expanding their beachhead. The Second Front is a reality.

June 18, Sunday. The Luftwaffe has practically disappeared from the skies. But the Allied air forces are all over the place and show an amazing aggressiveness. They bomb and strafe anything that looks military. They hit civilians too.

The mood in Brussels is one of high expectation and the question on everybody's lips is: "When will we be liberated and at what cost in lives and destruction?" Downtown is extremely quiet. All troops on leave - and Brussels is or was a favorite "resort"- have disappeared.

June 19, Monday. Father is now on night duty because most troop movements are made at night to avoid the terrible fighter-bombers.

Since June 6, the day of the invasion, there has been intense rail activity in troop and equipment transportation. From visual observation and the study of shipping documents, Father learns that most trains originate in the Cologne area and Belgium's Limburg province. The Cologne trains carry mostly guns, tanks, spare parts and so forth; the Limburg line convey troops with some of their equipment. Father suspects they come from Beverloo; this area was before the war an important Belgian Army training base and now a refitting area for Panzer divisions. The Panzer reserve unit that has recently moved from Beverloo to the Pas-de-Calais, via Brussels and Lille is the SS Panzer Division "Adolf Hitler."

June 20, Tuesday. The British Minister of Home Security, a Mr. Morrison, has released the following statement:

"The enemy has begun to use his secret weapon, the pilotless aircraft. The damage it has caused has been relatively small, and the new weapon will not interfere with our war effort and our sure and steady march to victory.

"There is no reason to think that raids by this weapon will be worse than or indeed as heavy as the raids with which the people of this country are already familiar and have borne so bravely."

I take note of this new German weapon announced, time and time again, by Hitler and Goebbels. It is my intention to get additional information on this "pilotless aicraft."

June 21, Wednesday. Cherbourg is isolated and thousands of troops are trapped in that city. The Cotentin peninsula has been sliced in two by the U.S. Ninth and 82nd Airborne divisions on a line from Montebourg to St. Jacques-de-Nehou up to Barneville. If they can take Cherbourg, the Allies will have a good port for the flow of troops and equipment to the battle line.

The rest of the Normandy front is rather static, the Germans opposing a dogged resistance to all attacks. A drive by the American forces, south of Isigny, has taken them to a point which is only six miles from St. Lô. Further east, on the front Tilly-Caumont-Caen, the British and Canadians have a very tough job against Rommel's four Panzer divisions (or more?) facing them.

June 22, Thursday. Radio Berlin and its affiliates in occupied countries are gloating over the new German weapon being used against London. It is called "Vergeltungswaffe 1 or V1. The British call it the "pilotless plane."

The keynote of Big Mouth's (Goebbels) propaganda is that the new weapon is a reprisal for Allied raids on German cities. "The feeling of hatred and the glowing wish for revenge inspiring the German people was lit by our enemies by their mean terror crimes."

The German radio added that dense smoke clouds cover wide stretches of Southern England. "Kingsley and Bromley seem to have been particularly hit and large fires were observed at Sevenoaks and Sutton."

June 28, Sunday. Cherbourg has fallen to the Americans but the town is in ruins and the port has been destroyed and not likely to be used by the Allies for some time.

June 29, Monday. They came at dusk last night, fewer of them, and much lower than usual. Soon after the alarm sounded you could hear the deep throbbing hum of their engines and the higher pitch tone of their protectors, the fighters. But the latter had nothing to do because no Luftwaffe fighter showed up. Instead, the FLAK guns went into action just above the house, shooting so violently that we hastily went down to what we think is the strongest part of the cellar because of the vaulted ceiling. We could hear the shrapnel cascading on the roof and see it sparkling on the sidewalk and the cobblestones.

Then the bombs fell but further north, away from the neighborhood. The FLAK increased in intensity; the noise of exploding bombs, bursting shells and gun reports was loud and frightening. Thirty-five minutes later the monotone all-clear sounded and all was calm again. The northern part of Brussels has again been hit but I have not been called up and there is no hard information.

June 30, Tuesday. I don't know whether last night's bombing was particularly severe but there are no streetcars this morning and there is no way I can walk to school.

Finally, at mid-morning, I am lucky enough to catch one at the terminal, down the avenue; it must be the first one to circulate because in no time at all it is chock-full and I understand how sardines feel in their tin can. And, in my case, there is no oil to smoothen the asperities of sharp elbows and an assortment of purses, bags, bundles and briefcases.

I extricate myself with great difficulty at the Porte de Schaerbeek and reach school at around eleven o'clock, only to find out that classes have been suspended until further notice.

The target of last night's attack was the railroad center of Schaerbeek/Haren, only three miles away from our school, as the crow flies. A few stray bombs have fallen nearby and as the end of the school year is only two weeks away, the municipal authorities have decided to close all schools in the vicinity, including ours.

The final exams will take place in one week's time at the rate of one exam in the morning and one in the afternoon. There will be no end of the year ceremony.

July 2, Monday. Father has seen the report on the bombing results of Schaerbeek/Haren.

Damage to buildings: extensive. Rolling stock: only limited losses. Railroad beds repairs and rail replacement completed in less than 22 hours. Troop movements diverted south via Louvain,

Nivelles, Mons and Valenciennes; in the north, via Kontich (near Antwerp), Dendermonde, Oudenaarde and Courtrai. No significant delays suffered, except for civilian traffic.

July 3, Tuesday. I advise Fr. Capart that I can join his Youth Center by July 15 for three weeks, that is until August 5, "si Dieu nous prête vie," briefly translated: "God willing."

July 5, Thursday. The slugging match in the Caen-Tilly area is still going on. It appears that Rommel has taken personal command of the seven Panzer divisions facing the British. In other words, from his perch as "Inspector General" he has descended to the task of commanding officer of tactical troops, the only thing he is very good at. The Americans have cleared the Cherbourg peninsula of all German forces and all resistance above the line La-Haye-du-Puits/Carentan has ended.

On the Eastern front, the Soviet offensive is continuing unabated. The Russians are advancing towards north Poland and Lithuania, after the central front collapsed, through three gaps at Vitebsk, Mogilev and Bobruisk. Tanks and shock troops are pushing along the road to Warsaw after storming a German strongpoint at Slutsk. A little more to the north other units are trying to encircle Minsk, the last big German-held base before Vilna.

July 8, Saturday. Very busy with exams and not much time to keep abreast of the war. I note, however, that Minsk has been retaken by Soviet troops.

There is news also from the Italian front. The Fifth U.S. Army has advanced swiftly toward the "Gothic Line" and it is now 16 miles from Livorno and 35 from Florence. This last city has been declared an "open city" by Hitler,because, says Berlin Radio, of "the irreplaceable treasures" contained in the town. I don't know how they will manage this because Florence is very much within the German fortification system stretching from Livorno across the peninsula to Rimini!

July 10, Monday. The British forces have, at long last, taken the city of Caen, the préfecture of the département of Calvados. It is a gateway which could lead to Paris, 145 miles and Berlin, about 650 miles away. But the Russians in Minsk are even closer to the German capital.

I was present at school by 9:30 a.m. this morning and found myself the only one to take the last two exams; the rest of the class has not shown up. I am all finished by noon; I say goodbye to the teachers I can find, and to Fr. Huysmans the school principal, who is convinced that the war will be over before Christmas.

I hope so because everything is fast falling apart. Travel by train is almost impossible; even the streetcars are unpredictable and the timetables are no longer respected. When the tram appears you have to shoehorn yourself into it, even before the alighting passengers have a chance to get out. Heated words are exchanged and all civility has disappeared.

The soldier on R & R has gone too. What is left are the garrison soldiers, guarding the regional headquarters and services spread around town, plus the heavily armed security company protecting general Baron Alexander von Falkenhausen, the military governor.

July 16, Sunday. I am now at Tourneppe, at the Youth Center not seen since last August. Outwardly not much has changed but all the leaders I met last year are gone except for Herman Bouton who receives me warmly.

The place is more crowded, Herman explains. This situation has led to the use of two wooden buildings with fourteen beds each, situated in the woods at the bottom of the hill. I will be in charge of them at night. More details later. I make the acquaintance of the new leaders and try to find out, on my own, who the "réfractaires" are and who are the university students here to help. Fr. Capart is in Brussels on one of his money-raising tours for the Youth Center and will be back in a day or two.

I meet his deputy Fr. Joseph Masson, who is a missionary in Ranchi, India, northwest of Calcutta. He was on sick leave when the war left him stranded here. He is very impatient to go back to his mission post, of course. I found him studying Sanskrit, certainly an excellent intellectual exercise, recommended to all. As I show enough curiosity, he proceeds to give me Lesson No. 1 in this Indo-European Indic tongue, in use since 1200 B.C., and the most important religious and literary language in India. I have the feeling this first lesson will also be the last.

From Sanskrit the conversation turns, I don't know how, to the influence of Greek hellenistic art on Buddhist sculpture of the third century B.C., transmitted later to China and Japan. We end up talking about Alexander the Great, whose name signifies "Guardian of men" (356-323 B.C.) and his famous expedition which brought Hellenism all the way to Khodjend and the confines of China, as well as to the Himalaya mountains and the Indus.

"I regret, I say, that no one in the entourage of Alexander kept a diary recording these momentous events."

"You are mistaken," is the answer. "At least four personages, close to the young monarch kept records. One was Eumenes (friend), his secretary, the historian who later published the "Ephemerides," the official version of the conquest. Three other members of the expedition also published their memoirs: Aristobulus (best counsel), a Greek, one of the technicians of the army; Ptolemy (the warrior), the future king of Egypt; Callisthenes (most excellent), Aristotle's nephew, a trained philosopher and historian. His account covers the first four years of the expedition."

Our discussion brings back memories of Greek history studied five years ago already. I have always preferred the Greek world, genial and artistic, to the Roman juggernaut, orderly and ruthless.

July 17, Monday. My duties are very much like the ones I had last year, except that at night I go down the hill with a group of 25 boys, who are lodged, as I have said, in two wooden dormitories near the rear entrance of the property. They are numbered Dorm I and II, the first situated closer to the road. The interior is spartan: six beds on one side and eight on the other; a chair, a washstand and a wooden chest at the foot of each bed for clothes and sundries. That's all.

My own accommodation is a little more luxurious consisting of a roomy alcove surrounded by a wooden wall two meters high (6 feet) with bed, washstand, a small desk, a chair and a wardrobe. A small desk lamp is the only light source for reading. The rest of the building is lighted by blue-tainted bulbs to conform to blackout regulations. They are sufficient to move around and even recognize faces but of no use for manual work or reading.

Dorm II is isolated further away from the road. Its isolation made it the place of choice to shelter the fourteen Jewish boys hidden here among the other kids. It is hoped that in case of a roundup the Gestapo, finding the main building in order, will not look further.

July 20, Thursday. Fr. Capart is optimistic about the progress of the war. I know he has serious sources of information I don't want to inquire about. He tells me that, with a few exceptions, the Allied troops are short of battle experience but they are immensely superior in manpower and equipment. The Germans, skilful warriors, are opposing a dogged resistance but their best troops have been killed or are fighting in Russia. All they have now, in the West, are elite Panzer and Panzer Grenadier divisions but not enough of them, plus replacement units consisting mostly of very young recruits and older veterans, always hard to find.

The Youth Center is in good shape, the civilian authorities do their best to find and supply scarce food supplies. However since the beginning of the invasion the latter have slowly been easier to find. This is because the black marketeers, feeling the war might end soon, are releasing some of their hoarded goods to the civilian sector. They are offering them at much lower prices, allowing the Ministry of Health a bigger share of the official stocks used to feed the children most at risk.

July 22, Saturday. Very early on Friday morning, the German radio went on the air:

"Achtung! Achtung! we are broacasting an important announcement. An attempt to murder the Führer has failed. The Führer is not hurt."

After the reading of the official statement the announcer went on:

"The German people will learn with deep gratitude and satisfaction that the life of our Führer has not been harmed by this criminal attempt.

"Providence has protected the Führer from an attack made by an enemy who has so often made use of murder, and who thought he could obtain by murder that which he could never attain through honest fighting. For every German this abortive attempt must be a warning to intensify our war effort."

Hitler's own official announcement says:

"Hitler received slight burns and concussion but no serious injury. He at once began to work again. He then received Mussolini for a long meeting, which had been previously arranged."

We discuss this stunning news among the leaders and come to the conclusion that this attempt to blow up Hitler must be the work of disgruntled top Nazi officials or high-ranking officers who have access to Hitler's headquarters. We all agree it is unfortunate it didn't succeed. It surely would have had a great influence on the future conduct of the war.

July 24, Monday. My group of Jewish boys, young men really, is a model of courage in adversity, the more so since they cannot show, in any way, the big trouble they are in. They have to be carefree, joyous, easy-going, boisterous at times, as is normal at their age. They are not allowed to be taciturn, despondent, worried, at least not in front of their young comrades. They have to blend perfectly within the whole group and not show, at any time, that they belong to the Jewish race. No Jewish Scriptures nor books; no discussions of Jewish matters; perfect indifference concerning Jewish news.

I discuss this with Fr. Capart who proceeds to enlighten me about the real situation of the Jews in our country.

The Persecution of the Jews

Hitler has been a virulent anti-semite since way back in the Twenties, identifying the Jew as the cause of Germany's defeat and her subsequent economic and social troubles. The program of his Nazi party, the NSDAP, of February, 1920 states: "None but those belonging to the people may be citizens; none but those of German blood may belong to the people. It follows then that no Jew may belong to the people."

In *Mein Kampf*, Hitler repeats this assertion asking for the elimination of Jews from all public employment and for other restrictions.

When he came to power, in January 1933, this anti-Semitism immediately became an integral part of Hitler's governmental policy and the systematic persecution of the Jews began. When the Nazis overran Belgium they, at first, didn't bother the Jews, Belgian or foreign. However, in June 1942, Himmler ordered a crackdown and set quotas for their deportation from Nazi-occupied countries.

There were, in 1940, about 80,000 Jews in Belgium, plus an

unknown number of foreign ones, from Germany and other countries, who had fled Nazi persecution. Since July, 1942 onward, each Jewish family has to face difficult decisions. Those with children have to decide whether to keep them or place them in safety somewhere. Countless parents, at first, entrusted their children to the care of Christian families; then, believing that they had overreacted, had taken them back and found themselves arrested with their children. Numerous families have rejected entirely the notion of separation, choosing to face the future together. "Even if we are deported, life in relocation 'Umsiedlung' camps cannot be all that bad. And at least, we will be able to face the difficulties as a group".

From several sources it is possible to piece together how the roundup of Jews is carried out. As explained before, the SS or their collaborators, appear in the middle of the night and order the victims to get out of their house or their apartment without delay. They are allowed to take only one suitcase with the bare necessities. Everything else has to stay behind. They have to "voluntarily" renounce any claim on their house, in writing, and then they are taken to the freight station for "shipment" to camps in the East.

Despite the secrecy, some disturbing news is filtering through. Reliable reports have it that Jews are being killed in these camps. The Underground Press, which is the voice of the Resistance in Belgium, France and Holland, divulged, about the end of 1942 and early 1943, the existence of a Vernichtungslager in a Polish town with a complicated name, Osciewczim or something. It even mentioned that the Jews are killed by asphyxiation and other means.

This grave disturbing news has been transmitted by Belgians and Dutch alike to their respective governments in exile as well as to the British Foreign Office. The reaction? Very negative. The reports are labeled a gross exaggeration of what actually happens to the Jews in the camps. Certainly no picnic but on average they are not treated too badly...

I don't understand. They are given undisputed facts. Why don't they listen ?

Time for me to join my flock waiting to go down to the dorms. I intend to pursue this conversation within a day or two.

July 24, Wednesday. Hardly a day goes by without hundreds of bombers and fighters flying high above us, day and night, on their way to Grossdeutschland. Its cities must be piles of rubble. Big Mouth Goebbels is very mad. He calls the raids "terrorist attacks on the civilian population". But who started the war?

In the last few days, Belgium has had its share of air attacks, north, south, east and west, but mostly west. The coastal area is hit almost daily. The beautiful medieval center of Courtrai has been destroyed. North of Brussels the industrial area of Vilvoorde, as well as the airfields of Evere and Grimbergen, have received the visit of bombers and fighter-bombers. The Germans call the latter *Jabos* a slang term for Jagdbomber.

July 29, Saturday. We get additional news concerning the assassination attempt against Hitler. It is now known that Claus von Stauffenberg, a colonel on the General Staff, has placed a bomb in Hitler's conference room at Supreme Headquarters. But Hitler, as by miracle, suffered only minor injuries; he resumed work and later received Mussolini.

Hitler spoke on the radio on July 21 at 1 p.m. "A small clique of ambitious, dishonorable and criminally stupid officers," he said, "who have nothing in common with the German armed forces and above all, with the German people, have formed a plot to remove me. A bomb, planted by a Colonel von Stauffenberg, exploded seriously wounding several members of Hitler's staff, one fatally. This very small gang of criminals will now be ruthlessly exterminated".

Oberst (Colonel) von Stauffenberg was arrested in Berlin, where he had fled after the attempt, court-martialed and shot soon after, with other unnamed accomplices.

13

August 1 – September, 1944

August 1, Tuesday. Fr. Capart continues his analysis of the Nazis' attempt to remove the Jews to camps which are either awful ghettos or worse, extermination camps. He tries to explain how, at first, Himmler worked at eliminating the Jews from all public activity in Belgium, France and Holland.

The Hounding of the Jews

It all started some time in January, 1941. The Occupant announced that all persons of Jewish blood or Jewish mixed parentage (descended from two wholly Jewish grandparents) have to register with the civilian authorities in their town of residence. A few weeks later, those who registered were told to exchange their normal ID card for a yellow one with a black "J" in the middle of the front panel. (Belgian ID cards are light green in color and consist of three panels.)

At that point, the harassment started. The Jews were forbidden to hold public office and all Jewish civil servants had to resign or retire. Later, all Jews were ordered to register with their regional or national Jewish Council.

Things started to get worse in 1942. On April 24, all Jews were compelled to wear the yellow star on their right breast. A new regulation removed them to designated cities and to live, segregated in a few streets, under a Jewish Council serving as the representative of the Jewish community with the Nazi masters and lords.

A few months later, Jews were forbidden to exercise certain professions: teacher, doctor, lawyer, dentist. They were also barred from sending their children to public or private schools; they had to organize their own.

The "yellow star" regulation became more severe. From then on, it had to be sewn not pinned on articles of clothing. It had to be worn not only on the streets but also in gardens, open areas and open doors.

Then came the time when Jews had to surrender their bikes; furthermore they could no longer practice open air sports such as swimming, canoeing, rowing, tennis, football (soccer) fishing, etc. Shopping in non-Jewish shops was allowed only between 2 and 5 p.m. when practically everything was sold out, and grocery- as well as butcher- and fish shops are off-limits to them.

Around October, 1942, the Jewish Councils were under heavy pressure to come up with the names of Jews which, in groups of 300 or more, were designated for "transport", that is deportation to camps in the East. Later the number of call-ups oscillated between 1100 and 1200 which is the size of a "train load".

At present, not many Jews move about freely. It is estimated that about half of the 80,000 Belgian Jews have been deported or are awaiting transportation in transit camps. The other half is in hiding. Compared to other countries like France and Holland this can be considered a "success". And it can be attributed to three factors:

1) The relatively small number of Jewish people living in the country versus the total population of about eight and half million.

2) The dogged resistance of the Belgian people against the Occupant who, day after day, sabotage, delay, confuse, in a myriad subtle ways, the Nazi and military system in Belgium. This resistance as practiced by civil servants allows the Jews to be provided with "genuine" false papers which helps them to blend in the population with little risk of discovery.

3) The fact that our country is occupied and governed under military not direct Nazi rule. It is known that the Wehrmacht, which can be extremely harsh and brutal towards our people, is often at loggerheads with the Gestapo, the SS and other Nazi organizations. The Army doesn't care about the Jews one way or another but, with the present fighting in Normandy, the generals don't want to divert trains to transport the Jews to places unknown when they need every locomotive and every railroad car for their troops and equipment.

August 2, Wednesday. The BBC French program has announced the capture of the town of Avranches by the troops of General

Patton's Third Army. The announcer calls this important event as "La Percée d'Avranches". He explains that the Americans have broken through the German defenses and are pushing south toward Rennes, in Brittany. Great news!

August 3, Thursday. Among the group of Jewish boys we call Dolphins, because they live submerged, one of them, by the assumed name of Max D., stands out. He is, so to speak the unofficial spokesman for the little flock. We get along very well and have become friends.

He is about 16 years old, very intelligent and well educated. It is a pleasure to exchange ideas and conduct discussions on all kinds of subjects: Literature, religion, philosophy, the war - you name it.

He is normally very upbeat and carefree but sometimes, at night, out of sight of his non-Jewish companions, he sheds this appearance and shows every sign of being very discouraged and even depressed. I know why. Like his friends at Dorm II, he was separated from his family with hardly the time to say goodbye and is now utterly alone. There is no possibility of contact with the members of his family; he doesn't even know what happened to them. His only hope is to see them again "after the war", at pre-determined places, the homes of non-Jewish friends and acquaintances. In the meantime: no news, no letters, no phone calls, no visits, just dead silence...

Max' parents are non-practicing Jews. As a consequence he never received a religious education. Now he attends Mass every day at our little chapel, not as a convert to Catholicism but to find, in religion, spiritual strength, consolation and peace. He has taken hold of a Bible and discovered "The Law and the Prophets", which he reads with studied attention every morning. He loves the Psalms, especially Psalm 22 (23) which is also my favorite. From time to time, at night, we slowly recite this short hymn, only six verses, starting as follows:

Dominus regit me / Nihil me deerit
Le Seigneur est mon berger / Rien ne saurait me manquer
The Lord is my shepherd / I shall not want.

Here I sit with this young man, on the stoop of the dorm, a friendly presence, as the tears roll down his cheeks, thinking no doubt of his parents and siblings, with no knowledge of their fate and not much hope to see them again soon - or ever- immersed in his sorrow "too deep to tell" (Aeneid. II, 3). I don't utter a word; there are no words for black despair; there is almost no defense against the apparently victorious forces of Total Evil.

I think of the thousands upon thousands of persecuted people, in Belgium and in Europe, who, tonight, face the same Evil. And I reflect about those who have decided to help them, at the risk of their lives, without any afterthought, simply because it is the decent thing to do. The Good Samaritan was not out on the Jericho road seeking opportunities for dispensing charity; he was presumably bound on his own business, but confronted with the plight of the robber's victim, he did the thing any Christian or, yes, any decent man would do.

August 4, Friday. It is my last day at the Youth Center. With days full of activities, time has passed *comme un éclair* (flash of lightning), as they say in French.

There is also daily a lot of animated talk and speculation when we pore over maps, picking out the towns mentioned in the communiqués, and about the great news from Normandy which gets more exciting by the hour.

The fact is that the German front has collapsed. American tanks, fanning out in strength from the northeast corner of Brittany, have reached Rennes, key to all communications to the Brittany peninsula and St. Malo. The Yankees took Avranches on Monday; today they are in Rennes, 45 miles to the south.

It is always interesting to hear from the German side. Sertorius, a serious commentator, within limits of course, stated last night: "The Americans' stabs from Avranches in a southwesterly and southerly direction, gained a fair amount of ground after crossing the Sélune. They may have as an objective a breakthrough to the mouth of the Loire."

More interesting news. In the last few days, persistent rumors had it that Field Marhal Rommel had been injured while directing the battle of Normandy. Now Berlin has at last admitted the fact adding that, for the time being he is "out of the war."

Here is what the German News Agency announced last night: "Field Marshal Rommel met with a car accident as the result of an air raid in France on July 17. He suffered injuries and concussion. His condition is satisfactory."

Tonight, before "lights out", Max hands me a farewell note penned in a beautiful almost print-like handwriting:
"The Lord will guard you from all evil
He will guard your life
The Lord will guard your coming and going
Both now and forever." (Ps. 121, 7-8.)

This is my prayer for him, tonight.

August 5, Saturday. I leave early to catch a train for Brussels. This means of transport is a lot faster than the inter-urban tramway. I bid my goodbyes to all and slipped a note to Max in exchange for his of yesterday.
The Lord answer you in time of distress
The name of the God of Jacob defend you
May he send you help from the sanctuary
From Zion may he sustain you...
May he grant what is in your heart
and fulfill your every plan. (Ps. 20, 1-3, 5.)

My decision to travel by train was a mistake. It should be avoided nowadays. All the fun you can expect is cancellations, delays, shunting to a side track and waiting, air raid alarms, breakdowns. The railroad system is on its last legs due to its overuse by the Nazis. However, the crowding and the unscheduled stops notwithstanding, I arrived home in one piece. I did not fail to observe during this trip, like in all earlier ones that, at each slowdown or stop, people are anxiously scanning the skies looking for marauding fighters. The latter have acquired quite a reputation for aggressiveness far superior, because of higher speed and armament, to the one the Stukas enjoyed in 1940.

August 7, Monday. The big news of yesterday might finally mark the turn of the tide after nearly five years of war.
On the Western front, American tanks have not only reached the outskirts of Brest, at the tip of Brittany, but have reached the river Loire; the great peninsula, with its vitally important ports of Brest, Lorient (with its U-boat bases) and St. Nazaire, is cut off. For his

261

part, Montgomery has burst through German defenses and the Nazis have to swing back with the Caen area as an hinge.

On the Eastern front, the Russians have smashed across the frontier of East Prussia and, for the first time, the Allies are fighting on German soil.

In Italy, Florence has been liberated.

August 9, Wednesday. Mr. W. pays us a visit. He has been coming more often lately. He is quite excited about the breakthrough in Normandy and looks rejuvenated.

He brings with him two pieces of information and an assessment.

In addition to the V1, which we call now the Flying Bomb, the Germans have come up with two additional secret weapons. *First,* a double plane, a small one, the nose of which is filled with high-explosive, mounted on a Messerschmidt 109. This robot can be released in flight and remotely controlled to its target by the pilot of the 109. *Second,* a robot tank which has made its appearance in the Canadian sector of Normandy; it is the size of a small truck and is guided by a driver who takes it as far as he can, gets out and directs it by wireless. The tank is supposed to release, by radio signal, a salvo of explosives, turn around and waddle back.

The efficiency and success of these new weapons is not known.

As to the assessment handed to me by Mr. W., it looks like the summary of a report he wrote himself or received from some other source.

"The supreme event of the last few days is the collapse of the German front in Normandy because, in strategic importance, it exceeds all the great happenings in Eastern Europe: the assault on Warsaw, the occupation of the Gulf of Riga and the invasion of East Prussia.

"Since the initial landings and until a few days ago, the Allied forces in Normandy occupied no more than a bridgehead. Now that bridgehead has vanished and in its place we see a true Second Front established, from which operations are in full swing.

"The Normandy door, the door to the whole of Western France, has been burst in at its lock, Avranches. But even more important than this bursting is that a gap has been created in the German strategic front in the West, a gap extending from the Gulf of St. Malo to the Mediterranean.

"For, as has been proven, if the Germans have not force enough to hold a front of one hundred miles, it may be assumed that they are not in a position to hold one of greater length, unless they can place between themselves and their enemy an obstacle of such strength that it will lend power to their waning numbers.

"Only one such obstacle exists within reach. It is the river Seine. Can the Germans withdraw to it? Or can they be prevented from doing so?

"As regards the first: should Rommel, or whoever is now directing the German forces in Normandy, successfully carry out their fall back, then indeed it will be one of the most remarkable retreats in history.

"Should the answer be that the retreat cannot be stopped then the decisive moment in the Battle of France is approaching that will knock the foundations from under the feet of every other German army corps, division and brigade now in France."

August 10, Thursday. Mother is a practical philosopher, sort of. With eight children (five still at home) you have to be. She knows, for example, that every piece of positive news has a negative side. She is, of course, delighted by the turn of events in Normandy but feels that the Allies' success in France might push the crux of the battle into Belgium and get stuck here for an indefinite period. In that case, she fears, the supply of food will stop altogether and we might have to survive on what we can hoard now or face starvation.

In other words, Mother is preparing for the worst and has started storing provisions to last for at least three months. We have a good amount of potatoes growing in the garden together with French-style green beans, carrots, leeks and salads. We have also a fair amount of dried peas and beans.

Fruit has been plentiful this year, especially apples and pears. We are planning to pick them and line them up on shelves and any plane area we can find in the house. They will also last for about three months at the rate of two (one apple, one pear) per day, per head.

The old pump has been repaired and now gives us a supply of

non-drinkable water which, if need be, can be purified. Coal has been squirreled away together with kerosene which Father has "liberated" from the Nazi-controlled railroad. We have to deal also with the almost daily electricity cuts and the gas turned on for only one hour at noontime and another at six or seven in the evening.

The situation is not satisfactory in the departments of grains and meat. We have about 65 kilos (143 lbs.) of flour which would mean 140 grams or 5 oz. of bread per head on a 90-day basis. Father is working hard at doubling this amount by visiting a few friendly farmers who, sensing that the war might come to an end, are not so reluctant to part with some of their precious reserves. Not much can be said about the meat supply: it is almost non-existent. We have a dozen live rabbits and one ham. This is not so bad if we can get additional flour. We eat very little meat and no fish except for herring in season. We might add two or three rabbits and father will try for another ham. And other fats? No fat! Their price is astronomical and mother prefers to replace them with more affordable products.

For Father feeding the family is a daily battle; for Mother, an exhausting struggle. We try to help as much as we can.

August 12, Saturday. The Germans have tried a counterattack at Mortain in an effort to stop the American offensive by splitting the front in two but they have failed.

Now, in a sensational thrust, the Americans are at the gates of Chartres, some 50 miles from Paris, threatening to envelop von Kluge's entire Normandy army, leaving it with only the Seine as an escape route. A secondary column of Americans has reached Chateaudun, 22 miles southwest of Chartres, in an astonishing race to the east.

The German military leaders are now on the point of taking their major decision in Normandy: whether to fight it out to the bitter end or to retreat. Their front line is being forced into an impossible shape. In other words, the Germans are threatened with the old-fashioned pincer movement.

The top arm of the pincer is the British and Canadian drive to Falaise. From the American spearhead at Le Mans and Chartres to north of Falaise, the line forms as it were the mouth of the bag, a gap from Le Mans, according to my map, of 72 miles. And the whole of the Wehrmacht is in that bag.

August 13, Sunday. A few days after the opening of the Second Front, the National Bureau of the Scouting Movement advised all Troop leaders to be extremely careful not to antagonize the Occupant in any way. Troop outings should be avoided and scout uniform not worn. Meetings should be held indoors. This week came the order to suspend all activities. So, we obey.

August 14, Monday. There are more troop movements in and around Brussels. I avoid going out so as not to be caught in any last ditch roundup. I stay inside listening to the radio, taking notes and studying maps. I venture outside only at dusk, for an hour or so, with brother Michel.

Lucien, who is not quite fifteen but looks thirteen (he is very, very thin) can move around more freely. His job is to go out and stand in line for food, one hour or two, until he is relieved at the last moment by Mother or sister Léona, who do the buying.

There is not much to buy however and the quality is, well, abysmal. Bread for example is now a mixture of flour and something else we call "edible sawdust", which might be barley, potato- or chestnut-flour, whatever. It is very soggy, so much so that if you slam a slice against the wall it will stick to it. We don't, of course, we eat it, very slowly, because it is rather indigestible.

In Grossdeutschland, every boy and girl in the Hitler Youth has been mobilized for Germany's war production or for the battle lines. This decree, announced by Berlin radio came at the end of "last ditch" call-up orders for the defense of the Reich, to fill the need for "hundreds of thousands" more workers and soldiers. Whole age groups of Germany's exempts find themselves with their exemptions canceled and under orders for front-line service. Domestic servants are sent to factories or to priority households. Every foreign maid or cook will be drafted into armament works.

The new decrees were issued by Goebbels as "Trustee for Total Mobilization" in what he calls "scraping the bottom of the barrel".

August 16, Wednesday. The Allies have invaded Southern France along the Côte d'Azur (Riviera) coast. The landing was successful but it is too early to get concrete information.

I don't understand this move. Of course, I am only a civilian, a nobody in this time of war. But let me ask very respectfully: "Why attack from the south when all these troops and equipment could be used in the West of France pursuing the Germans, or getting ready to move when the front becomes so extended that their help will be greatly needed?...."

Father, back on night duty, mentions intense troop movements from sunset to sunrise. During the day, for fear of Allied bombers and fighters, the Germans stay under cover except for local activities.

August 18, Friday. As the Allies approach Paris, our country becomes more and more an important strategic platform for the Germans and a choice target for the Allied air forces.

Yesterday, early in the afternoon, I was on duty with the Défense Passive, as I am now officially on vacation and therefore availaible. There had been air raid alarms in the morning but nothing happened. We had another one around 1:30 p.m. This time we could hear the planes approaching and they were coming directly at us. We scrambled for safety as the first bombs started falling. The action was north of us and a little to the west. It was short but intense, and the noise terrific. The FLAK, mute so far, started barking adding to the bedlam. The din was frightening and as the *Bombenteppich* or carpet-bombing was falling closer, shaking the building, we ran to the basement as far as we could go.

Suddenly the bombers veered away; the FLAK fell silent. We climbed onto the roof and looked out towards the town. Someone said he could see houses burning, but there was so much smoke that one couldn't really tell what had happened. We are soon on our way towards the scene. The streets are so blocked by fallen down masonry that no vehicle can get through and we have to walk, shouldering our equipment.

We meet the first people scurrying around, disheveled and smelling of smoke. There is an eerie silence soon broken with the cries of wounded and frightened people. We go to work, staggering among piles of glass and rubble.

Our first duty is to look for the wounded and to bring them to the first-aid station. When we find dead people, some of them horribly mangled, we carry them out gently and line them up in any convenient place along the sidewalk, covering them with any type of cover available. Special crews will soon come by, look for identification and bring them to an improvised morgue nearby.

By this time, we are covered from head to toe with a very fine white powder that makes breathing through our gauze-masks laborious. I must admit that I am pretty much shaken up but fortunately, after a while, the brain shuts off and on we go on with the job.

As we pursue our efforts, the sirens start to howl again. Soon after, the FLAK resumes its organ concert, fortissimo. We run for cover and, as there is no decent shelter available, we decide to lie down in a small park, flat on our face against a low wall. To our surprise only three planes appear, flying rather low. Stragglers probably, having been shot up and trying desperately to get back to base. One of them must have jettisoned its bombs because all of a sudden I hear violent explosions close by.

I push my nose deeper in the lose ground as a shower of dirt, bricks, stones and sand rains upon us. A brick or a stone falls upon my left ankle but fear has anaesthetized my nerves. I feel nothing. A few seconds later I hear a low whistle and a thud close to my head. I lay very flat against the wall protecting me from most of the raining debris.

The planes are gone. The FLAK has stopped its noisome banging and barking. At first there is total silence. After a while I lift my head above the wall and see nothing but a thick yellowish fog made of very fine particles of cement, plaster and other matter, moving slowly to the left by the breeze. I readjust my mask, rather dirty by now, for I know this milky cloud can be deadly. It is what kills people trapped in cellars; it penetrates the lungs and chokes them to death.

A few shadows are moving around and I try to get up. My left foot, however, doesn't respond and, crawling, I sit on the wall feeling completely drained. My ankle is swelling a little and starts to hurt. I massage it softly and decide that nothing is broken. Looking up I get a glimpse of a shiny object a few feet away. I approach it on all four and discover a jagged piece of metal, oval in shape, a little smaller than my hand. It is a bomb fragment embedded only inches away from where my head had been, two inches or so sticking out, still hot but cooling off rapidly and very shiny.

The chief approaches and I show him the piece of metal. Been lucky, he concludes. Only a few inches! To my surprise, a few minutes later, the fragment is covered with a layer of rust and now looks like an old piece of junk...
"A chemical reaction," opines the chief. I wrap it in my handkerchief and, as it is too big for my pocket, I clutch it in my left hand.

I am helped to first aid where the nurse confirms that nothing is broken and proceeds to bandage the ankle for support. I have however a hard time standing on just one foot, so they decide to send me home in one of the ambulances, by way of the hospital Brugmans, with a few wounded who don't seem in any danger but look very scared .

Mother almost had a heart attack seeing the ambulance stop in front of the house; she was soon reassured but remains very doubtful about my involvement in Civil Defense.

Last night, evidently as a result of the previous day's experience, I woke suddenly to find my body almost entirely covered with a rash that, by morning, has entirely disappeared. I will have to consult the doctor about this occurrence.

August 20, Sunday. After days of operational silence, it has now been announced that the tanks of General Patton are barely 20 miles from the Seine River; their possession of the high ground between Dreux and Chartres means that there can be no sustained defense except on the river before Paris.

Interestingly enough, the news is confirmed by the German News Agency announcing that the German High Command has given up the Battle of Normandy as lost.

The following statement was made by Max Krull, the agency's military correspondent:

"The Normandy front has been liquidated by the Oberkommando der Wehrmacht (OKW). German forces are withdrawing in an easterly direction.

"The cards now are being dealt for a new game. Fast Allied troops meanwhile are trying to overrun the German forces on their march back, if possible to encircle them again. An attempt of this sort is being made at Dreux where thrusts in several directions, including Paris, are being made."

It seems to me that the Wehrmacht is more and more truthful about the situation in the West. Their communiqués are not just pure propaganda and this brings me to think that Goebbels is no longer in total control of information in Germany.

August 21, Monday. The Allies have won a decisive victory in Normandy. The Germans are defeated. Most of the enemy divisions, including crack SS formations are trapped in the pocket formed between Argentan, west of Flers, north to Condé-sur-Noireau and then east to Falaise. On my map the mouth of the bag is about 14 miles wide and the depth around 30 miles. It is clear that there is a complete disorganization of army elements trying to get away between the immediate battle area and the Seine.

In Southern France, the bridgehead is now more than one thousand square miles. Allied troops are within six miles of Toulon, on the road to Aix-en-Provence, and have occupied Draguignan, to the east.

Note. The Germans in Normandy have used another new weapon in the form of the Royal Tiger tank. According to German sources this tank weighs 65 tons, has 15 cm (six inches) armor and is 7 meters (23 ft.) long. I don't think the Allies have anything they can use to oppose this monster.

August 22, Tuesday. Allied tanks are across the Seine, west of Paris. This has been announced by Radio Berlin and confirmed later by the OKW. This advance, if continued, will menace the flying bomb (V1) and the long-range guns of the Pas-de-Calais coast, 140 km to the north.

West of this crossing, the British Second Army and the Canadian First Army have reduced the Falaise pocket and are threatening to overtake and overwhelm the German divisions between Argentan, the Seine and the Channel.

Last minute. Patton's Third Army has reached the outskirts of Paris at Versailles and Fontainebleau. In Paris itself it is reported that dozens of armed clashes are taking place between French underground fighters and German troops.

It has also been announced that General de Gaulle has landed at Cherbourg. It is expected that he will move his government from Algiers to Paris as soon as the capital has been freed.

August 23, Wednesday. Radio Brussels, under German control, now views the ongoing bombing of Belgium as "invasion bombing". The Germans believe that Allied landings will be made somewhere on the Belgian-Dutch coast in an effort to finish off Germany before winter.

The German High Command spokesman, Generalleutnant Dietmar, has this to tell to his country and the world:

"The gravity of our situation cannot be disguised. Events in the west have taken a turn that places a burden of heavy anxiety on the German people.

"Under the conditions in which we have to fight on the Western front, where the enemy's aerial superiority makes our every movement a harsh and ticklish business, the difficulty of the task is redoubled.

"The most important basis of our resistance remains the steadfast will of the German soldier to go on fighting.

In the east we know that the worst is not yet over. Perhaps also in the west we shall be compelled to fall back to a new and more narrowly confined base for our conduct of the war. Let us face this issue without flinching."

I note that General Dietmar doesn't even mention Germany's dear and infallible Führer, Adolf Hitler! The idol with feet of clay?

August 24, Thursday. Great news from the battlegrounds of France! A column of General Patton's tanks, whose movements have been a secret since the capture of Orléans, are now reported past Sens, about 60 miles southeast of Paris and 170 miles from the German border!

Further west, in the Seine area, Patton's tanks have reached Beauvais, an important rail junction north of Paris. The Canadians have reached Deauville and Lisieux has fallen. The German army is again caught in a pocket between the Allied troops and the Seine.

In the streets of Paris, guerrilla fighters with grenades, rifles and machine guns are attacking the German garrison. Radio Paris has been silent for the last four days but Radio Lille has broken a 12-hour silence to broadcast a German High Command appeal to Parisians to return to work and to maintain public services.

There is a rumor that Maréchal Pétain has been arrested by the Nazis and brought to Belfort in eastern France.

August 25, Friday. Radio Brussels, last night, had an explanation for the German retreat in France and Russia.

"Since the Germans have developed an astonishing series of new weapons, and since these will appear in great masses very soon, the German General Staff has decided to retreat on all fronts in order to limit losses until the time for their use arrives.

"Germany could launch most of these new weapons straight away but she prefers to wait until the war has reached the highest climax."

By the way, Deauville was liberated yesterday by Belgian troops, fighting under Canadian Army Command.

In Paris there is no full confirmation of the capital's liberation announced in General Koenig's communiqué yesterday. Allied troops are believed to be pouring into the city on their way northward.

In the south, U.S. troops have captured Grenoble and are now 30 miles from Lyons. Far behind them, the Allies are in Marseilles and the net around Toulon is closing.

August 26, Saturday. Paris is clear of Germans!

The German commander surrendered unconditionally yesterday.

It was the Allied Armies greatest day! In the past 24 hours they have:

* Fought their to way in Paris.
* Broken through the last defense line in the German pocket, west of the Seine.
* Penetrated to Troyes and Rheims, a town situated less than 30 miles from the Belgian border and about 150 miles from Germany.

Mr. W. paid us a visit today. He announces flatly that the Germans are preparing their exit from Brussels. General von Falkenhausen had been recalled to Berlin in early August; he might have been involved in the plot against Hitler. General Richard Jungkraus, a Nazi, has taken his place but, hopefully, he will not last very long.

The way the Allied offensive is progressing, we discuss our chances of being liberated very soon. Everybody in town talks about it. But will the Germans stop their retreat, turn around and counterattack? Mother still argues that the Wehrmacht will fight in Belgium, perhaps around Brussels. Mr W. retorts that the Germans have no natural barrier where to establish a defensive line except in the Ardennes and along the Meuse, the Albert Canal and the Scheldt at Antwerp.

And so we have the Nazis defeated and exhausted with shorter lines of supply on the one hand, and the Allies victorious and exhausted with longer lines of supply on the other. Furthermore soon the Wehrmacht will be fighting for the Heimat on its own soil.

August 28, Monday. On the German radio, a few days ago, pep talkers and front reporters told German troops in France:

"We must hold out against the enemy assault, we must try to stop their tanks, never mind where, until the new weapons are ready. Then we shall have the upper hand again."

Among the new weapons like the V1, the Royal Tiger tank, the robot tank, etc. there is more and more talk of a flying robot which Hitler calls the Vergeltungswaffe No 2 or V2. The Führer tells his troops time and time again, through his mouthpieces, that if only they will fight on a little longer V1s and V2s will bring Britain to her knees.

It seems that the morale in the Wehrmacht is now largely founded on rocket philosophy, on the dreadful things the V1s are supposed to be doing in London add on the much more terrible devastation promised for the V2s.

What this V2 is exactly, only the German military experts and a few Nazi officials can tell us. All we know is that it is a "rocket" several times more powerful than the flying bomb or V1, used at present. Since they cannot be aimed accurately at a target, they are nothing else than terror weapons.

August 31, Thursday. On the Eastern front, Rumania has quit the Axis, joined the Allies and declared war against Germany. The Rumanian communiqué says that the fascist government of Marshal

272

Antonescu has resigned, replaced by a Liberal government.

In Bulgaria, as a result of the fast-moving situation throughout the Balkans, the government has requested the German troops stationed in the country to leave immediately. Hungary has a new government and general mobilization has been ordered throughout the country. Ribbentrop is said to be in Budapest for negotiations with leading politicians.

September 1st, Saturday. The German retreat is not a coordinated movement from one position to another but more of an "each man for himself" scramble. This we know. But not much else, for the Allies do not report the names of places reached or the location of forward elements in any area of the front to avoid giving useful information to the enemy. And so we are left in the dark, depending solely on rumors, phone calls and the German news that also can be rather vague.

The town of Brussels is in a state of subdued excitement. It seems that people are expecting great events like, *mirabile dictu* (marvelous to relate), the liberation of the capital.

The bombing of military and not so military targets in Belgium is growing in intensity. Brussels has been hit several times during the past two weeks but I cannot be of any help to the Défense Passive because of my bruised ankle. It is healing satisfactorily but I cannot walk on it for any length of time.

Courtrai has been bombed for the third time year this year; the last raid was particularly severe. As mentioned earlier, much of the beautiful medieval center has been destroyed, alas! More than two thousand buildings, including many historic monuments, have been destroyed or damaged.

September 2, Saturday. The Wehrmacht is abandoning Brussels. All German civilians and administrative military personnel have left town. In the southern suburbs, German troops are erecting and manning strong points but it doesn't seem they want to make a stand here, just delay the enemy.

We learn that the Americans have crossed the Belgian border at Bettignies, coming from Avesnes and Maubeuge. There is heavy fighting in and around Mons.

THE LIBERATION OF BELGIUM HAS BEGUN!

A little further to the west, the British are pushing fast in the direction of Arras and Lille. The German front has completely collapsed except for rearguard actions. Unbelievable progress!

I learn that Louvain has suffered a terrible bombardment. I place a call to a friend who confirms that the Place Foch has been destroyed as well as parts of the rue de Namur, the rue de Diest and many other sections of town. Loss of life is heavy.

September 3, Sunday. The churches are full and after Mass everyone is milling around in great trepidation, exchanging the latest gossip. It is quite difficult to get solid information. Most of it is hearsay or pure fabrication. We know however that the "Yankees" have liberated Mons, and American spearheads are approaching Charleroi moving in an easterly direction. The telephone system is still working and people from liberated towns are calling their relatives or friends to let them listen to the staccato of machine guns or the roar of thundering tanks.

In the afternoon, the agitation gives way to feverish excitement with the news that the British have occupied Tournai and are now proceeding full speed in a northeast direction on the road to Brussels. There is no doubt at present that the Tommies will reach the capital before sundown. Absolutely incredible! Nobody will ever forget these last hours of anxious wait which slowly dissolve into an almost uncontrollable burst of emotion, more than flesh and blood can bear. Brother Michel is running up and down the street and visiting friends and acquaintances, enjoying freedom again after months and months of being cooped up at home.

It is around five or six o'clock that, according to reports, the advanced elements of the 11th British Armored Division, commanded by Major General George Roberts, reached the southern suburbs. The sun was inclining to the west, sinking into a misty horizon, with just a few jagged clouds towards Koekelberg.

The first patrols, followed by tanks moved cautiously through the suburb of Uccle without encountering any opposition. The streets were empty, with people impatiently watching behind closed doors and shuttered windows.

The Germans were waiting on the great thoroughfares. Fighting erupted on the Boulevard de Waterloo and around the Palais de

Justice, which has been gutted by fire, its massive dome destroyed. Street fighting occurred at the Place St. Jean, very near the magnificent Town Hall that, however, has been spared. As the British advanced, the fighting spread to the Park near the Royal Palace as well as the Place du Trône, not far away, and at the entrance to the Bois de la Cambre.

With brothers, Michel and Lucien, and sisters, Léona and Marie-Thérèse, I went, later at night, to the Basilica of Koekelberg where one has a great view of the city. It is not very far from home but it is hard on my ankle.

We are not alone on this "plateau". Quite a number of people move around aimlessly in the semi-darkness as the moon illuminates the landscape. There is not much to see. From time to time we hear mute explosions and flashes of action. Further south we can perceive a glimmer of what seems to be a raging fire. Perfect strangers speak to vague shadows, hungry for hard news. But there is no news. Only a repetition of what we already know, the confirmation of our impending liberation: the British are in town - the Boche is out, at last!

Quite elated, we return home under the veiled moon that reminds me of Virgil in one of his immortal verses:
Now daylight left the sky, and the mild moon
In mid-haven, rode her night-wandering car. Aen. X, 216-7

September 4, Monday. It has been a bustling night with most of the neighborhood in the street, talking loudly, and laughing and toasting each other until the wee hours of the morning. I slept through it all and woke up early in excellent mood, which brought to mind another quotation of the great master Publius Vergilius Maro:
Soon early Dawn,
Quitting the saffron bed of old Timotheus,
Cast new light on earth." Aen. IV, 587-88.

After a good breakfast to celebrate - we can afford it as we don't have to hoard for a siege - I join the crowd already swelling on the Place Reine Astrid. It is a warm September day; the sky filled with a luminous powder of dawn is now deepening into shades of blue.

The square is in a festive mood and festooned with Belgian flags flapping lazily in the breeze, with here and there, the brighter colors of the Union Jack and the Stars and Stripes.

One of our neighbors is zigzagging around the block on a very old bike without mudguards or light; no brakes either; he slows down by rubbing his right foot against the front wheel. His face makes me think of the back of a London taxicab. At present, this particular face is flushed with the spirits absorbed during the night and it looks like it will soon detonate into a thousand fragments.

In the western corner of the plaza, a small group is assembled in a ring around a lady leaning on a bicycle. She has just arrived from downtown with the latest news. In a nutshell: the British, with a Belgian contingent, have occupied the center of the city yesterday evening and, after a few sharp clashes have forced the enemy rearguard to take the road toward Louvain. I watch the lady as she speaks and find her eyes as lovely as her complexion. It dawns on me that she is very beautiful, not just nice to look at.

Nobody has gone to work although a few shops are open, offering their miserable goods. Public transportation is at a standstill and no one cares. The people of Brussels giddy with delight, has spontaneously declared this Monday, a day of celebration.

By mid-morning the street empties as the word has gone out that Free Radio Brussels will resume broadcasting at ten o'clock. After a rousing Brabançonne, our national hymn, the first on the sound waves in fifty-two months, comes military communiqués, announcements and local news. Also the latter details of yesterday's skirmishes downtown.

The one o'clock broadcast brings the news that the same flying column, which liberated Brussels yesterday, has now reached the suburbs of Antwerp encountering very little resistance so far. This will complete the sealing off of the Channel coast. The German army is retiring eastward on both sides of the Louvain road, in two long columns, in not very orderly fashion. In their hurry to get away, the Germans are ignoring all military rules of spacing their vehicles on the roads. They are wheel to wheel, riding on horse-drawn guns, on limbers, in trucks, requisitioned cars, on farm carts and on bicycles. And above them, swarms of fighters and fighter-bombers to strafe and bomb this utter confusion.

Further south, the Americans are now in the vicinity of Nancy.

Later in the evening, mother inquires: "What do we do with the Reichmarks the Germans imposed us as legal tender in Belgium?" My answer is: nothing! They are not worth a penny. This will be the last act of piracy in the drama of the thorough exploitation of our national economy. It does not however affect our family too much, as we have always shunned this *monnaie de singe* or phony money.

September 5, Tuesday. We still live in a dream and have not yet come back to the realities of life. We don't comprehend yet that we are free. No more curfews, no round-ups, no checkpoints, no line-ups against the wall, no hateful Bekanntmachung (proclamation) announcing new restrictions or the execution of hostages, no odious German signposts (they have disappeared overnight). Sure, the war is not over and we now want to help the Allies the best we can, share in the burden of achieving final victory and start rebuilding our moribund economy and our destroyed cities: an enormous undertaking.

We don't think about reconstruction yet or anything else. Just the inexpressible joy of being free again which drives some of our normally dour and dull neighbors to dance in the streets and shout themselves hoarse as soon as a contingent of Tommies, rushing to the front, drives by in the vicinity.

Reality will make itself felt very soon. We are now under Allied military control until our government is ready to come back from England and the legal civilian authorities are back in place. Public transportation is operating again but with unexplained delays. Nobody notices. It is now possible, with more than a little patience, to go downtown and greet the British columns: an endless convoy of tanks, guns, tractors and all kinds of combat vehicles and supply trucks thundering by along the Boulevards on their way north and east, among ever-renewed popular rejoicing. People are lined up, three of four deep, on each side of the road, waving and shouting. Some, waving a Belgian flag, a Union Jack or an American flag occasionally jump on a slower tank or any convenient vehicle.

The great event today is the liberation of Antwerp by the same

Armored Division, the 11th, reinforced by the 53rd British Division. The port is of great strategic significance, provided the mouth of the Scheldt is also free of Germans. I understand that the Belgian Secret Army has secured the port installations and handed them to the Allies virtually intact. If true, this is an impressive feat indeed.

I wonder why the Wehrmacht didn't fight for Antwerp? Disorganization among their troops, demoralization and the speed of the Allied advance?

September 6, Wednesday. Mother is now happy "squandering" our food reserves in the sense that we eat almost our fill. With potatoes mostly. Father is on the outlook for ham and other fats. He says the liberation has released tons of meat on the black market, renamed the "free" food supply system.

The situation is complicated by the uncertainty as to the future of our currency. The Allies have brought their own Belgian notes and our government-in-exile, soon to return here, has announced plans calling for the "stabilization" of the national currency. We have now to contend with Belgian (war) money, worthless Reichmarks, Allied script and soon new Belgian banknotes. A nice mess in perspective!

The Allies are still progressing further east but there is an unmistakable stiffening of German resistance. The British are consolidating in Antwerp and seem to have reached Breda, just across the border in Holland. In the west, the Canadians, or rather the Polish troops, are approaching Bruges. Further east, the First U,S. Army has crossed the Meuse at Namur and is pushing toward Liège. And in France General Patton's Third Army is pouring across the Moselle River near Pont-à-Mousson, on its way to Germany.

I forgot to mention that General Montgomery, as of September 1st, is now Field Marshal Montgomery!

September 8, Friday. It is now a race to see which of the three Allied armies will reach first the borders of the Reich: the British Second Army could push towards the Siegfried Line via Maastricht; the U.S. First could do the same via Arlon and Luxemburg and, of course, Patton can smash his way through Lorraine and Metz.

Yesterday morning Field Marshal Montgomery drove into

Brussels in pouring rain. (Today the weather is fine.) At first, the crowds in the cafés and restaurants at the Grand'Place, they are still celebrating, did not recognize the gray-green, unmarked car until it stopped in front of the Town Hall.

The Marshal got a terrific reception and people rushed up cheering and shouting. He didn't stay very long however and he soon was on his way to the front. And the good burghers of Brussels went back to their favorite occupation: eating pommes frites and drinking strong beer.

The Pierlot government will be back from London soon. The Parliament reconvenes on September 19 for the first time since May, 1940.

September 12, Tuesday. We had another sunny day, and a fresh and cool easterly breeze blew over liberated Belgium. Last night, the sky was starlit and cloudless. The barometer has been high and steady for the last 24 hours.

The Allied troops are now fighting on German soil. Yesterday, General Hodges' U.S. First Army smashed its way five miles into the Reich, north of Trier. The border was crossed from Luxemburg and Arlon. Trier, in the heart of the Siegfried Line defenses, was founded as Augusta Treverorum by Emperor Octavianus Augustus around 20 B.C.; it became the capital of Gaul from 297 until early in the fifth century.

General Patton's U.S. Third Army, driving through Lorraine, has captured, intact, many miles of the Siegfried Line along the Luxemburg frontier. Almost at the same time, General Patch's Riviera Invasion Army linked up with Patton's Third at Cambernon, 16 miles west of Dijon.

September 18, Monday. An aerial caravan of 1,000 huge transports and troop-carrying gliders carried out yesterday's onslaught on Nazi-occupied Holland. A strong landing was made at noon on the north bank of the Rhine, between Arnhem and Nijmegen, and other landings were made near Tilburg and Eindhoven.

So far everything seems to go well but we must expect a delay of twenty-four hours before the situation can be assessed.

September 20, Wednesday. General Dempsey's Second Army is

engaged in heavy fighting on the southern bank of the Rhine, close to the Dutch towns of Nijmegen and Arnhem, three miles from the German border.

With this news comes also the report that the Germans are massing for an attack to cut off the spearhead of Dempsey's armor driving to Nijmegen. This concentration is apparently on the German border.

At Nijmegen, reached after crossing two of the great water barriers, the Maas and the Wilhelmina Canal, the Second Army is 330 miles from Berlin, 10 miles nearer than the Russians at the Warsaw suburb of Praga.

When Dempsey's tanks cross the Rhine and link up with the paratroopers at Arnhem, Germany's last defense line will have been turned.

September 21, Thursday. Mr. W., whom we had not seen for about three weeks, has shown up today in a very triumphant mood. It is now official that he has been very active in the Resistance. specializing in intelligence service and in escape routes to England for political figures, secret agents, Jews, and airmen who had been shot down.

I am not surprised by this news because of Mr. W.'s access to sensitive information. But I had no idea he was involved in escape routes.

I try to get details but Mr. W. wants to keep his secrets to himself. All he has to say is that he was part of the line organized from Brussels via Roubaix and Paris, ending in Lyons. There the escapees were passed on to Portugal overland across the Pyrenees and Spain.

September 22, Friday. Mother has decided to celebrate our liberation by preparing a big banquet for the whole family. Father has made the tour of his farmer friends for flour, eggs, cheese as well as fruit and he has killed two rabbits. Mam is busy in the kitchen; sisters Léona and Marie-Thérèse are preparing, in utmost secrecy, "the greatest dessert ever concocted in this world..." The dining room is decorated with the flowers of our garden; all traces of "blackout" have disappeared, although officially it is still in effect, but nobody cares. In the meantine, we, the boys, set the table and play cards until Father's return from work.

All is ready. Mother insists that we dress in our best clothes. We celebrate the end of fifty-two months under the Nazi boot and this is a private festivity never to be forgotten.

We start with a short but very solemn prayer to thank the Lord for protecting the family during this long war and with a prayer for the safety of all the the POWs and forced laborers, especially uncle "Seph", still in Germany.

This banquet is the best meal we had since the month of May, 1940. It opens with consommé, crêpes de volaille, salade verte, light and delicious as they should be. Then comes the pièce de résistance: the lapin aux pruneaux or braised rabbit with prunes, my favorite dish, which is a delight accompanied by two Pommard bottles, one of the best red Burgundy.

A short interlude to let our stomachs rest a bit which is also the occasion for us, the children, to offer mother a simple but beautiful golden necklace, as a token of our love for her courage and fortitude which she has shown during these times of trouble. She accepts it proudly with big tears rolling down her cheeks. Father is not forgotten, he gets a big pipe "not to be smoked indoors".

It is now time for dessert which Léona and Marie-Thérèse unveil with great pride. It is composed of those lustrous Flemish pastries which look like a congealing of sunshine and air. They vanish on the palate immediately they are tasted and become a memory almost before there is time to isolate them as an experience. We applaud the pastry cooks, especially Marie-Thérèse, as it is her first try at haute cuisine. She acknowledges our ovation blushingly and I notice that my little sister has become a young woman with a high and agreeably curved forehead, balanced by prominent cheekbones, a slender but resolute oval of jaw line and a strongly molded chin. Her mouth is small but fully lipped, with precisely set, small, white teeth. Her eyes are the best part of her visage: large, warm brown, luminously friendly under slender arched brows...

We feel a need for some exercise. It has been a day of low clouds and late summer squalls but, as we we walk toward the park, in the last hour of the day, we find the world transformed. The sun has emerged, the wind has fallen to a mild breeze, which gently stirs the yellow roses and carries their fragrance, fresh from the late rains.

September 23 Saturday. Belgium is a free and independent

nation again. The Parliament has reconvened, the first meeting since May, 1940, in liberated Brussels.

Prime Minister Pierlot stated that King Léopold III, now held in captivity in Germany is to return to the throne of Belgium. As Chief of the State, Léopold will resume his constitutional prerogatives and the Monarchy will remain, says Mr. Pierlot.

Except for a few towns around the mouth of the Scheldt River, still held by the Germans, to deny the Allies the use of the port of Antwerp, all of Belgium has been liberated. I therefore wish to end this diary, begun in earnest when the Boche invaded our country. The long wait for freedom is over.

...

At dusk, I take my bike and head for the Chaussée Romaine, the Roman Road, as I did in early August, 1940.

The evening is pure and calm, the coloring of the sky and earth such as no painter could reproduce. A rosy flush of sunset still glows in the heavens, bathing the landscape in amethystine light of incomparable transparency.

The September moon, mellow and golden, rises beyond the stately homes and shines down on us with a weird and shadowy effect. A melancholy silence reigns undisturbed at this hour. The plane trees struggle up the gentle hillside forming patches of intense gloom.

Soon darkness rules supreme in this secluded spot. The trees and the wind hold their unending converse. The transient ebullience of this day is quenched, obliterated by the gentle grip of the night.

Now, if ever, the martyred souls of the present war, joined by the ghosts of long gone invading armies, quit their tombs to haunt the scene of their last earthly pilgrimage:

Our world has passed away
In wantonness o'erthrown
There's nothing left today
But steel and fire and stone.
Rudyard Kipling